Athletic Conditioning

Edited & Compiled by:

DR. U.C. GUPTA

KHEL SAHITYA KENDRA

7/26, Ansari Road, Darya Ganj, New Delhi-110002

Ph.: (O) 65190343, 42564726 (M) 9811088729

Published by:

KHEL SAHITYA KENDRA

7/26, Ansari Road, Darya Ganj, New Delhi-110002
Ph.: (O) 65190343, 42564726 (M) 9811088729
E-mail: khelsahitya1@rediffmail.com
Website: www.khelsahitya.com

ISBN – 978-81-7524-391-0

PRINTED IN INDIA

Laser Typeset by:

JAIN MEDIA GRAPHICS

C-4/95-A, Keshav Puram, (Lawrence Road),
Delhi-110035. (Mobile) 9911151534

Printed by:

NEW GYAN OFFSET PRINTERS

Shahjada Bagh, Delhi-110035

PREFACE

The approach to rehabilitation after injury must include an accurate appraisal of muscle strength to determine areas of local weakness. The results of muscle testing are evaluated in terms of muscle strength on opposite sides of the body. A full range of motion is equally important and limitations when compared to the opposite side give rise to the possibility of further injury. Unless strength and range of motion are accurately determined the athlete is not fully protected against further difficulty.

The cause of the weakness or limitation may be a medical condition requiring further attention. If so, it is brought out for the athlete's own well being. Where correction of the weakness involves further exercises of a special type, these exercises have been detailed.

The present book entitled ***Athletic Conditioning*** critically discusses all the necessary and essential facts of Athletic Conditioning. The entire book is precisely arranged and enhanced into eighteen comprehensive chapters containing relevant informations pertaining athletic conditioning. The book discusses briefly important topics viz., The Musculo-Skeletal System, The Nervous System, Agility and Power, Metabolism, Effect of Altitude, Neuromuscular Skill, Fitness and Health, Strength Training, Rehabilitation, Physical Conditioning etc.

It is hoped that the book will be found useful for evaluators, physical educators, physiotherapists, sportsmen and sportswomen, athletes, prospective coaches, students & teachers of Physical Education & Sports.

— Dr. U.C. Gupta

Contents

1

THE MUSCULO-SKELETAL SYSTEM

Basic to the study of conditioning is understanding of the musculoskeletal system, for this system is responsible for motor movements.

Membrane Potential

Every cell of the body has a membrane surrounding its cytoplasm which controls what goes in and out of the cell. The discussion in this section will be limited to the membrane potential of muscles and nerve cells. The cell membrane surrounding a muscle or nerve cell is thin and elastic, and is composed of protein and lipid material.

The membrane is organized into three layers, the two outer layers which are composed of protein, and the inside layer composed of lipid. The outside protein layer makes the membrane hydrophilic while the lipid layer in the centre makes the membrane impervious to lipid-insoluble substances. There are numerous pores in the membrane, but they are so small that only tiny molecules such as water and urea can pass through them. There is an electrical potential in the membrane of nerve and muscle fibres.

This potential gives the fibres the capacity to transmit electrical impulses, or of becoming excited. The membrane potential is actually the result of an excessive accumulation of negative ions on the inside of the cell and an accumulation of positive ions on the outside of the cell.

It seems obvious that the concentration of ions inside and outside the cell membrane would remain equal unless some force upsets the equilibrium. In the cell there is such a force called the sodium pump, which pump large quantities of sodium ions out of the cell into the fluid surrounding the cell.

This is an active transport mechanism, which means that it works against the concentration gradient of the cell, and it requires energy to function. At the same time, it also pumps potassium ions into the cell. However, since the cell membrane is at least 100 times more permeable to potassium than it is to sodium most of the potassium ions tend to diffuse back out of the cell because of the concentration a gradient. This tendency is counteracted by the—75 to –85 mV membrane potential created by the sodium pump where the negative charge inside the cell tends to attract the positive potassium ion.

Therefore, potassium ions remain in the cell primarily as a result of the negative charge in the cell and partially from the potassium pump mechanism. As long as the membrane of a nerve or muscle fibre remains undisturbed, resting potential exists. However, when something changes the permeability of the membrane to sodium, a rapid change in membrane occurs called the action potential. The action potential can be by electrical stimulation, chemical stimulation, mechanical damage, and by heat and cold.

The first part of the action potential is called depolarization. This is thought to be associated with the loosening of calcium ions from the interior of the membrane. When the calcium ions are dislodged, they can no longer effectively resist sodium and, therefore, sodium ions rush into the membrane in ever-increasing numbers, and this dislodges still more of the calcium ions. So much sodium rushes into the cell that the potential actually.

This is called the reverse potential. As more and more sodium ions enter the cell, their positive charge repel additional flow. The calcium binds back to the pores in the interior of the membrane, and the action potential ceases.

Meanwhile, the cell membrane becomes re-polarized. Potassium ions respond to the inflow of sodium ions by leaving the site of high sodium concentration. The outflow of potassium is the most important mechanism for the re-polarization process. The return of the membrane to a resting potential is caused almost entirely by the outflow of potassium ions and not by the sodium pump, which would be much too slow to re-polarize the membrane at the required speed. Of course, as soon as possible, the sodium pump expels the sodium ions, and the potassium ions are exchanged to the inside of the membrane once again.

In muscle cells this action potential triggers the contraction mechanism so that the muscle fibre contracts. In nerve cells the action potential causes a propagation impulse to travel down the nerve cell to transmit information to other body parts. Apparently the action potential at a particular point along the membrane causes an increased permeability to sodium in adjacent sections of the membrane, and the action potential spreads in all directions like circles in water caused when a rock is thrown in.

This transmission of the depolarization process along a nerve or muscle fibre is called an impulse. Each muscle or nerve fibre has its own threshold of excitation. This refers to the amount of stimulation necessary to cause the membrane to depolarize. It should be obvious, however, that one the membrane depolarizes, the depolarization process will travel over the entire membrane.

This is referred to as the all-or-none law and it applies to all nerve and muscle fibres. To state the all-or-none law another way, it means that if a fibre responds to a stimulus it responds completely; otherwise it does not respond at all.

Roles of Muscles

A muscle may contract fully or partially with maximum force or less. It may contract isometrically or isotonically, singly or as a member of a group. Also, muscles may act in different roles and changes quickly from one role to another. At any given time a muscle may play the role of agonist, antagonist, stabilizer or neutralizer.

Neutralizer

A muscle plays role of neutralizer when it equalizes or nullifies one or more actions of another muscle. In order to neutralize each other, two muscles just cause opposite movements. For example, the pectoralis major an the latissimus dorsi both contribute to adduction of the humerus.

In addition, the pectoralis flexes the humerus while the latissimus dorsi extend it. When the two muscles neutralize each other's function of flexion and extension, the result is adduction. Neutralizing actions similar to this occur in almost all movements of body segments.

Antagonist

A muscle is antagonistic to a movement when it must relax to allow the movement to occur. Antagonist muscles cause actions opposite those caused by the agonist muscles. The triceps brachii is antagonistic to elbow flexion. Therefore, the triceps must relax to permit flexion.

In elbow extension the triceps are agonistic and the biceps are antagonistic. In other terms, agonists and antagonists cause opposite movements. Generally, extensors and flexors are antagonistics to each other, as are abductors and adductors, and medical rotators, and lateral rotators.

Agonist

A muscles is an agonist when its contraction contributes to the body movement. For instance, in flexing the elbow, the biceps brachii is a mover, as are seven other muscles in this case. Some muscles may cause more than one action in a particular joint and some cause movements in more than one joint.

Stabilizers

In order for a segment of the body to move, the part on which it moves must be stabilized. For instance, when the arm moves at the shoulder joint, the shoulder girdle must be held firm by the contraction of muscles in that region. Without being stabilized the shoulder girdle would move, and thus reduce the effectiveness of the arm action.

Similar examples could be given. During motor performances various body parts are often stabilized by the contraction of skeletal muscles.

Coordinated Action of Muscles

Motor muscles almost always act in group rather than individually. Whenever a major motor movement occurs, many muscles contract and numerous coordinations take place. Those agonistic to the movement contract concentrically, and they must be coordinated with each other to produce maximum contractile force. At the same time the muscles antagonistic to the movement must relax to permit the movement to occur.

Simultaneously numerous other muscles contract isometrically to stabilize parts of the body on which the active segments move, and these contractions must be coordinated with the agonists and antagonists.

Many other contractions are required to neutralize undesired actions of some of the contracting muscles. In order for a well-coordinated movement or series of movements to occur, all of the various muscles involved must act in their respective roles with precise timing. Hence, when we attempt to improve skill, we try to perfect the coordination of the contractions of the many different muscles involved, and at the same time we attempt to relax better those muscles antagonistic to the desired movements.

Kinds of Muscles

There are two basic types of muscles in the human body, smooth and striated. Striated muscles is of two type, skeletal and cardiac. Thus it can be said that three types of muscle exist: smooth, cardiac, and skeletal.

All three types possess the basic characteristics of muscle tissue: extensibility, the ability to stretch; elasticity, the ability to return to normal length when the stretching force is removed; excitability, the ability to be excited by stimuli; and contractibly, the ability to apply tension when stimulated.

The different types of muscle have some characteristics in common, but they differ in several ways. For instance, the contractile process is the same in each, but the speed of contraction, duration of contraction, and purposes which they serve differ greatly. Each muscle is especially suited in both structure and function to its particular task.

Smooth muscle is innervated by the autonomic nervous system and cannot be controlled voluntarily. It is located in the walls of the internal organs other than the heart, such as the blood vessels, intestines, alimentary tract, and stomach. Smooth muscle is characterized by smooth-appearing muscle cells are much are slender and tapered towards both ends.

The cells are much smaller than those found in skeletal muscles. Each cell has a single nucleus located about midway along the fibre. Compared with skeletal muscle, smooth muscle possesses (i) great ability, (ii) more sensitivity to temperature and chemical stimuli, (iii) greater ability for sustained contraction, and (iv) more sluggishness in its movements.

Cardiac muscle forms the walls and partition of the heart. Like other muscle tissue, it is composed of thousands if fibres. The most striking characteristic of its fibre are (i) they are involuntary, meaning we contract; (ii) they are striated, similar to skeletal muscle; and (iii) they are arranged in syncytia, meaning they appear to be interconnected with each other. Recent discoveries have shown that the fibres are actually separate in structure but function as syncytia.

Skeletal Muscle

All motor movements of the body involve contractions of skeletal muscles. As a result of their contractions, made in correct sequence and with sufficient force, man is able to walk, run, swim, throw objects, breathe, and perform numerous other movements.

There are more than 400 skeletal muscles, each of which is shaped differently. In almost every case muscles appear in pairs on the two sides of the body. Skeletal muscles are voluntarily controlled by nerve impulses transmitted from the central nervous system.

Contraction

A muscles has the capacity only to contract or not contract. When it contracts, the muscle always applies tension toward its middle. This may result in a concentric contraction, meaning the muscle shortens, or an eccentric contraction, meaning that while it applies tension the muscle gets longer because the resistance is greater than the tension.

A muscle is said to contract isotonically when it either shortens or lengthens, and thus movement occurs, or isometrically when no movement occurs because the tension is not sufficient to overcome the resistance against the muscle.

A muscle can contract with varying degrees of force at any particular time, and the amount of force is voluntarily controlled. The contractions may range from very mild to maximal. The force of contraction at a given time is controlled by two variables: (i) the number of motor units that are activated, and (b) the stimulating frequency or rate.

The fibres of a skeletal muscles are organized into motor units, with each consisting of a motor neuron and all muscle fibres innervated by that neuron. A motor nerve fibre originates in the central nervous system and enters the skeletal muscle which it serves. Near its end the nerve fibre separates into many branches, each of which is attached to a muscle fibre.

When the motor neuron transmits impulses, the impulses pass through the branches of the neuron and go to all the muscle fibres in the motor unit. All the active muscle fibres within the motor unit respond in unison.

The muscle fibres in a motor unit are not grouped together but are dispersed throughout the muscle. Therefore, if a single-motor unit were to contract, it would appear that the total muscle experienced a mild contraction. If additional motor units contract, the muscle applies greater tension.

When the central nervous system provides a stimulus to a particular upon whether the stimulus is enough toe exceed the threshold of the nerve fibre. If the threshold is exceeded, impulses are transmitted through the fibre. If the threshold is exceeded, impulses are transmitted through the fibre to all the muscle fibre which it serves.

When the impulses reach the nerve endings acetylcholine is released, causing depolarization of the cell membrane and a rapid influx of calcium ions. This excites the entire muscle fibre and caused it to contract.

The contraction actually results from interaction between the layers of myosin and actin filaments which causes the actin filaments to be pulled inwards among the myosin filaments, thus thyrogenic the fibre. Once the calcium ions have been released into the interior of the muscle fibre, the contraction will continue until they are removed.

Within the muscle fibre is a substance called relaxing factor, which has a natural affinity for calcium ions and combines with them within a few hundredths of a second. This action neutralizes the calcium and caused the muscle fibre to relax. Following is a more detailed explanation of what actually happens when a muscle contracts.

It has been found that during contraction, the length of the A-band remains constant. The length of the I-band, however, changes according to the change in length of the muscles. Since the A-band consists primarily of the thick myosin filaments, it is assumed that these filaments remain a constant length.

The H-band varies with the increase or decrease of muscle length, and with the increase or decrease of the length of the I-band, but the distance from the end of one H-zone through the Z-line to the end of the next H-zone remains the same.

Because of this relationship, it has been concluded that when the muscle changes length, the two sets of filaments slide past each other. When the muscle shortens greatly, the needs of the filaments meet, and heavy areas can be seen under and electron microscope.

The sliding action of the filaments is probably linked to the action of the cross-bridges located on the myosin filaments. Each myosin molecule is thought to have one bridge. Huxley postulated that the bridges could oscillate, hooking up with specific sites on the actin filaments pulling them a short distance, and them returning to their original configuration, ready to hook up with another active site of pull the actin filaments a short distance farther.

This scheme explains many of the observed phenomena of muscle contraction, and it is presently accepted as the most probable explanation of contraction.

The energy source for the movement of the bridges is supplied by ATP, a high-energy chemical compound present in all muscle tissue. This compound is produced by the mitochondria, organelles found in all cells which are specifically responsible for the energy production of the cell.

What causes the bridges to connect to the actin filaments so that contraction can occur? When impulses arrive at the muscle fibre from a motor-nerve, they are conducted into the fibre through a portion of the sacrolasmic reticulum called the T-tubule.

The T-tubule is a narrow tubule running transversely through the muscles fibre between two somewhat larger channels called terminal cisternae. These three structures are commonly referred to as the triad. The triads carry the action potential quickly into the innermost parts of the myofibrils.

A much finer system of tubules extends lengthwise along each myofibril between the triads. Calcium is normally bound to the fine reticulum along the sides of the myofibrils.

When the signal passes through the reticulum, calcium is mobilized in the form of calcium ions, which initiate chemical reactions between the myosin and actin filaments causing them to gain an affinity for each other, and thus contraction occur.

The calcium ions remain in the myofibrils for only a short time because of the strong affinity the reticulum has for the ions. The reticulum, or some chemical on its surface, is the relaxing factor.; that is, it causes the muscle to relax by binding the calcium ion.

The specific and detailed chemical reactions involved in contraction are not known at this time. However, there are some facts that give insight into the process. First, for contraction to occur, ATP, magnesium and calcium ions must be present. To break the linkage, the fibres must be free from Ca^{++} ions, they must have Mg^{++} , and they must have ATP.

Second ATP is probably located on the actin filaments as the muscle awaits contraction. Third, myosin is probably an ATP-base in the presence of calcium ions. In other words, when calcium comes into the fibril, myosin is able to release energy from ATP to cause contraction.

This energy probably develop strong electrostatic charges along the actin filaments, and these attract the oppositely charged cross bridges of the myosin filaments.

Thus contraction takes place with the filaments overlapping each other as the muscle shorten.

The importance of ATP to both contraction and relaxation should be stressed. If contraction occurs until the supply of ATP is depleted, the linkages stay locked, and the muscles goes into sustained contraction. An example of this situation is the rigidity of muscles after death. If ATP is added, the muscles can again relax.

It is generally known that as the speed of shortening increases, the tension exerted by a muscles decrease. This can be explained by assuming that the cross-bridges form their attachments at a given rate. There is only a certain period of time available for a bridge to become attached as the actin filaments slide past. Therefore, if the speed of contraction were increased, the number of effective bridges would be decreased and the tension would decrease.

The total energy of a muscle over a given distance increases with the tension or load on the muscle. This can be easily explained if we realize that as the load increases, more active sites must be activated. Since more ATP is used when more sites are activated, the energy cost for an increased load would naturally be greater.

Structure

Skeletal muscles come in a great variety of shapes and sizes: long and slender; short and chubby; round, flat, or fan-shaped. The fleshy portion, known as the belly, tapers into tough fibrous tissue at the ends called tendons. Most muscles are taper into only one tendon at each end.

Examples are the sartorius and rectus femoris

muscles. A muscle is known as a biceps when it is divided at one end to form two tendons. The muscles in the front of the upper arm is such as muscle. A triceps divides into three tendons at one end and has three points of attachment. The triceps branchii, in the back of the upper arm, is an example.

Skeletal muscles attach at both ends either directly or indirectly to the skeletal system. The attachment nearest the midline of the body is the proximal attachment. The attachment farther from the midline is the distal attachment.

When the muscle contracts it does not pull mostly on the distal end, but rather it pulls toward its middle, exerting equal force on the attachments at both ends. Which bone moves as a result of the force depends on the relative stability of the bones at the time. Stability of a bone at a given time is determined, to a large degree, by muscles acting as stabilizers.

Most skeletal muscles are single-joint muscles, meaning they cross only one joint and cause movement in the joint only. Examples are the soleus, which crosses only the ankle joint; the gluteus maximum, which crosses only the hip joint; and the pectoralis major which crosses only the shoulder joint. Some muscles cross two of more joints, and are thus known as multi-joint muscles. Examples are the biceps brachii, which crosses the elbow and shoulder joints; the sartorius, which crosses both the hip and elbow and shoulder joints; the sartorius, which crosses both the hip and knee joints; and the flexor digitorum profundus, which crosses the wrist joint and the three joints of each of the four fingers.

The basic unit of skeletal muscle, as in any tissue, is the muscle cell or fibre, a long cylindrical structure containing numerous nuclei. The nuclei are located immediately under the cell membrane.

In some muscles, the fibres are thought to be shorter than the muscle as a whole, and must be connected to each other, and the bony surfaces they moved with a network tough connective tissues.

The connective tissue around the cell, just outside the cell membrane, is called endomysium. Groups of muscle fibres are know as fascicles and are visible to the eye. The muscle as a whole is surrounded by a layer of connective tissue called epimysium.

This connective tissue network binds together the single contractile units and of units, and it integrates their actions while allowing a certain degree of freedom and autonomy among the cells.

Each muscle fibre is innervated by a branch of a motor nerve and is fed by a rich network of capillaries, which surround the fibre in such a way that they can accommodate the changes in shape during contraction that they can accommodate the changes in shape during contraction. A nerve fibre and all the muscle fibres it serves compose a motor unit.

Most of the interior of muscle fibre is made up of myofibrils, the protein contractile elements of the cell. About 90% of the substance of the myofibril is represented by the three proteins, myosin, actin, and tropomyosin. The banded appearance of striate muscle is due to the arrangement of the actin and myosin filaments.

The dark area is anisotropic and the light area is isotropic. These terms refer to the optical properties of the tissue. The central region of the A-ban d is often less dense than the rest of the band and is known as the H-zone.

The dense A-band consists of overlapping thick and thin filaments, while the lighter I-band consists of thin filaments alone, and the H-zone consists of thick filaments alone. The I-band is bisected by a dense narrow line, called the Z-membrane or Z-link. From one Z-line to the next is called a sarcomere.

A myofibril cut on a transverse of cross section shows a hexagonal pattern with the thick filaments in the centre of thin filaments in a repeating pattern throughout the muscle. The two kinds of filaments are linked by a system of cross-bridges which play in important role in muscle contraction.

Mechanics of Movement

All motor movements of the human body result from the actions of body levers, which are moved by muscular forces. The following points will help to explain the coordinated actions of levers and muscles.

(i) In the body a bone or combination of bones composes a rigid bar known as lever.

(ii) The joint is the fulcrum, the point around which the lever rotates.

(iii) The application of force is at the attachments of the muscles which produce the force when they contract.

(iv) Resistance against the movement is caused by the weight of the body segment plus any external weight or force.

Muscles furnish the force, and levers constitute the simple machines that cause muscular force to be useful in motor movements. In some cases the leverage can be improved by making certain adjustments in the mechanics of the movements. For the most part, levers of the body have relatively short effort arms, and long resistance arms.

Such levers are known as speed levers because they are adapted to sweeping-type fast movements at the expense of the application of great force.

Levers are of three types, first class, second class, and third class. A first-class lever is one where the fulcrum lies between the effort and the resistance.

2

THE NERVOUS SYSTEM

Through the nervous system a person is able to interpret and respond to the events of his environment and to coordinate the functions of his organs and muscles to accomplish the various tasks of life. In essence, the purpose of the nervous system is communication.

All body movements, both external and internal are coordinated by muscles are unable to contract; consequently, the organism is unable to function or even survive. The timing with which impulses arrive at particular muscles determines skills. Physiologically, the coordination of movement into exact patterns is a highly complicated process.

From the standpoint of function, the nervous system is divided into two parts: autonomic system and voluntary system. The autonomic system is responsible for the automatic functions of the organs. While this system is of utmost importance to the functions of the organs. While this system is of utmost importance to the functions of life it is only of secondary importance in the preparation for athletic performance.

The voluntary system is the part of the nervous system over which we can exercise conscious control, but which often operates below the conscious level. This is the portion of the system which controls the skeletal muscles.

Structurally, the voluntary system is divided into the central nervous system and the peripheral nervous system. The CNS includes only the brain and spinal cord, and the PNS includes all of the other nerve tissue in the voluntary system. The tissue of the PNS is distributed in all areas of the body and connects with the CNS at various levels along the spinal column.

Control of Motor Activity

In addition to the transmission of impulses across motor neurons, motor activity is dependent upon (i) the coordination of impulse from sensory organs throughout the body, and (ii) information from the higher centres where memories of previous experience are stored and conscious movements are initiated.

Higher Centres

Certain portion of the central nervous system are much involved in motor performances. This is a discussion of those parts and other processes.

Most of the cranial cavity is occupied by the largest section of the brain called the cerebrum. The surface of cerebrum is known as the cortex. The cerebral cortex appears to be the seat of voluntary movement. It orders gross muscular actions, but relies on lower levels of the CNS to control the details.

The cortex is responsible for consciousness, perception, and memory , interpretation, and reasoning. A combination of these functions results in what is known as judgement. The exact response, is probably based upon the success or failure of similar to be rejected.

The more extensive and well established its store of memories, the faster and more accurate will be its responses in terms of muscular actions. If the particular situation at hand is a near duplicate of successfully handled situations of the past, the response will probably nearly duplicate past responses. But if the problem is unique or only rarely nearly duplicate past responses, but if the problem is unique or only rarely experienced, the chances of responding quickly and correctly are considerably lessened. In the latter, case the judgment of how to respond will be based on the most nearly related experiences.

All of this indicates that children should be provided with opportunities for experience in a great variety of basic movement patters before their interests become too specialized. Otherwise, overall skill development will be limited. Extensive experience in motor movements will undoubtedly cause development of the nervous system which will result in increased success in a variety of motor movement pattern.

The parts of the cerebral cortex directly concerned with motor movements are the sensory cortex, motor cortex, and pre-motor cortex.

The sensory cortex is the terminating area for most of the afferent information coming from the various sensory receptors. Interpretation of the sensory impulses takes place in this area. On the basis of the interpretation action is initiated.

The motor cortex provides stimulation to individual muscles and to small muscle groups. A single shock of near-threshold level from an electrode in the motor cortex area usually elicits a discrete motor movement such as a flick of the finger or a deviation of the lip.

The muscle groups of the body are represented in this area according to the discreteness of the movement required. Thumb and forefingers, lips, local cords, etc. have large representation, while the areas for postural muscle activities are relatively small.

A large shock in this area, however, may result in a coordinated limb movement to move that limb to a fixed "final position." Changing the position of the electrode minutely could cause that limb to change to another "final position" demonstrating that the motor cortex does have coordination function as well as single response functions.

The pre-motor cortex produces impulses for complication movement. It has been found that loss of function in this area of the brain destroys the sequence and timing of complex movement patters. Many coordinations are basically repetition so the performance of the pre-motor area is not as complex as it might seem. But still it is the key area of the brain so far as motor performance is concerned.

The most important differences between the motor cortex and the pre-motor cortex are the functional differences. When first learning a skill in which conscious attention must be given to each action, the origin of the movements very likely shifts to the pre-motor cortex. However, the motor cortex still acts as a relay station fibres passing through it from the pre-motor cortex.

The Interior of the cerebrum is composed mostly of white matter which links cerebrum to all the levels of the spinal cords. This while matter provides fast and often direct impulse conduction from the higher centres of the central nervous system to the various junctions in the spinal cord, and vice vera.

The nerve fibres composing the white matter are bundled together according to common functions; the bundles are called nerve tracts The afferent bundles are ascending tracts and transmit sensory impulses are descending tracts which conduct impulses from the higher centres to the motor nerves.

In addition to the white matter in the interior of the cerebrum, several clusters of gray mater, called nuclei, are present. Little is known about the functions of some of these clusters. However, the largest and probably the most important relay centre for both motor and sensory impulses. It has extensive connections with the cortex.

The cerebellum is not in the main line of impulse travel between the cerebral cortex and the spinal cord, but it is tied to the main tracts through a series of collateral nerve endings. As far as motor performance is concerned, the function of the cerebellum is to modify motor impulses and thereby contribute to the perfection of the desired movements. An indefinite a movement nor will he be able to make needed adjustments as the movement progress.

He will exhibit extreme inaccuracy, overcompensation, and a marked jerkiness in movement. In fact, the cerebellum can predict from the present state of the muscles and joints what will occur as the movement progress, and distribute signals which prevent errors in the movement pattern.

The brain stem is the direct connection between the brain and the spinal cod, and thus impulses pass through it in both direction. The functions of the brain stem are more directly concerned with atomic responses than with responses involving the voluntary nervous system. Part of the stem governs the rates of respiration and heart beat.

Some authorities think inhibitory impulses originate in the cerebrum, but most neural experts claim they originate in the brain stem. The inhibitory impulses produce conditions which make it necessary for more facilitative impulses to arrive in order to excite a neuron in the spinal cord. If this phenomenon did not exist with a normal degree of efficiency, we would experience unwanted contractions, and perhaps the inability to stop contractions short of complete fatigue.

Thus, motor activity is influenced by the sum of all of the information reaching the motor-neuron from both the higher centres and the sensor organs. The descending impulses from the higher centres of the brain, including those voluntarily evoked, are modified on the basis of information from the receptor organs because of the many possible alternatives available through the synoptic system of interneurons within the spinal cord.

This coordination of motor information makes possible the movement pattern associated with athletic performances.

Sensory information

Much information comes to the motor neuron from sensory organs by way of the sensory nerves. Sensory organs are located in and around the muscles, in the skin, and in various other kinds of tissue. One of the most important sensory organs is the muscle spindle.

Each spindle consists of a connective tissue sheath containing several intro-fusal fibres. These sheaths are parallel to the regular muscle fibre or extra-fusal fibres and are large enough to be visible to the naked eye.

The muscle fibres in the sheath have a central, heavy nucleated area called the nuclear bag, which has lost is striation and is unable to contract. Whenever the muscle is stretched, the nuclear bag is stretched, and nerve endings, found entwined around the nuclear centre of the spindle, called annulospiral endings, are excited. From these nerve endings come large type A nerve fivers which carry information concerning the stretch of the spindle to the dorsal root of the spinal cord.

On each side of the annulospiral endings are flowerspray receptors, which transmit on smaller nerve fibres than the type a fibre used by the annulospiral endings. The function of the flowerspray receptors is thought to be the same as that of the annulospiral endings except that a much greater stretch is required to excite these receptors.

The impulses from the spindle are monosynaptic, and they are transmitted back to the same muscle from which they came. The striated portions of the muscles in the spindle are innervated by gamma fibres from the ventral portion of the spinal cord, as opposed to the large alpha efferent or motor neurons which transmit to the extra-fusal fibres.

Contraction of the two end portion of the spindle will cause the centre portion to stretch and excite the annulospiral endings of the spindle. Such a mechanism is called a servomechanism, and it allow the body to contract and arm or leg to a predetermined length in a coordinated movement. The spindle also functions to measure muscle length, the extent of stretch applied to the muscle, and the rate the stretch is applied.

How well the muscle spindle function in the quadriceps muscle can be tested by tapping the patellar tendon. This stretches the extra-fusal muscle and spindle, which excites the annulospiral endings. In turn, this results in a feedback of information to the extra-fusal fibres to shorten their length.

Another important sensory organ is the Golgi tendon apparatus. It lies between the fibres of a tendon and is excited by high tension on the tendon. Its function is to detect too much load on the muscle and to protect the muscle from injury.

Excitation of this organ sends a signal on a large type A fibre to an inhibitory interneuron which inhibits the contractions of the muscle being stretched.

Pacinian corpuscles also function to inform the higher centres of the body's position. Because of their presence, a person is able to tell where his body parts are without visual information.

Neurons

Cells in the nervous system are called neurons; in other words, neurons are nerve cells or fibres. Neurons exhibit the properties of irritability and conductivity. When a cell has irritability, it will respond to a stimulus, and if it passes the response to other cells, it has conductivity.

The responses conducted by neurons are known as impulses. There are three types of neurons; sensory, motor, and internuncial. Sensory and motor neurons relay messages to and from the central nervous system.

If a sensory neuron receives a stimulus the

information usually terminates in a specialized area of the brain where it is interpreted. On the other hand, a stimulus may originate in the brain, travel through motor neurons, and terminates in a muscle causing the muscle to contract. Some sensory impulses may travel to the spinal cord and there may transfer to motor neurons and arrive at the muscle without any brain involvement.

Sensory neurons are different from motor neurons, but they both have the same basic components. Each neuron has a soma or cell body with its nucleus and cytoplasm and several short processes called dendrites and as long process called the axon.

These processes are functionally very important because through them the neuron is able to accomplish the task of passing information from one area of the body to another.

Spinal Nerves

Extending from the spinal cord and 21 pairs of large nerves, called spinal nerves. Each one is about the size of a pencil and contains thousands of individual axon. The axons in a spinal nerve vary in length, with the longer axons being several feet and the shorter ones hardly measurable. The larger axons are capable of conducting over 2000 impulses per second.

There is a tendency to confuse the term "nerve" with "neuron" or "nerve fibre." Neurons are the basic cells in the nervous system and include the axon and the cell body. Nerves are groups of axons.

The cells bodies of motor neurons are located in the anterior horn of the spinal cord, and their axons group together and extent, via the spinal nerves, to the muscle fibres. Sensory neuron cells bodies are located near the posterior side of the spinal cord in the dorsal root ganglion. However, their axons originate in specialized sensory receptors throughout the body and carry information up the spinal nerves to the spinal cord.

Thus, the spinal nerves are groups of axons from both motor and sensory neurons which function much like a cross-country telephone cable, with messages travelling both ways in the communication process.

Interneurons

All sensory and motor nerve cells in the body can be classified functional as excitatory neurons. However, in the gray matter of the spinal cord, there are short neurons called interneurons which can be either excitatory or inhibit nerve cell transmission by hyperpolarizing the membrane. Others inhibit nerve cell transmission by hyperpolarizing the cell membrane.

The obvious importance of an interneuron system which can inhibit as well as excite is that information from other areas an be modified to suit the needs of the organism by either passing it along the pathways or stopping it from being transmitted.

For example, the inhibition or blocking of nerve impulses to those muscles in opposition to a desired movement is of utmost importance to the efficiency and speed of that movement. The process of inhibiting contractions is mostly automatic and is don at the subconscious level.

However, it can also be done consciously to some extent. Ordinarily, with additional practice of a movement the inhibition of the antagonistic muscles becomes quicker and more complete, and the movement becomes more efficient and effective. Thus, the nervous system can either excite or inhibit muscle activity depending on information received from the higher centres or from receptor organs.

Motor Neurons

Special attention is devoted to motor neurons because they carry impulses to muscles. The motor neuron, like other cells is surrounded by a cell membrane which is metabolically very active, and which provides a barrier between the intracellular and the extracellular fluid so that a membrane potential of electrical difference between the inside and outside of the cell can be maintained.

The potential difference between the inside and outside of a typical motor neuron has been measured at about –70 milli-volts. When the ions rush through the membrane and it becomes depolarized.

The axon of a motor neuron is enclosed in an insulated sheath called the neurolemma or sheath of Schwann, and the larger axon also have a myelin sheath. It is the myelin sheath that is responsible for the white colour of the nerve tissue in the brain, spinal cord, and many peripheral nerves.

The sheath of Schwann and the myelin sheath are interrupted at regular intervals by structures called nodes of Ranvier, which are small insulated areas almost 500 times as permeable as the membranes of some unmyelinated fibres.

Since the myelin sheath is an excellent insulator which prevents almost all flow of ions from the cell membrane, the depolarization of myelinated fibres occurs at the nodes of Ranvier, instead of continuously along the entire fibre.

Its conductions from node to node is thought to be the explanation for the high transmission rate of myelinated fibres, and probably conserves energy for the axons since only the nodes need to depolarize. It is this property which allows information to be transmitted the length of the axon at the speed of up to 100 meters/sec.

Motor Units

As the axon of the motor neuron approaches the muscle fibres, it loses the myelin sheath and branches to contact the muscle cells it innervates. The motor neuron, with all of the muscle cells innervated by its branches, is referred to as a motor unit.

The number of muscle fibres innervated by the motor-neuron depends upon the quality of movement expected of the muscle. Usually, slow-contracting muscles, such as the soleus, have several hundred muscle fibres in a motor unit, while fast-contracting muscles, such as those controlling the eye, may have as few as ten to fifteen fibres in each unit. Impulses which travel along an axon of a motor neuron will activate all the muscle fibres in the motor unit almost simultaneously.

The Fewer fibres included in a unit, the finer will be the gradation of the contraction which is possible. The fibres of the motor unit will very likely be scattered among the fibres of other unit in the muscle.

Establishment of Skill Patterns

The correct and efficient functioning of the nervous system is the key to motor skills. A coordinated act is the result of each movement occurring in the correct sequence and timing and with the right amount of force. When a highly coordinated movement occurs, It appears smooth and rhythmical.

Of course, motor movements occur only as a result of muscular contractions, and under normal conditions skeletal muscles respond only to nerve impulses. Therefore, when a coordinated movement occurs, it is the result of nerve impulses reaching the proper muscles with sufficient intensity at the correct time.

The contractions of the muscles then cause the movements which constitute the skilled performance. The key to improving coordinations is development of the nervous system.

Neural Junctions

In this section will a discussion of the nerve-nerve and the nerve-muscle junctions.

Synapses

A synapse is a junction between two or more neurons. There junctions operate much like the motor end plates, with a release of a chemical which causes depolarization of the fibre to which the message is being passed. Information is passed from one neuron to another via the synapse which connects them.

The body is able to regulate in activity of motor neurons by the amount of chemical released at the synapses. For instance, if enough of the vesicle at the end of one neuron release their chemical, the membranes potential of the connecting neurons will be reduced to a critical value, and depolarization will occur.

However, sometimes the amount of chemical liberated is insufficient to cause depolarization, but it does lower the membrane potential. This is called facilitation, and it prepares the neuron to fire more readily if a second volley of impulses arrives while the membrane is still facilitated. If this occurs because of repeated impulse volleys from the same synapse, it is called temporal summation. If several synapses are in proximity to each other, their combined effort is called spatial summation.

Acetylcholine has been identified as the transmitter substance in some synapses. Located close to synapses is a supply of the enzyme cholinesterase which inactivates ACh to allow the membrane potential to be restored quickly (re-polarized).

Motor End Plate

The branches of the nerve fibre contact the muscle fibres at motor end plates. Small knob-like processes containing vesicles of acetylcholine fit into depression on the muscle sarcoplasm called synaptic clefts. When impulses arrive at the end plate, the vesicles release their ACh, and depolarization of the membrane occurs.

Another chemical, cholinesterase, functions to inactivate ACh almost immediately so that the membrane can again re-polarize.

3

AGILITY AND POWER

Agility

Agility is often represented by the terms "manoeuvrability," "mobility," and "shiftiness." It is the ability to change direction of the body and its parts rapidly. Agility is combination of several athletic traits, including strength, reaction time, speed of movement, power, and coordination.

It is demonstrated in such movements as dodging, zigzag running, stopping and starting, and changing body positions quickly.

Agility is both general and specific. Examples of general agility are as follows: football running back who eludes would-be tacklers by shifting and dodging while he runs; a soccer player who cleverly manoeuvres the ball past his opponents as he zigzags down the field; a basketball player who darts past his opponent, stops quickly to leap into the air for a shot; a another as he does a complex routine; or a skier who gracefully zigzags down a slope continually shifting the body parts to maintain balance and to manoeuvre.

Specific agility may be demonstrated in the rapid manoeuvre-ability of the hands and arms, as in playing a piano. Some athletes have "good hands" or "quick hands," meaning their hands and arms are highly manoeuvrable, which enables them to handle a ball or other object with unusual proficiency.

Factors which Influence Agility

Several factors relate to agility in different ways. Following are points of information about the different factors:

Somatotype

Tall and lanky people tend to lack agility, as do obese or pear-shaped individuals. Conversely people of medium highest or shorter who are well muscled tend to be highly manoeuvrable. To related to somatotypes, it can be said that mesomorphies, and meso-ectomorphs tend to be agile, while ectomorphs and endomorphs tend to be less agile. However, there are exception to this rule.

Age and Sex Type

Young children increase steadily in agility to about the age of 12, when they enter the "awkward years" of fast growth. During this period of about three years, their agility tends not to increase and may even decrease.

After the rapid growth period is over, agility increases once again at a rather steady rate until maturity is reached.

Boys are only slightly more agile then girls during the years before puberty. After puberty boys increase in agility to a level considerably higher than that of girls.

Overweight

Excess weight detractors directly and significantly from agility. It increase the inertia of the body and its parts, and it reduces the speed of muscle contraction, thereby causing changes in direction to be less rapid.

Fatigue

Fatigue detracts greatly from agility, because fatigue has a diminishing effect on the components of agility, such as strength, reaction time, speed of movement, and power.

How to Increase Agility

Agility either, general or specific, can be improved by increasing the athletic components which constitute it. Coordination involved in the specific movements is by far the most important component of agility. If a person is poorly coordinated (awkward), he will lack agility regardless of the other traits he possesses.

Therefore, great emphasis should be placed on developing coordination in the movement patterns essential to the given performance.

Improvement of the other components of agility offer limited, but worth-while, opportunities. Therefore, only the application of the components to agility is discussed here.

Some people lack enough strength to control the inertia of the body in motion effectively. For example, great leg strength is needed to abruptly stop a 200-point body in motion at 20 mph. Thus, it is apparent that variability of the body. Power, which is demonstrated in projecting the body, is an important contributor to agility, because in the absence of adequate power the body cannot be projected rapidly in any direction, nor can it be accelerated rapidly. Fast reaction time is essential in game situations where a performer must respond quickly to an external stimulus with an act of agility.

For example, he reacts to immediate game situations, or to the moves made by his opponents, or to immediate game situations, or to the moves made by his opponents, or to signals given by his team-mates. Slow reactions detract from one's manoeuvrability, while improved reaction time enhances agility. In addition to fast reactions, an agile performer displays, fast movements, which often enable him to outmanoeuvre his opponents

A normal amount of flexibility is essential to full ranges of motion and to smooth, graceful, and effective movement. However, it seems doubtful that more than normal flexibility would improve agility.

Even though the components mentioned above form the basis for ability and have potential for improving agility, it should be recognized that the best way to improve agility in specific movement patterns is to practice those patterns correctly over and over, and to do so at high speeds. This approach emphasizes the development of specific coordinations, the prime component of agility and at the same time contributes to some of the other components.

Significance of Agility

Agility is very important in all activities involving quick changes in positions of the body and it parts. Fast starts and stops and quick changes in direction are fundamental to good performance in practically all court games, such as basketball, tennis, badminton, and volleyball, and in many field games, such as soccer, football, speedball, and baseball.

These games require running agility. Gymnastics and diving also depended largely upon rapid body movements and quick changes in body position.

Conversely, there are some activities which do not depend on agility to any large degree. Examples are track-and-field events, and swimming.

The importance of agility in athletic performances can be summarized by saying that in certain activities it is fundamental to good performance, and may even be the most important single characteristic, while in certain other activities agility is practically non-contributing. In the majority of activities, performance will improve with increased agility.

Power

Power is a combination of strength and speed. As staged by De Vries, if two individuals can each lift 100 pounds a distance of three feet, but one can do it with twice as much speed as the other, then he is twice as powerful. Likewise, if the two individuals move at the same speed, but one works against twice as much resistance as the other, then he has demonstrated twice as much power.

Factors which Influence Power

Several factors relate to power and influence it in different ways. Following are brief discussions of these relationships.

Somatotypes

The available evidence shows that mesomorphs are more powerful for their size than either endomorphs or ectomorphs. This is partly accounted for by the fact that mesomorphs have higher proportions of muscle tissue per body weight. Decathlon performers seem to be consistently mesomorphic in body type. Endomorphic types are apparently more powerful than ectomorphs.

Age and Sex Type

These factors have essentially the same relationships to power as they have to strength.

Weight Training

It has been argued that weight training has a slowing effect on movement, and thus reduces power. Research does not support this idea. Conversely several studies support the ideas that (i) weight training does not reduce speed, and (ii) weight training can contribute to increased power.

Brown and Reley, using college freshmen basketball players, reported that weight training increased the vertical jump more than a general physical education program. Knudston learned that girls improved in the vertical jump after six weeks of weight training. Similar result were obtained by Mitchell, Ness and Sharos, Capen, Chui, and Hopkins.

Several studies indicate that weight training has a favourable effect on speed movement. Chui reported that times for the 60-yards sprint improved after three months of weight training. Meisel found weight training to be superior to other sports classes for improving speed for a 10-yard run. Hairabvedian also concluded that weight training was desirable for increasing running speed. A study by Masley and others indicated that weight training was superior to volleyball for increasing speed of movement and muscle coordination. Other researchers, namely, Calvin, Kut, and Usinitz and Keeney, also reported that weight training improved muscular coordination.

Overweight

Excess weight restricts speed, and thereby reduces

power, especially in performances where speed is the primary component of power.

The weight tends to reduce speed in the following ways; (i) fatty tissue in the muscles creates friction, and thus reduces the rate and efficiency of muscle contractions; (ii) the additional weight is dead weight, and thus increases the resistance against body movements.

How to Increase Power

It is possible for a person to be extremely strong and still not be extremely powerful; conversely he able to move rapidly against very light resistance and still not be able to overcome heavy resistance rapidly.

Thus, he maybe strong but not very powerful, or he may have great speed and not be very powerful. If, however, he possesses great strength combined with great speed of movement, ten he is powerful. Examples are seen of some person who are very strong, but lack the speed necessary to throw far, jump high, or strike hard.

Some other individuals can move with great speed against little resistance but have such limited strength that they cannot work effectively against heavy resistance.

Power can be increased by increasing strength without sacrificing speed, by increasing speed of movement without sacrificing strength, or by increasing both strength and speed. Usually the best approach for increasing power is to increase strength.

However, speed, the other component of power, can also be increased a limited amount as a result of training. The relative emphasis that performer puts on the development of strength and speed will depend upon the nature of the power performance for which he is in training. Both strength and sped can be emphasized by applying strong force through rapid movements.

The Strength Component

In considering the strength component of power, it must be remembered that under normal conditions a muscle contracts against some resistance, even if the resistance is only the weight of the body segment being moved. Because of this, strength can influence the rate of contraction. If all else remains equal, as muscles become stronger, the resistance against their contractions has less retarding effect on contractile speed.

Several research studies support the claim that power can be increased by increasing strength. Berger and Henpderson found that the relation ship between power and both static and dynamic leg strength was highly significant.

It was concluded that neither static nor dynamic strength was more related than the other to leg power. Several other studies support this claim. Start et al. stated that power is related to speed than to strength.

The Speed Component

In considering the speed component of power, recognize that the task to increase contractile speed of the mover muscles. Muscles contract at different rates in different individuals. Also, in the same individual, muscles differ rate in of contraction.

For instance, postural muscles tend to contract more

rapidly. In addition, there is a relationship between the size of different muscles and their speed of contraction; the smaller muscles tend to contract faster than the larger ones. However, there are exceptions to these rules.

Contractile speed, and, therefore, movement speed, is highly specific to muscles and muscle groups. For example, person A may have faster leg actions while person Y has faster arm actions.

Moreover, person X's arm extensor muscles may contact fast while his arm flexors contract at a relatively slow rate. In other words, speed varies with individual body movements. Although a person is a slow runner, he may have very fast arm and finger movements and vice versa. The following factors influence the speed component:

Muscle Length

If all else is equal, a longer muscle will produce proportionately greater speed than a shorter one. Assume that muscle X and Muscle Y contract at the same rate per linear inch of muscle, and that muscle X is fie times as long as muscle Y.

In this case muscle X will contract five times as far as in a given period of time simply because it is five times longer.

Coordination

Improved coordination of muscles can increase speed of movement because as the several mover muscles become better coordinated, they can cooperatively overcome external resistance with greater speed. Furthermore, when muscle contractions are well coordinated the contractile force one muscle arrives at the peak velocity of the previous force; consequently, the second force is more effective. Also, as the agonists and antagonists become better coordinated, the antagonists furnish less resistance to the movements.

There is evidence that antagonist muscles often relax more slowly than agonist muscles contract; thus ability to relax antagonist muscles may be an important factor in movements speed. If increased speed is practised at rates equal to or exceeding those used in performance.

Temperature

Hill claims that speed of contraction can be increased approximately 20% by raising body temperature 2^0 C, and that speed of contraction is diminished two to three times by a reduction in temperature of 10^0C.

The magnitude of this claim lacks sufficient evidence, but it is well established that increased body temperature does improve rates of contraction to some degree. Apparently such increase is due to decreased viscosity in the muscles.

Much work is required to raise body temperature measurable amount, and is one argument in favour of warm-up.

Muscle Efficiency

The efficiency of muscle contraction can be increased by training, and this may result in creased contractile speed. For example, if fatty tissue within a muscle is eliminated, or if viscosity is reduced, the result is greater efficiency and faster contraction.

If flexibility of resistance to movement, resulting in greater speed. Also, reducing neural inhibitions as a result of training will allow the performer to call voluntarily upon greater number of available motor units. The more motor units involved, the more quickly the resistance can be overcome.

Significance of Power

Power is demonstrated in athletic performance by the ability to project an object or the body through space. In projecting an object, the object might be thrown, kicked, or struck, and the power is determined by the more force to the bat at a faster rate, the bat will develop speed faster and will have greater velocity when it meets the ball.

In turn, the ball will be struck harder and will go farther. Thus, a powerful hitter is one who applies great force at a fast rate. A similar analysis could be made of the contact is broken, and that velocity is determined by the amount and rate of the force applied to the ball.

Shot putting depends more on pure power than nearly any other activity. If the angle of projection is constant, then the distance the shot will travel is related directly to its final velocity. Thus, the prime objective of the shot putter is to have the shot moving as fast as possible. To achieve this he must apply maximum force at maximum speed over as much distance as possible.

Similar examples of power could be given in the case of any throwing, kicking, or striking activity where maximum distance or maximum striking force is the objective.

In demonstration power by projecting the body, the key to success is still the correct combination of force and speed. In jumping, the performer attempts to move the body and rapidly as possible in the correct direction at the moment contact with the surface is broken. This final velocity is directly dependent upon the performer's ability to apply great force rapidly.

Sprint running is greatly dependent upon power because it is essentially a series of body projections. When one considers the prevalence of running, jumping, throwing, kicking, and striking in athletics, the significance of power performance becomes apparent.

Even though power always involves the components of strength and speed, it is interesting to note that different kinds of events require different combinations of the two components. Power events involving light resistance place emphasis upon speed, while performances against heavy resistance depend ore upon strength.

For example, consider the throwing events in track and field. The power needed in the 35-pound weight throw mostly is dependent upon strength. Speed is not a great limitation because even a very strong person will be unable to contract the muscles rapidly against 35 pounds of resistance.

However, speed is still a contributing factor. In putting the 16-pound shot, speed is of greater relative importance, but strength is still the predominant component of power, because the resistance is still relatively heavy. In throwing the college discus, speed contributes more and strength contributes less than in putting the shot.

The javelin throw is the throwing event that depends more on speed and less on strength than any of the other events, because the javelin is the lightest of the implements. In summary, it can be said that power performances involving heavy resistance depend greatly upon strength, while performances against lighter resistance depend more upon speed. In performances against very light resistance, speed is by far the more important of the two components of power.

4

METABOLISM

Metabolism is the process by which foods are broken down and converted into energy, and the energy is stored by the body. It involves numerous chemical reaction and some complex process.

Measurement of Metabolism

Metabolism can be defined as the "sum total of all the chemical reactions of the body," and it is expressed in units of heat. A calorie is the amount of heat needed to raise I gram of water I degree centigrade. The kilocalorie or Calorie is equal to 100 calories, and is commonly used to express energy expenditure of the body in heat units.

Oxygen Debt

During light exercise, the energy stored in the muscles plus the oxygen supplied by the cardiovascular system completely covers the oxygen needs of the body. However, at higher work levels, it is thought that the anaerobic energy scheme is used in ever-increasing amounts because the body is unable to provide sufficient oxygen to run the oxidative energy source.

As the anaerobic processes increase, lactic acid is produced. Of course, the more severe the work load, the greater the need for energy through the an aerobic process, and the amount of lactic acid in the blood increases.

As lactic acid is produced by the glycolytic pathway, it slowly diffuses into the blood stream and is carried throughout the body. Even though it is buffered by the blood, large quantities cause a decrease in the bloods pH, and can finally slow down or stop the metabolic processes.

Following work, about 85% of the lactic acid is re-synthesized back to glycogen, mainly in the liver, using the other 15% for energy for the conversion. Some lactic acid is also re-synthesized in the kidney, and some is used directly by cardiac muscle.

The re-synthesizing process appears to be enhanced during recovery by mild exercise, if the exercise is of low intensity os more lactic acid is not produced.

The anaerobic sources of energy can be divided into two general areas: lactacid and alact acid. The lactacid portion refers to the energy which can be produced through glycolysis with a production of lactic acid.

The alact acid portion refers to the stored energy available in the muscle such as ATP and CP, along with the stored oxygen bound as myoglobin which can be used to provide an immediate source for oxidative pathway. The alact acid portion is probably used in a very short period of time, and is restocked quickly following anaerobic work.

An oxygen debt, then, occurs whenever increased work creates a metabolic need for greater amounts of oxygen than can be supplied by the cardio-respiratory system. This can, of course. Occur at the beginning of light exercise if there is a flag in the metabolic processes.

However, this will be paid off quickly during the exercise itself if the body is able to reach a steady state. During high-intensity work, the oxygen debt will continue to build until work ceases. It will then be paid off during the recovery period. The maximum oxygen debt would probably be somewhere near 15 litres of oxygen; 4 litres to the alact acid portion and about 11 to 12 litres to eliminate the lactic acid.

It seems obvious that a person with great aerobic power or great ability to transport oxygen to the cells will have a much lower oxygen debt for a given workload than a person who is unable to supply a large quantity of oxygen to his cells.

Maximum Oxygen Uptake

The maximum oxygen uptake is perhaps the best indication of the ability to do high levels of cardiovascular work. Most physiologists standardize the VO_2 max by dividing by body weight in kilograms to get millilitres of oxygen per kilogram of body weight per minute. Outstanding distance runners, cross-country skiers, and other endurance athletes have VO_2's in the neighbourhood of 70 to 87 ml/kg/min.

This indicates that their cardiovascular system is able to provide large quantities of lactic acid. Therefore, they are able to produce energy using the more efficient energy-producing pathway for a longer period of time.

A strand pointed out that greater oxygen uptake potential is probably an inherited factory. Gains of only 10 to 20% in VO_2 can be achieved as a result of training programs. This means that a person whose VO_2 max is only 40 to 45 ml/kg/min may never be able to reach the necessary uptake levels needed to become an Olympic athlete in an endurance even.

Direct Colorimetry

Since the amount of heat released from the body is indicative of the metabolic rate, any means used to measure this output would be a good measurement of metabolism. To measure the amount of heat released from the body directly, a subject is placed in a large insulated chamber where the heat from the both warms the air of the chamber.

The air in the chamber is kept at a constant temperature, however, and the warm air from the body is forced through pipes in a cool water bath. The rate of heat gain by the water bath is then equal to the total heat output of the body.

This method has several disadvantages: (i) the equipment is expensive and difficult to use; (ii) the equipment is very inflexible and cannot be used except under ideal laboratory conditions; and (ii) the test could not be used as maximum work test without much difficulty. For these reasons, other methods of colorimetry were developed.

Indirect Colorimetry

Since all of the metabolic process of the body use oxygen and produce carbon dioxide, the energy is directly to the quantity of the respiratory gases consumed and expelled. If these gases are collected and measured, an estimation of metabolic rate can made. There are two basic ways that these gases can be measured: (i) closed-circuit colorimetry, and (ii) open-circuit colorimetry.

Closed-Circuit Colorimetry

The closed-circuit system is so named because the

subject breathes directly into and out of tank through a two-way valve with no access outside air. The expired air passes through a container of soda lime, which absorbs all of the CO_2 produced.

As the CO_2 is absorbed, the total volume of the tank decreases, and the amount of decrease is recorded on a revolving drum. The problems with the closed-circuit system are (i) the volume of the drum is sallow too small to be used during any kind of exercise, (ii) the resistance is too great, and (ii) the accuracy is poor.

Open-Circuit Colorimetry

The most commonly used method to measure metabolic rate during exercise is the open-circuit method. A subject works on a bicycle ergometer, or some other work device and air is expired through a high-velocity, low-resistance valve into some type of collecting apparatus such as a Douglas bag, or meteorological balloon.

The expired air is then analysed by either chemical or electronic analysers to determine the percentage of oxygen and carbon dioxide remaining in the air. The total volume of expired air can be measured by passing it through a gas meter, and the volume of inspired air can be computed from the percentage of nitrogen in the expired air.

Since the percentage of oxygen and carbon dioxide is always constant in the inspired air, the amount of oxygen used or carbon dioxide produced can easily be calculated by multiplying the percentage times the volume of both inspired and expired air, and determining the difference.

There are several new devices on the market to

measure oxygen consumption during work. One of these, the metabolic rate monitor, contains an oxygen sensor unit in a small portable motor, which senses changes in oxygen concentration.

If the concentration of oxygen decreases, the motor speeds up to re-establish the original concentration. The motor speed is metered and calibrated to indicate oxygen usage by the body.

Production of Energy in the Body

The final products of carbohydrate digestion are glucose, fructose, and galactose, with glucose being by far the most abundant of the three. Before these food particles can be used by the body, they must be processed through metabolic pathways to produce ATP. They are transported through the cell membrane with the help of insulin which is secreted by the pancreas.

Immediately upon entering the cell, the sugar molecule is captured by the cell through a process called phosphorylation, which means that a phosphate molecule is attached to the sugar molecule. This process is irreversible except in the liver where specific enzymes are available to break off the phosphate molecule so that the sugar molecule can be released into the blood stream again for energy several hours after a meal.

Glucose, then, can be used immediately for energy, or it can be stored in the form of glycogen for future use. Liver cells and muscle cells are both capable of storing large amount of glycogen which can be used in the energy schemes of the body during athletic performance.

Glycolysis

By far the most important pathway for the metabolism

of glucose is through glycolysis and the oxidation of the end products of glycolysis. The glycolytic energy scheme functions without oxygen and spoilt the glucose molecule to form 2 molecules of pyruvic acid.

Energy is required in the initial states of the pathway, but later, ATP is synthesized from the process for a net gain of 2 molecule of ATP for each molecule of glucose that starts through the cycle. Four hydrogen atoms are also released during the process.

During intense work, or when the body is unable to supply oxygen to the cell in sufficient quantity, the glycolytic pathway is able to supply energy for muscular contractions. However, this process is very inefficient as compared to the oxidative pathways and yields a by-product called lactic acid, which is extremely detrimental to performance.

It sufficient oxygen is available, lactic acid is not formed in large quantities, and the end product of glycolysis is shouted to the Krebs cycle, with the release of 4 more hydrogen atoms. In the Krebs cycle, the end product of glycolysis is processed through a series of enzymes thought to be located on the cristae of the mitochondria. These enzymes are probably arranged in sequential order so the products of the reactions can be relayed from enzyme to enzyme as the chemical reactions occur which produce 2 more ATP molecule, 16 more hydrogen atoms, and some carbon dioxide. The 4 hydrogen atoms from glycolysis, the 4 from pyruvic acid breakdown, and the 16 and the 16 from the Kerts cycle yield a total of 24 hydrogen atoms.

The Hydrogen-Electron Transport System

After the hydrogen atoms have been released from

the glycolytic pathway and the Krebs cycle, they must be oxidized to provide the rest of the energy gain from the breakdown.

This is accomplished in the hydrogen-electron transport system, where a series of oxidative enzymes change hydrogen atoms to hydrogen ions, and dissolved oxygen to hydroxyl ions. These two products then combine to form the water of metabolism. The enzymes responsible for this process are also thought to be bound in the mitochondria of the cell.

It is in the hydrogen-electron transport system that the majority of the energy from the degradation of glucose is produced. Twenty of the 24 hydrogen atoms from glycolysis and the Krebs cycle yield energy at a ratio of 3 ATP molecules for each 2 hydrogen atoms which enter the system.

The other 4 hydrogen atoms enter the H-E transport system for a 1 ATP for 1 hydrogen exchange to held 4 more ATP. Thus, the total yield of this system is 34 ATP molecules. This, combined with the 2 molecules of ATP from the Krebs cycle and the 2 molecules of ATP from glucose entering the system.

The net efficiency of the system in about 44% since 1 mol of glucose contains 686 kilocalories and yields 304 kilocalories of energy stored as ATP. The energy not stored as ATP is released as heat.

Lipids can enter the Krebs cycle easily to produce energy. Normal 18-carbon fatty acids are split off into 2 carbon units to enter the Krebs cycle almost exactly like the end product of glucose through glycolysis. A normal 18-carbaon fatty acid will yield a net gain of 130 ATP.

Although proteins are not an important source of energy, they too can be used to run the Krebs cycle. For example, alanine, a typical amino acid, is pyruvic acid when dominated and can enter directly into the cycle at the same level as pyruvic acid from glycolysis.

Phospholuconate Pathway

This is another important pathway for the breakdown of glucose, and it is responsible for as much as 30% of the glucose breakdown in the liver. Although not a highly efficient pathway, its importance lies in the fact that it can provide energy independently of the Krebs cycle. This would be an important source of energy in case of some abnormally of the Krebs cycle.

The Basic Source of Energy

All energy as we know it comes from the sun. The sun loses mass in accordance with Albert Einstein's formula, E - mc^2, to produce energy which reaches the earth at a rate of about 2×10^{13} kilocalories per second. The chloroplasts of plants provide chlorophyll, which uses some of this energy to break down water to hydrogen and oxygen.

Some of the hydrogen released from its breakdown goes through a respiratory chain and produces energy in the from this breakdown goes through a respiratory chain and produces energy in the form of plant ATP.

The rest of the hydrogen combines with carbon dioxide to form carbohydrates and release oxygen into the atmosphere. The plant carbohydrates have stored energy in their chemical bonds. It is this source, either directly or indirectly, which provides energy for man.

Digestion is the basic process used by man to

convent food into energy. The purpose of digestion is to break down large un-absorbable molecules to small molecules which can be absorbed through the intestinal wall and into the blood stream to be carried to the cells throughout the body.

The three basic foods used by man be classified into carbohydrates, fats, and protein. Carbohydrates enter the body at the mouth, where they are attacked by ptyalin which hydrolyses the starches into maltose. There is little activity in the stomach toward carbohydrates, but in the small intestine, they are worked on by several pancreatic analyses which break the particles into glucose, fructose, and galactose.

In these forms, carbohydrates are absorbed through the intestinal wall into the portal vein, and through the sinusoids of the liver. Here some are stored as glycogen to be released later as the body needs energy. The rest are transported directly to the cells of the body to be used as an immediate energy source.

Fats are not broken down very much in either the mouth to the stomach. However, in the small intestine, bile from the liver emulsifies the fat molecules so that enzymes can act on their surfaces. Pancreatic liposes complete the process by breaking the emulsified fat into fatty acids, glycerol, and glycerides. Fat particles are carried from the intestine through the lymphatic system as chylomicron and are dumped into the blood stream near the heart.

Protein goes through the mouth with little action. However, in the stomach, the particles are hydrolysed or broken apart at their peptide linkages by pepsin and gastricin, enzymes which work well in the acidic environment of the stomach. These particles then pass into the small intestine were they are treated by chemicals from the pancreas and small intestine were they are treated by chemicals from the pancreas and small intestine and are broken into small units to yield amino acids and small polypeptides.

The input of proteins is important because the body is unable to produce certain amino acids from other ingested food, so they must be provided from ingested protein to replace those used up by the body.

After the digested food particles have entered the blood, they are carried throughout the body to the cells where they are oxidized, and the energy released is converted to ATP.

ATP is an essential chemical compound found in the cytoplasm of cells. It is composed of adenine, ribose, and three "high-energy" Phosphate radicals. The amount of energy stored in each of these bonds is approximately 8 kilocalories, which is sufficient energy for almost any chemical reaction in the body. If the energy level of ATP were lower than that required by a chemical reaction, that chemical reaction could not be energized by ATP.

ATP is the basic energy source for all activity and, when needed, is broken to adenosine diphosphere and adenosine monophosphate. ADP and AMP are re-synthesized by the energy schemes in the body. Because of this relationship, ATP is sometimes referred to as the "energy currency" of the body.

Another important chemical which provides stored unit is creatine phosphate. The bond energy in CP is even higher than in ATP. However, CP cannot be used directly y the cells as a source of energy, but it is used to re-synthesize ATP from ADP.

Creatine phosphate is much more abundant in the cells than ATP and is used immediately to regenerate ATP during heavy work in order to keep the concentration of ATP at a constant level. CP is very important during muscular work because it can re-synthesize ADP to ATP much more quickly than the schemes discussed below.

5

EFFECT OF ALTITUDE

The choice of Mexico City as the site of the 1968 Olympics aroused a tremendous interest in the effects of altitude on athletic performance. It stimulated much discussion among physiologists and athletic coaches and caused considerable on problems related to performance at high altitude.

After all the medals had been distributed to the victorious, it became obvious that the effects of altitude, although apparent, were not as severe as many experts had predicted.

Physiological Adjustment to Altitude

Several changes occur to the physiological systems which help them adjust to the decreased atmosphere pressure at high altitude. Some of these changes take place immediately, and other require several weeks. Each of the changes occur for the purpose of overcoming the negative effects caused by the decrease in oxygen pressure.

The chemo-receptors in the aortic arch and carotid sinus are sensitive to either decreased oxygen pressure or increased CO_2 production. They stimulate ventilation rate and depth upon exposure to reduced oxygen pressure at high altitude in an attempt to provide sufficient O_2 to the alveoli.

However, the increased ventilation tends to "blow off" CO_2, causing the blood to become more alkaline and lowers the partial pressure of carbon. During normal works, the PCO_2 of the blood increases and causes an increase in respiration. At altitude, the decreased PCO_2 inhibits rather than aids the stimulus for increased ventilation from the lowered oxygen pressure, and only small net increase in ventilation occurs initially.

Another factors related to the decreased PCO_2 is the O_2 dissociation curve. The oxygen dislocation curve shifts with changes in acidity or alkalinity of the blood. The shift in the curve for alkalinity is favourable for increasing the oxygen saturation of the blood.

Within a week or two the respiratory centre becomes less sensitive to the decreased PCO_2, and the kidneys re-adjust the blood pH to a normal range by reducing the blood bicarbonate level.

This latter adjustment could decrease the buffering power of the blood and may negatively affect anaerobic capacity. However, the respiratory centre then can respond fully to the reduced PO_2, and pulmonary ventilation may increase by as much as 100%.

The large increase in respiration rate increases alveolar oxygen pressure, which increases the diffusion of oxygen to the blood from the alveoli. However, blood O_2 saturation levels never reach those experienced at lower altitudes.

When an athlete moves from sea level to an intermediate altitude, there is a significant initial increase in heat rate at rest and during sub-maximal work. This is followed by a steady decline over a ten-week-period to normal sea level rates.

The heart rate pattern is followed closely by the cardiac output, except that sea level values will usually not be reached, even after a ten-week adjustment period. These adjustments are necessary to maintain cellular oxygen levels with the decreased alveolar oxygen tension.

The cardiac output and heart rate will be greater at altitude for any given sub-maximal work load than for corresponding work at sea level. Although the initial adjustment in cardiac output is brought about primarily by heart rate, stroke volume takes on a greater portion of the cardiac output as the intensity of the work increase.

Maximum cardiac output, stroke volume, and heart rate are affected very little at intermediate altitudes, but the maximum heart rate is reached at a lower work level. Maximum oxygen uptake is reduced by about the same value as the reduction in the arterial saturation. With a cardiac output which was 100% of sea level values, oxygen uptake during maximum work was reduced to 72% when the arterial oxygen content was reduced 75%.

At extremely high altitude, the cardiac output may be reduced significantly, with the decrease due primarily to decreased heart rate. Pugh et al. reported decreases in cardiac output from 22 to 25 litres per minute at sea level to 16 to 17 litres at 19,000 feet. This reduction occurred because of a reduction in heart rate from 192 to 135 beats per minute and a small reduction in stroke volume.

After only a few days at high altitude, the haemoglobin concentration increases due to a decrease in plasma volume. Later, real increase occurs in both haemiglobin and haematocrit which increase the amount of oxygen the blood is able to carry per unit of volume.

Of course, the increased red blood cell percentage also increase the viscosity of the blood which, in turn, increases the cardiac work at a given heart rate.

There also seems to be an increased capillarization during acclimatization to altitude, along with vasodilation in those areas where gas exchange is needed for optimal functioning. This provides a source of oxygen closer to each cell even with are relatively lower oxygen tension.

In a summary statement at an altitude symposium, Dr. Bruno Balke mentioned the following compensating mechanisms which are used by the body to restore "normal" aerobic capacity : (i) an increase in pulmonary ventilation for any given level of work; (ii) an increase of cardiac output for any sub-maximal work load brought about primarily by increased heart rate : (iii) reduced maximum oxygen uptake, usually related to the reduction in arterial oxygen content; (iv) initial haemoconcentration because of reduction in plasma volume (v) a gradual increase in red blood cell count and haemiglobin content in the blood; (vi) an increase in myoglobin, the oxygen carrying pigment in the muscle; (vii) a vasodilation in the areas where oxygen is needed of capillaries per unit of tissue.

Effect of High Altitude

As man ascends to higher and higher altitudes, the total of the atmosphere decreases because of the decreased weight of the column of air above him. Since the percentage of each of the gases in the atmosphere remains the same regardless of altitude, the partial pressure of each of the gases decreases proportionally to the total pressure decrease. Of course, when the oxygen partial pressure is reduced, the endurance for work by man decreases.

This decreased ability can be demonstrated by comparing the performance in the 1968 Olympics at Mexico City with previous Olympic and world records.

The cause of the reduced performance in endurance events is that the reduced oxygen pressure at high altitude reduces the arterial saturation of the blood, which in turn decreases the amount of oxygen available to the cells to be used for the production of energy.

At sea level, the alveolar oxygen elevation of 10,000 feet, it is reduced to 63 mm Hg; at 20,000 feet, to less than 40 mm Hg. Luckily, the arterial oxygen saturation does not decrease at the same rate as the alveolar partial pressure because of the flattening of the oxygen dissociation curve at moderate altitude partial pressure.

Even though the partial pressure of oxygen in the alveoli drops rapidly with increasing altitude, the saturation level of the blood remains fairly high up to about 10,000 feet. Above this point, the situation falls rapidly to 70% at 20,000 feet, 50% at 23,000 feet, and only about 20% at 30,000 feet. Because unconsciousness usually occurs between 25 and 50% saturation, pilots and mountain climbers are required to use oxygen at altitudes over 20,000 feet if activity is carried on for a very long period of time. Oxygen is often used at altitudes much lower than 20,000 feet because of the effect of hypoxia on the body. These effects include drowsiness, mental fatigue, and headaches. All of the adjustments made by the body upon exposure to altitude are for the purpose of increasing the amount of oxygen delivered to the cells as the alveolar O_2 pressure drops.

Not all of the effects of altitude are detrimental to athletic performance, however. The reduced density of the air decreases the resistance of the airways to the flow of air into and out of the lungs. This allows larger volumes of air to be breathed during work with no significant increase in ventilation cost. Of course, this does not make up for the reduced partial pressure oxygen, but it does allow the body to adjust somewhat to the requirement for more oxygen during heavy work.

The positive effects of decreased air resistance are also noticeable on spring activities, jumping events, and other high-velocity events which do not require extensive aerobic involvement. Performances in these activities are sometimes phenomenal. Take, for example, the long jump record of 29 feet 2½ inches set by Bob Beamon in Mexico City at the 1968 Olympics. This performance might not have been achieved at a lower altitude.

Air is usually cooler and dryer at high altitude. Cooler temperatures can aid performances involving prolonged heavy work but, at the same time, the dryer air can increase the water loss from the respiratory system causing discomfort to the performer.

There is no doubt that aerobic capacity is reduced with increased altitude. This clearly demonstrated in the Pan-American Games at Mexico City in 1955. At 7370 feet, running times were about 10% longer than at sea level for distances over 1500 meters.

There seemed to be no effect on the events under

400 meters. The body is able to provide energy for short periods of time without large quantities of oxygen. Any activity which can be completed before the depletion of readily available energy stores in the body will not be affected by the decreased oxygen pressure at high altitude. Those events requiring energy from the oxidative systems are affected significantly.

Training Guidelines

The following guidelines can be used when working with athletes involved in aerobic events at high altitude. No acclimatization is necessary for athletes involved in anaerobic events, such as short races, jumping and throwing events.

(i) There seems to be no evidence that performance is improved by training at a higher altitude for a performance at a lower altitude, with the possible exception that the anaerobic processes of the body may be improved slightly by high-altitude training.

(ii) Athletes who live and train at high altitude do not perform better at high altitude than athletes who train at sea level and then acclimatize themselves to the high altitude. Athletes who train at high altitude do not perform better at sea level than athletes who train at sea level.

(iii) There may be individual differences in ability to acclimatize. Some athletes may be more vulnerable to the effects of high altitude than others. Some athletes will require longer of time to adjust.

(iv) The time necessary to acclimatize is related to the preceding training state of the individual athlete; a well-trained athletes will acclimatize more quickly than an untrained person.

As a general rule, however, the acclimatization period should probably starts two to three weeks prior to the competition in aerobic events.

5. Training programs similar to those used at sea level can be used for training at high altitude. However, the coach and athlete should be aware that fatigue will set in earlier. Less intense work-outs of shorter duration will stress the system maximal at high altitude.

6. Man has the ability to adjust to higher altitudes and can perform more successfully after a period of acclimatization. Pugh states that man can probably acclimatize to altitudes in excess of 28,000 feet if sufficient time and proper procedures are used.

6

EFFECT OF MALPRACTICES IN TRAINING

Frequently the difference between winning and losing in athletes is half-stride, a fraction of a second, or a near miss. Incorrect training practices can often cause this difference. Even a champion who violates training could be better if he were of such malpractices.

The place of alcohol, nicotine, drugs, and caffeine beverages in the diet of athletes deserves regular attention, because new knowledge about the effects of these substances continues to become available.

Caffeine

Caffeine is the alkaloid consumed daily million of people in coffee, tea, coca, and cola. It is known for its mild stimulating effects. When used in moderation, caffeine beverages are apparently harmless. However, caffeine is a toxic drug, and if injected into the blood stream a small amount can be fetal.

If injected into a muscle, caffeine causes temporary paralysis, severe convulsions. With all of these reactions one would assume that caffeine beverages are dangerous. The reason these toxic effects never occur in a an individual who drinks such beverages is that caffeine diffuses into the blood stream and then is removed from the blood to the kidneys where it is excreted.

Caffeine acts mostly upon the blood vessels, hear, and nervous system. Mild doses cause general vasoconstriction with simultaneous dilation of the coronary artery, increase the contractile force of the heart, and cause an increase in the heat, and cause an increase in the heart rate.

The temperature of the stomach increases along with an increase of hydrochloric acid secretion. Mild doses may cause an increase in metabolic rate up to 25%, stimulate the central nervous system, and accelerate the respiratory rate. In small doses it acts beneficially upon the psychic processes.

Two research studies indicated that mild doses will increase work output and postpone the onset of fatigue evidence that caffeine has no influence on performance.

Exercise physiologists and other expects on conditioning generally agree that caffeine beverages are not ergogenic aids. However, they also generally agree that moderate consumption of caffeine beverages has no detrimental effects on conditioning and performance provided they do not interfere with a well-balanced diet and adequate sleep.

Nicotine

The effects of cigarette smoking on athletic conditioning and performance have been well established in recent years. As a rule, coach are against smoking, and rightfully so. According to the Community on the Medical Aspects of Sports of the American Medical Association, it is unwise for a young man who has ambitions to excel in sports to begin smoking or to continue the habit if he already has started.

The Committee noted that while the effects of tobacco vary in different people, the following conclusions seem warranted:

(i) Research shows that puffs of cigarette smoke can decrease the conductance of the airway into the lung by 30% in resting subjects. This can seriously limit maximum ventilation required for vigorous athletic events.

(ii) In certain persons, the constricting effect of tobacco on the blood vessels contributes to the development of circulatory disorders.

(iii) In smoking, some carbon monoxide may be absorbed, thereby reducing temporality the oxygen-carrying capacity of the blood.

(iv) Habitual smoking with inhalation irritates the delicate membranes of the throat and lungs. This induces chronic cough and renders the throat more susceptible to infection.

(v) Habitual smoking when the stomach is empty tends to produce digestive disturbances and distress.

(vi) Habitual smoking sometimes leads to irritability, a reaction more likely to occur in young people.

It is known that icotine constricts the blood vessels, raises blood pressure, and increases heart rate. There is little doubt that this affects athletic performance negatively, particularly in strenuous sports.

Smoking inhibits the flow of gastric juices and the onset of hunger pangs, and thus interferes with nutritional patterns.

The role of tobacco smoke as a factor in lung cancer cannot be ignored by those professionally concerned with health and fitness. Statistically, it has been shown that a heavy smoker is 42 times as likely to develop lung cancer as a non-smoker.

Since there is no evidence that smoking does anything good for athletes and much evidence to the contrary, it seems prudent for the coach to vigorously enforce a no-smoking rule. A coach who issues a no-smoking edict hinders its effects if he himself smokes.

Alcohol

It has been the practice to exclude alcohol from the diet of athletes. But strict adherence to this rule has been difficult to enforce, especially among professional athletes, because it is argued that moderate drinking has no effect on disease, general health, or length of life. In view of this, let us analyse some points that relate specifically to athletics.

(i) Alcohol is not a stimulant as some people believe. It is a narcotic, and a such it suppresses the functioning of the organism. It gives a temporary sense of well-being, but over a period of time it acts as a depressant to both mind and body.

(ii) It saps energy and greatly increases fatigue. The reason for this is that alcohol slows removal of lactic acid from the cells, and the accumulation of lactic acid is very prominent in fatigue.

(iii) Alcohol seriously interferes with the functioning of the nervous system. It disturbs the protective lipids and dehydrates some of the moisture in the body which is os essential to proper functioning of the nervous system.

(iv) One of the most serious effects of alcohol is on the cerebrum of the brain which directs thoughts and actions. Alcohol interferes with the messages which are received from the sensory nerves and also reduces normal inhibition.

(v) Alcohol interferes with both voluntary and reflex movements of the body, and it drastically upsets the teamwork between mind and muscles; that is, coordination.

(vi) It affects reaction time actively and reduces ability to make sound judgments quickly.

(vii) Habitual use of alcohol leads to poor eating patterns and eventual malnutrition.

(viii) Its use is often associated with loss of sleep and loss of normal social inhibitions, both of which are important to athletes.

There is no doubt that strong alcoholic drinks are detrimental to both conditioning and performance, and there are no arguments in favour of athletes using such beverages. Thus athletes should refrain front the use of alcohol, and coaches should strictly enforce rules against its use.

Narcotics

According to common usage of the term, there are three classes of Narcotics : opium and its derivatives, cocaine, and marijuana. There is some support for the addition of barbiturates and alcohol to this list.

Opium relieves pain and produces a false sense of well-being. It produces depression of the central nervous system and induces sleep. It reduces body secretions except those of the skin.

A larger dose can depress respiration and thus cause death. Morphine, heroin, and codeine are all derivatives of opium. Heroin also has effects similar to those of opium and is the most dangerous drug having no medical uses. Probably 75% of all confirmed drug addicts use heroin.

Cocaine is a powerful, quick-acting drug capable of producing strong addiction. Unlike most narcotics which act as sedatives, a moderate dose of cocaine actually stimulates the central nervous system, accelerating respiratory and circulatory rates.

Take in excess, cocaine can produce psychotic symptoms of great excitement and peculiar sensations of creatures crawling on the skin, commonly referred to as "cocaine bugs."

Marijuana is a relatively mild intoxicating drug to which people tend to become psychologically addicted rather than psychologically addicted. Records show that its use leads towards the use of more harmful drugs.

There are no arguments in favour of athletes using narcotics and there are very strong arguments against their use but people in general, and especially by athletes. Therefore, it should be firmly concluded that there is no place for the use of narcotics in athletic training or performance.

Sedatives

Sedatives generally reduce nervous system activity, produce a state of relaxation, and depress the actions of the vital organs. They are basically sleep-producing drugs. The most commonly used of this group are barbiturates, of which there are at least 20 different drugs.

Under proper medical supervision, the barbiturates serve a useful medical purpose. However, to use these drugs indiscriminately as an easy an easy, quick method of reducing conscious activity of the brain is very unwise.

The danger in using barbiturates indiscriminately lies both in development of a dependency upon them and the possibility of over-dosage. There is no argument in favour of using sedatives in connection with athletics except under medical supervision.

Amphetamines

Amphetamines produce effects similar to those caused by the activity of the sympathetic nervous system. On most people the immediate effect is an increase in alertness and faster reaction.

Because of the stimulating effect of amphetamines, there has been some interest in determining whether athletic performance can be improved by their use. Melodically speaking, recommended. However, no legal restrictions exists for the use of mild stimulating drugs.

The best evidence presently available indicates that amphetamines do not produce superior performance, but do tend to cause the participant to perceive that is performance well.

7

SPECIAL PREPARATION FOR PERFORMANCE

There are several elements in the preparation for performance which deserve special attention. They are nutrition, pre-competition procedures, making weight, and warm-up.

Making Weight in Athletics

In some sports, such as wrestling and boxing, competition is organized into divisions by body weight. The advantages of competing in the lowest possible weight class are obvious.

For mature athletes, "making weight" is not a large health problem due to experience which has set a percent as to their normal weight. However, many cases of excessive weight loss of high school boys have been revealed, involving as much as 15 pounds.

This practice should be avoided, because such weight loss can be obtained only by drastic changes in water metabolism, and this causes changes in kidney and cardiovascular functions.

In secondary school athletes, a 5% weight loss is the outside limit of prudence, and it is likely that even this amount is too great for some boys.

The American Medical Association's Committee on Medical aspect of Sports has stated that there are frequent excuses for the need for weight loss in such sports as wresting in order to balance the squad's representation in all weight classes and to gain an advantage by getting a boy pitted against a lighter opponent.

The committee further states that the desired modification of weight should be accomplished over an extended period of time, so the change is in body composition. It is possible to add muscle and lose fats and keep one's weight constant.

Weight loss by cutting calories is defensible only if the athlete has enough nutrients and energy reserves to meet the requirements during practice and meets. The A.M.A. committee suggests periodical medical examinations and a general year-round conditioning program.

It also suggests four to six week of an intensive conditioning program before the season, followed by a weigh-in. This weight should be the minimal effective weight. All during this program the body should keep himself in state of nutritional readiness.

Many coaches cause athletes to bring about the desired weight loss by profuse sweating and abstaining from food liquids for several hours before weighing in for competition. Weight losses up to 10 pounds were measured without any negative effects in six college wrestlers. Weight losses were induced by a procedure usually considered orthodox by wrestling coaches; food and water were withheld.

The wrestlers wearing heavy sweat suits worked on

the mats and alternated this with sitting in a heat room. This can abnormal loss of weight is regained in part after weighing in, as a result of acting and drinking. More than 5 pounds may be gained in few hours.

Singer and Weiss, in a study of ten college wrestlers, concluded that a wrestler may lose up to 7% of his body weight without adversely affecting strength, cardiovascular endurance, and general performance.

In summary, it should be pointed out that there are two important problems associated with dramatic short-term losses in weight; (i) The athlete might be weakened considerably as a result of lack of nutrition, and this might more than offset the advantage of competing in a lighter weight class. (ii) Excessive abstinence from the consumption of fluids combined with profuse sweating can result in partial dehydration, which will adversely affect several body functions and may result in illness.

These problems are less serious among mature athletes then teenagers. Thus, coaches should be extremely cautions in the practices they encourage among young athletes.

Warm-Up

The question is often asked, "How important is warm-up to performance and the prevention of injury, and if it is important which type of warm-up is best?" Several points of argument in favour of warm-up have been stated by athletic performance experts. They advocate the importance of warm-up on the basis of the following claims.

(i) Warm-up help to prevent injury.

(ii) Warm-up increases the rate and force of muscular

contraction.

(iii) Warm-up related to the particular activity improves the necessary coordinations.

(iv) In endurance activities, warm-up brings on second wind more readily. Second wind results from adjustments of body systems to the additional demands placed on them as a result of increased activity When second wind is reached, the supply has caught up with the increased demands.

During an extensive review of the research on warm-up, the authors found eight reports which support the idea that warm-pup is beneficial and seven reports which claim that warm-up has no effect on performance. No reports were found which indicate that regular warm-up is detrimental, and no reports supported the claim that warm-p up influences the occurrence of injury.

Unfortunately, some of the research was done under poorly controlled conditions, and some involved mild exercise routines which do not actually increase body temperature. These experiments have contributed to the confusion about the value of warm-up.

Most coaches and athletes seem to believe that warm-up is valuable and want their athletes to continue using warm-ups until further evidence is accumulated. The authors agree with this position. But, it must be recognized that indiscriminate warm-up may waste energy and result in limited effects on the effects on the essential muscles.

The warm-up should be specific to the activity being performed and should be increased in intensity as the performer becomes better conditioned. The timing of the warm-up in relation to the performance must be correct. Otherwise, the beneficial effects may be reduced or eliminated. Following are some important guides:

(i) Warm-up should be intense enough to increase body temperature and cause perspiration, but not so intense that it causes fatigue.

(ii) Warm-up should include some stretching and loosening exercise along with some heavy work.

(iii) It should include movements that are common to the performance. That is, runners should include running, whereas shot putters should included putting, and hurdlers should practice hurdling. This helps to prepare the specific muscle groups involved in the performance, and probably it sharpness the neuromuscular coordinations.

(iv) The warm-up should begin to taper off 10 to 15 minutes prior to the performance and end about 5 minutes before performance. This will allow recovery from any temporary fatigue without losing the effect of the warm-up.

Effects on Coordination

It is commonly believed, and rightfully so that performance of the skills involved in the activity will sharpen the competitor's coordination and timing. This implies that runners should include running in their warm-ups, whereas baseball pitchers should practice throwing, etc. The degree to which the sharpening of skills actually occurs is not clearly established.

Effects on Injury

Relative to the effect of warm-up on injury, several experts claim that failure to warm up may lead to tearing of muscle fibres. Hamola states that, as often as not, a pulled muscle occurs in the relaxed fibres, those antagonistic to the contracting fibres.

This happens because the opposing fibres do not yield to the pull suddenly placed on them by the rapidly contracting muscles. Morehouse and Miller support this idea by stating that the muscles most frequently torn because of inadequate warm-up are those antagonistic to the strong contracting muscles. These cold antagonistic muscles relax slowly and incompletely when the agonists contract, and thus retard free movement and hinder accurate coordination.

Morehouse and Rasch state, "The danger of injury is lessened when an athlete is thoroughly warmed up, which increases the speed with which he is able to react." They imply that this increased reaction helps to prevent injury.

Effects on Certain Performance Factors

Much of the research done on warm-up has been related to certain factors of performance such as the effect of warm-up on strength, speed, endurance, etc.

Strength—Two studies wherein total body warm-ups were used, produced evidence that warm-up will increase strength. Conversely, in three studies involving only local heating, no increases in strength resulted. In one of the studies strength decreased. On the basis of this information plus evidence which relates to power, of which strength is a part, it appears that strength can be increased a small amount by total body warm-up, whereas no increase in strength can be expected from local heating.

Muscular endurance—Massey et al. found that

warming up did not improve endurance and speed. Several other studies also support this claim. Conversely Asmussen and Boje found that certain types of warm-up did increase endurance and speed.

Thompson found that formal warm-up exercise improved swimming endurance. Grodijinobsky and Magel learned that vigorous warm-up improved performance significantly in the mile run.

Local heating was used all of the studies where warm-up was found to be of no value in endurance. Those studies that produced evidence in favour of warm-up involved total body warm-up.

Along with these findings it is interesting to note that there is good evidence that local cooling, which reduces skin temperature, results in better performance for the underlying muscles.

In essence, the rationale behind this is that cooling of the surface area results in less circulation near the surface, and thus a better supply of blood in the muscles beneath the surface.

Power—Merlino did one study and Pacheco did two studies which support the idea that warm-up will improve power as Hodkins found that warm-up will increase power as measured by throwing speed.

The studies that support the idea that warm-up improve swimming speed, running speed, and strength would add additional support to the claim that warm-up improves power, because swimming and running speeds depends greatly upon power, and strength and speed are elements in power.

Specific Skills—Jesnsen and Moregenegg

conducted a study wherein they found that warm-up improve performance in gymnastics. Thompson found that warm-up improved accuracy in basketball and bowling.

On the other hand, Hodgkins founds warm-up to have no effect on accuracy, and Van us et al. found similar results. The Evidence as to the effect of warm-up on skills is inconclusive.

Swimming—Carlile found that passive warming in a hot a shower improved swimming speed for 220 yards. Thompson learned that formal related warm-up drills improved swimming speed and endurance, but unrelated warm-up did no influence performance. DeVries found that swimming warm-up improved performance on the 100 yards swim. Miido's study also supports warm-up in preparation for swimming. There is little or no evidence to the contrary.

Running Speed—Blank and Simonson et al. found that total body warm-up has a favourable influence on running speed. Conversely, Mathews and Snyder found that warm-up did not improve speed on the 440-yard run, and Hipple obtained similar results relative to the 50-yard dash. Grodjinoblsy and Magel learned that warm-up did improve the 1-mile run; however, this is not a test of speed. The evidence relative to the effects of warm-up on running speed is conflicting and inconclusive.

Physiology of Warm-Up

Laboratory studies show that cooling of the body below normal temperature causes a loss of reaction time and contractile time and reduces excitability of the muscles. Supposedly, warming of the muscles will reverse these effects.

Hill found that increasing the temperature of muscle improved both contractile force that increasing the temperature of muscle improved both contractile force and contractile speed.

DeVries reasoned that warm-up which results in increased temperature of the blood and muscles should improve performance because (i) muscles would contract and relax faster, (ii) muscles would contract with greater efficiency because of lowered viscous resistance, (iii) haemoglobin would show effects similar to those of haemoglobin, (iv) haemoglobin would show effects similar to those of haemoglobin, (v) metabolic processes would increase, and (vi) resistance of the vascular bed would decrease.

Intensity and Duration of Warm-up

Burke has demonstrated that optimal combinations of intensity and duration are needed to bring about the desired warm-up effect. Too little work does not achieve optimal levels of temperature, and too much found that in a well-conditioned athlete a very heavy load can be used for as long as 30 minutes with ever-increasing muscle temperature and consistently improving performance.

Conversely, it should be pointed out that the typical high school boy ora poorly conditioned mature athlete will become exhausted prior to 30 minutes of vigorous work. Obviously the intensity and duration of warm-up must be adjusted to the individual. As a rule, one may look for signs or increased body temperature. In the normal environment, this is indicated by perspiration. For those who wish to be more scientific, an increase in internal temperature of 1 to 2 degrees is desirable.

Various Types of Warm-Up

Coaches and athletes should be acquainted with the different approaches to warming up.

Related and Unrelated—Related warm-up involves procedures that are included in the athletic activity itself, such as high jumpers practice jumping, basketball players practice shooting, dribbling, etc. Unrelated warm-up is a procedure to bring about the desired physiological changes without participating in the skills of the performance.

Research in this area is inconclusive, but it can be reasoned out that if the desired temperature changes can be achieved by a related warm-up, this would be preferable, because the practice effect would also result. However, in some athletic events related warm-up may be inadvisable or impractical.

Passive vs. Active—There is much evidence that any method of exercise which results in an increase in body temperature will have a favourable influence on performance. This has been demonstrated through the use of warm-up procedures such as running, calisthenics, etc.

But there is only limited evidence that passive heating such as hot baths, hot showers, Turkish baths, or diathermy is effective for increasing performance.

General vs. Local Heating—Several investigations have noted improvements in performance between 1 and 8% when the entire body was heated so that rectal and muscle temperatures were increased. However, the local heating of only the involved limb has resulted in earlier fatigue and less work output in that limb.

The explanation for the different effects of local and general heating probably lies in the fact that in local heating portion of the blood is drawn towards the skin to the detriment of circulation through the underlying muscles.

On the other hand, general heating of the entire body must exert some, or all, of the beneficial effects enumerated earlier.

Overload Warm-up—Overloading in preparation fora performance is not done frequently; however, it is common practice in baseball to swimming two or three bats in preparation for batting. This is done party to cause the better to feel loose and partly to practice the swimming action. Van Huss et al. showed that warming up by throwing an 11-ounce baseball resulted in significant improvements in throwing velocity of a regulation baseball.

The physiological involvement of this phenomenon has not been satisfactorily explained, and it is possible that psychological effects are involved.

Nutrition

Competitive athletes constantly seek methods of improving their conditioning and performance. As a result, many athletes seem to be easily influenced by the success of others whose training regimes may have included special dietary substance. But the fact is that the nutritional requirements of the athlete are not much different from those of anyone else.

There is no scientific evidence that athletic performance can be improved by modifying a basically sound and nutritious diet. Conversely and athlete can go downhill very rapidly if his diet is less than optimal.

Thus, an excellent diet is very important in athletic conditioning.

There is such great variety of nutritious foods that many different combinations can result in a sound diet, and the best diet for one athlete may not be the best for another. Individual difference exist in people's tastes as well as in their enzyme systems which are so necessary for digestion and absorption of foods. Thus, "one man's meat may be another man's poison."

In a brief statement, the best that can be said about diet of athletes in that it should be well balanced and nutritious, sufficient in quantity to maintain normal body weight, and composed of foods that are satisfying and not disrupting.

Such diet need not be supplemented with "fad foods," and it is doubtful that food supplements such as vitamins, wheat germ, and so forth, are of any additional value. On the other hand, if the diet is not sound in terms of its content and quantity, then food supplements may be beneficial.

Proportion of Different Foods

There has been much debate over the correct proportion of carbohydrates, fats, and protein in the athlete's diet. However, there has been only a limited amount of research on the topic, thus much common sense must be applied. It is known that the human organism prefers to burn carbohydrates for energy during muscular activity, although it is also capable of utilizing fats.

One litre of oxygen yields 5 kilocalories when burning carbohydrates and 4.7 kilocalories when burning fats. Because the burning of carbohydrates yields more kilocalories per litre of oxygen, it has been concluded that a person might be as much as 10% more efficient on a high-carbohydrate diet.

Studies show that endurance diminishes on a high-fat diet as compared to a high-carbohydrate diet. Astrand indicates that endurance activities require well-stocked glycogen reserves, which result from a high-carbohydrate diet.

He found that after a normal mixed diet and with an initial glycogen content of 1.75 gram/100 gram wet muscle, a workload of 75% of maximal oxygen uptake could be tolerated for 114 minutes. After three days of a diet consisting entirely of fat and protein, the glycogen concentration fell to 0.63 gram/100 gram muscle.

The standard workload could be maintained only for 57 minutes. After three days of carbohydrate-rich diet, the glycogen content was higher: 3.51 g/100g muscle, and the time on the same amount of work could be continued for 167 minutes.

What the subject could do only for less than an hour on a fat and protein diet, he could do for over 2½ hours when carbohydrate was added to the diet for three days.

Even though carbohydrates produce energy more efficiently, the exclusion of fats from the diet is not recommended. Aside from the important vitamins and essential fatty acids in fats, three appears to be a fat-contained factor that is necessary for the normal metabolism of carbohydrates. Fat has extremely high-energy value, even though the burning of it requires more oxygen.

The prime value of fat is associated with the fact that it contains fat-soluble vitamins, A, D, E, and K, and the essential fatty acids which cannot be synthesized by the body. Provide these dietary requirements are met, fat in itself is not an essential food. There seems to be accumulating evidence that too much fat contributes to the formation of high casserole levels, for in atherosclerosis.

Protein is needed mainly for building new body tissue. Only under conditions of starvation when the carbohydrate and fat stores have been depleted is the protein of body tissue consumed for energy. The protein molecule is made up of long chains of amino acids.

These acids, sometimes known as "tissue-building stones," are absorbed from the intestines and sent throughout the body, where their important functions of repair and formation of tissue, are initiated. During athletic training there is an increase of muscle tissue, hence additional protein is required for the formation of new capillaries, connective tissue, and sarcoplasm.

Pizzo tested college swimmers during morning practice sessions under three conditions; (i) with no breakfast or nutrition for a 12-hour period, (ii) with a regular breakfast, and (ii) with a fluid diet supplement high in simple sugars. Toward the end of the experiment, significantly higher nitrogen levels in the urine were discovered in those swimmers having no nutrition levels in the urine were discovered in those swimmers having no nutrition before practice. This indicates a higher metabolism of protein, meaning that possibly the muscles were using body protein for fuel.

As result of observations and reasoning, Morehouse and Millermade the following generalizations relative to the proportions of foodstuff: (i) a diet of 700 grams of carbohydrates, 150 grams of fats and 100 grams of protein plus adequate minerals and vitamins daily for long-duration events; and (ii) 350 to 411 grams of carbohydrates, 100 to 300 grams of fats, and 210 grams of protein, mostly meat, for speed and power events.

Best and Taylor recommended that for an athlete who utilize 3000 kilocalories daily, the correct proportion would be approximately as follows: carbohydrates—380 grams, fats—133 grams, protein—70 grams. Abrahams reports that Schenk studied 4700 competitors at the 1936 Olympic Games and found a daily consumption of over 7000 kilocalories with the following proportions: carbohydrates—800 grams, fats—270 grams, protein—320 grams.

When the available information is transposed into percentages, it appears that typically the athlete's diet should consist of about 65% carbohydrates, 20$ fats, and 15% protein.

If training is at usually high levels where muscle mass is likely to increase, the percentage of protein should be increased to as much as 20% with a proportional decrease in fats.

Quantity of Food

The total daily energy requirement for an active man may range from 3000 to 7000 calories, depending upon his size, condition, and the amount of work he performs. As the athlete work harder in his training, he consumes more calories and must have a proportionate increase in food.

He must consume enough food to meet his energy demands. If he eats less than this amount, he will burn his body tissues to make up the deficit, and he will approach “”staleness more readily. If he consumes more food than is needed, he will build up fatty tissue, with its accompanying mechanical and endurance disadvantages.

The best indicator of whether an athlete is consuming the correct amount of food is the amount of fatty tissue he possesses. He should be near normal weight for is body build, not too fat and not too thin. However, the degree of thinness that is desirable relates to the athletic even. For example, wrestlers and distance runners must be relatively fat free, while football and baseball players can carry a limited amount of fatty tissue without detrimental effects.

Principal Source of Carbohydrates, Fats, and Protein

No ordinary food is all carbohydrates, fat , or protein, but many foods are predominantly of one type. The following are some principal sources of the three foods types:—

Proteins.

Meat—beef, lamb chops.

Fish—Tuna, white, smoked, cod, blue, cat, trout.

Milk—skim, powdered.

Fowl—chicken, turkey

Soybeans.

Cheese.

Dried yeast.

Eggs.

Fats.

Certain meats—pork, mutton, goose, beacon.

Certain fish—salmon.

Cooking fats—animal fats and vegetable oils.

Magarine, butter, lard.

Whole milk.

Mayonnaise, salad dressing.

Nuts—peacans, almonds, peanuts.

Carbohydrates

Grain and cereal products—brads, cornbread, grain cereals.

Pastries—pies and cakes.

Fruits—bananas, grape juice.

Sugars—honey, candies, jams and jellies.

Vegetables—corn, potatoes, beans, rice.

Quality of Protein

The quality of the protein is equally as important as the quantity. All Protein foods breaks down to form amino acids, and these acids form the building bullocks for synthesis which results in the proteins found in body tissue. Of the 23 amino acids normally present in animal protein, only 13 can be synthesized in the cells.

The other 10 must be supplied in the diet, and they are called the essential amino acids. Supplying these acids is no problem fro those who eat meat and animal products. Regular consumption of "complete protein foods" such as milk, eggs, and meat solves this problem quite easily. For those who not eat animal products, the problem is more complicated.

Fad Foods

Some fad foods, such as sunflower seeds, kelp, raw meat, black-strap molasses, and other such substance, are sometimes claimed to have miraculous properties for improving performance. Typically, when these foods are tested scientifically, it turns out that the consumer performs well in spite of, and not because of, the particular food.

In rare cases when a person is sincerely dedicated to the value of the food, a psychological effect may be present. But, aside from possible psychological effects, there is no evidence that such foods have special value.

Floor Supplements

Many successful athletes content that their success is due in part to the consumption of food supplements. Because food has significance beyond the nutrients it provides, it is difficult to know whether an athlete receives psychological benefit from certain foods.

The results of research about food supplements must be interpreted with caution because much of the research has been done either by or under the auspices of companies that market the products.

Vitamins

At one time it was believed that the requirements for vitamins increased more rapidly than the increase in metabolism caused by exercise. But recent research shows that vitamin needs increase in about the same proportion as metabolism.

Thus, ingestion of larger amounts of food as daily work levels increase automatically provides the needed increase in vitamins. This statement assumes that the diet is well balanced and sound.

Some researchers have claimed that vitamin supplements improve performance. But when proper controls are applied, assuring that the subjects are on an adequate diet before the experiment, the improvements are no longer demonstrated. It appears that if a person is on a well-rounded and sound diet there is no need for vitamin supplements, but if the diet is not sound, supplementary vitamins might prove beneficial to either athletes or non-athletes.

It is recommended that vitamins be obtained from their natural sources rather than from purified synthetic source. However, vitamin C supplement might be an exception to this rule. Van Huss reports favourable results in the recovery rate of laboratory animals which had received vitamin C before exercising compared with those who had no supplements. Consilman states that, "All research seems to indicate an increasing need for vitamin C during the stress of a training program." Vitamin be excreted in the urine.

Minerals

As with vitamins, there is no scientific evidence that the need for minerals in increased any more than the need for food in general as a result of increased exercise. An adequate supply of minerals in apparently present in a well-balanced diet, but if the diet is not well balanced, then mineral supplements might prove beneficial.

Wheat Germ

Wheat germ is a rather complete food composed of a large number of nutrients. For this reason, some people have reasoned that regular consumption of wheat germ will assist in overcoming deficiencies in the diet.

This reasoning is based on the assumption that the diet does have some deficiencies. Cureton states, "Studies at the University of Illinois Physical Fitness Research Laboratory indicate that wheat germ, or its derivative what germ oil, aids those who consume it under proper conditions over a long period of time to enable the body to build up its glycogen reserve."

There is some indication that wheat germ contributes to low cholesterol levels, and low cholesterol has been associated with superior physical fitness. There is no evidence that harmful effects will result from consuming a reasonable amount of wheat germ on a regular basis.

Glycine

There has been some interest among athletes in the use of glycine to increase muscular power and endurance. Gelatin, which averages about 25% glycine, has been widely sold for this purpose. The basic idea behind this has been to promote endogenous cretin formation, presumably to enhance the supply of phosphocreatine in the muscles.

This idea is not substantiated by research results. However, there is no evidence that the consumption of a reasonable amount of glycine is harmful in the training diet.

In summary, it should be emphasized that if an athlete is on a sound diet, it is doubtful that any kind of dietary supplement will be beneficial to his conditioning and performance. Conversely, if he is not on a sound diet then certain supplement may be helpful.

Effect of Lack of Food and Fasting

The American Medical Association is opposed to "crash diets" for athletes. Its opposition is based on the idea that repeated periods of starvation and/or dehydration produce essentially the same pathological conditions that natural famine and voluntary food restrictions have produced.

On the other hand, many wrestling and boxing

coaches believed that rapid weight reductions up to about 7% of the body's weight are harmless and may actually aid performance. The two positions are not as incompatible as they seem.

The medical opinion relates to general health and the coaches' opinion to immediate effects upon performance. Small weight losses due to starvation do not cause appreciable changes in performance.

On the other hand, based on medical research, it must be concluded that submitting to several days of dehydration and/or acute starvation in order to "make weight" is inadvisable, especially for young people who are not physically mature.

An underfed person cannot sustain hard work as long as a well-fed one, because a substandard diet causes a reduction in the performance of the physiological systems. Especially those systems which deliver oxygen and removed metabolic wastes.

Another argument against excessive starving is the fact that as the demand for energy exceeds the supply, body tissues are consumed in the course of the activity. The depletion of body tissues impairs the functions of the organs of which these tissues are a part. Furthermore physical efficiency is lower when body tissues, instead of stored energy, are used as fuel.

It has been shown that after repetitive periods of fasting, people can tolerate fasting better. The blood sugar level becomes higher, and motor speed and coordination deteriorate less readily.

Meat Eater's vs. Vegetarians

The primary advantage of meat in the diet is that

meat is a good source of amino acids which are indispensable for life. Vegetarians can get along without meat if they use a variety of vegetables and fruits to assure an adequate supply of the essential amino acids. A meat diet, moreover, is more palatable to most people with the exception of dedicated vegetarians.

Reports stating that vegetarians have greater endurance than meat eaters should be discounted because there is no scientific evidence to support the idea that vegetarians are superior in any respect. Indications are that unless vegetarians eat a well-rounded diet of variety of foods they are likely to suffer from some sort of malnutrition.

Distribution of Meals

The athlete should have at least three meals each day. It is believed that frequent moderate-sized meals result in better efficiency, both psychologically and physiologically. Clarked et at. reported the effects of two meals per day vs. three meals per day upon Moslems fasting during Ramadan.

This is the month during which one meal is consumed before dawn in the morning and another after sunset in the evening. Athletic contests among Moslems resulted in better performances during the part of the year when three meals taken each day than during Ramadan.

Other Potential Aids to Athletes

Because only small differences in performance exist between champions and would-be champions, many athletes are interested in any aid they can find. This section includes important information about some potential aids.

Oxygen Inhalation

Oxygen inhalation has proven to be of very little value in athletics, whether it is breathed before, during, or after performance.

Experimentation shows that oxygen breathed before a contest has little effect, because oxygen cannot be stored successfully by the body. Any increase in oxygen saturation in the blood or lungs in quickly diluted by atmospheric air when the athlete begins his performance.

Oxygen breathed after the contest does not seem to speed up the elimination of anaerobic by-products, so is of very little value. Increasing the supply of oxygen during work does increase the maximum oxygen uptake, and reduces pulmonary ventilation, so it would be of some help for activities requiring a high energy yield. Unfortunately, oxygen equipment is heavy and awkward and could not be used effectively during performance.

Anabolic Steroids

The use of anabolic steroids by athletes attempting to develop high strength levels has become quite common. Anabolic steroids have been used clinically for some time for treatment of osteoporosis, fracture healing, burns, protein tissues building, myotrophy, muscular dystrophy, and so forth, because they increase nitrogen retention in the form of protein synthesis and because they decrease the rate of catabolism of amino acids. Based on their effects on clinical patients, steroids should stimulate muscle growth and strength increases in normal subjects.

There is strong evidence that anabolic steroids

accelerate increases in strength when administered with a high-protein supplement in the diet and in conjunction with a systematic weight training program.

However, little is known about the possible long-term side effects of steroids, thus athletes should extremely cautions about their use without the supervision of a doctor. Physically immature individuals should never use steroids because of possible acceleration of epiphyseal ossification and manifestations resembling macrogenitosomia redox.

Alkalizers

During high levels of work, the body depends heavily upon anaerobic process to provide energy for muscular contraction. The-by product from these processes, lactic acid, must be buffering by the blood to prevent a severe decrease in blood Ph.

This buffering action depends mainly upon the blood alkaline reserve. Early researchers found that the blood pH could be raised by the ingestion of alkaline salts. They theorized that if the blood was more alkaline before work, more lactic acid would be required to cause the pH to decrease to an intolerable level.

Researchers have produced evidence that would tend to support this theory. However, the theory only seems to apply to moderately trained subjects. Highly trained runners were not improved by the ingestion of these salts .

Procedures Before and After Competition

Research and much practical experience have lead to certain sound practices and producers associated with competition. Coaches and athletes should be well informed about these practices and procedures.

During Competition

During long-duration competition, such as basketball and soccer, athletes should be permitted to drink small amounts of water periodically in order to help replenish body fluids lost through sweating and to contribute to comfort. Large amounts of water should be avoided.

A few athletes choose to eat bits of candy or other quick-energy foods periodically during performance. Probably there is no harm in doing this; however, the value of it is questioned.

After Competition

After a long-duration performance, the athlete is usually thirsty and hungry. If profuse sweating has occurred, an immediate concern is the replenishment of body fluids. This is done best by consuming moderate amounts of water every fifteen to twenty minutes until the feeling of thirst and dehydration is satisfied.

The consumption of too much fluid at once will result in overfilling of the stomach and cause temporary discomfort. Consumption of large amounts of ice-cold fluids during or immediately after vigorous work is considered bad practice.

Following the performance, the athlete should eat a well-balanced meal of nutritious foods which are satisfying. It should include protein to replenish the body's supply of building material.

It should exclude (i) large amounts of slow-digesting foods such as fats, (ii) foods that tend to cause digestive disturbance, and (iii) foods which are unfamiliar to the individual.

The meal should contain enough bulk to satisfy the feeling of hunger, but not so much as to cause discomfort from overfilling. Once the athlete has recovered from the immediate excitement of the competition, and ample rest will prepare him for return to his usual living routine.

Pre-Competition Meal

Concern over the pre-competition meal has existed for many centuries. Records indicate that athletes of ancient times swallowed powdered lions' teeth to make themselves strong, and some ate lean both before and after competition believing to would build muscle mass, and thereby help them perform better.

Through the ages much confusion and many misconceptions have existed relative to pre-meet meals, and even today there is much disagreement about this matter.

There are two aspects to the pre-competition meal: physiological and psychological. From the physiological standpoint, the content, quantity, and timing are all important factors. Psychologically the performer must feel that meal was "right" to prepare him for his best effort.

The content of the pre-competition meal will influence the time it should be eaten. In turn the timing of the meal will influence its content. The idea is to have the athlete well nourished with an abundance of carbohydrates in the diet, and yet have the stomach empty or near-empty when the performance begins.

When vigorous exercise is performed while the stomach is full, the inspiratory descent of the diaphragm may be impaired. It is conceivable also that a full stomach may encroach upon the action of the heart during heavy exercise.

The consequent restriction of blood flow through the heart would reduce endurance.

The following guides are valid and should be helpful. Even when these aides are followed, much flexibility remains as to the exact content of the pre-competition meal.

(i) A substantial meal should be eaten three to four hours before competition. A small amount of fast-digesting carbohydrates may be eaten without harm as close as one hour before competition.

(ii) The pre-competition meal, and also the meal preceding it, should consist mostly of carbohydrates, with some protein and only a small amount of fats. Carbohydrates are fast to digest, and they replace the glycogen supply, thus providing quick energy.

The liver can store about 1500 calories of glycogen which can depleted in about one hour of moderate to vigorous activity. Protein foods digest reasonably fast and are valuable to performance, but their metabolism results in the production of acids, large quantities of which cause undesirable acidosis, and sometimes cramps.

The acid products of protein are exercised only through the urine. During heavy work, the functioning of the kidneys is greatly restricted, and this contributes to the accumulation of the acids. Fats are slow to digest and, therefore, retard gastric emptying. However, fats should not be totally omitted because they tend to satisfy hunger readily, and in long-duration performances they become increasingly value as a source of energy.

(iii) Foods that are distasteful to the individual should be avoided because they may cause stomach disturbance.

(iv) Foods that are irritating, such as roughage and highly spiced foods, should be avoided.

(v) Gas-forming foods should be eaten, such as cabbage, beans, applies, onions, etc.

(vi) Liquids are essential in the pre-competition meal, because the digestion, absorption, and assimilation of foods are dependent upon an adequate a supply of liquid. Coffee and tea are often because they ten d to give the athlete a "pick-up." But this lasts only a short while and tends to be followed by sluggishness.

Milk, which has been taboo on training tables in the past, is now considered acceptable in both the regular diet and in the-pre-competition meal. It is a valuable source of emulsified fats that are ready and available to the body, as well as a calcium source which acts as a catalyst in increasing the O_2 capacity of the blood.

Recent research indicates that no harmful effects result from drinking a moderate amount of milk three to four hours prior to competition.

(vii) The pre-competition meal that has traditionally been recommended is similar to the following: a 6-to 8-ounce broiled steak with fat removed, baked potato, green vegetable, toast and honey, fresh fruit, and two to three glasses of fluid. This is not a bad-pre-competition meal. The main criticism is that it may be too heavy in protein and too light in carbohydrates.

Pre-Competition Procedures

The rules which govern pre-competition procedures

are simple and well substantiated.

(i) The food eaten during the 24 hours prior to competition should be high in carbohydrates in order to build a near-maximal supply of glycogen in the liver and the muscles.

In order to avoid depletion of the glycogen supply, heavy work should be avoided during that 24-hours period, and only moderate work is advised for as long as long as 48 hours prior to strenuous competition.

(ii) During the 24 hours prior to competition, fatty foods and other extremely slow-digesting foods should be avoided. Also to be are heavily spiced foods and foods that tend to cause indigestion.

(iii) Any work-outs done within 48 hours prior to competition should emphasize the fine points of the skills involved and strategy and should not involve extremely heavy work.

(iv) Slightly more than the normal amount of rest during the 48 hours before competition is recommended, os the performer will feel fully rested and ready to compete. However, excessive rest or any other significant deviation from the normal living routine is not advised.

(v) The competitor should occupy himself in pursuits that are interesting and relaxing which tend to keep him from becoming to anxious about the upcoming competition. Emotional involvement over a period of several hours is fatiguing.

(vi) As much possible, without violating basically sound practices, and athlete should do those things which him to feel that he is "ready" for the competition.

8

ENDURANCE

Endurance is defined as "resistance to fatigue and quick recovery after." It is the ability to persist in strenuous activity. This definition may apply to the body as a whole, to a particular body system, or to a local are of the muscle system.

For instance, reference is sometimes made to total-body endurance, cardiovascular endurance, or muscular endurance. But regardless of how many different names we give to endurance, the loss of it always has the same result—the muscle cease to function effectively. The exact cause and location of the fatigue which causes the muscle failure are difficult to determine.

Factors Which Influence Endurance

The following factors relate to endurance and influence it in different ways.

Age

Endurance increases with age up to certain point, after which endurance decreases as age increases. Among trained individuals, maximum endurance usually occurs slightly later than maximum strength; the early 20s among women, and the middle to late 20s among men. Morehouse and Miller state that the age of

20.

They make these observations about the endurance of children: "The physiological system of younger children are apparently not as well developed to meet the demands of strenuous exercise as they become when puberty is reached. Children under twelve years of age possess a highly active sympathetic nervous system that predisposes to a high heart rate and an easily depleted capacity to utilize oxygen. "

These limitations on endurance gradually diminish as the person matures into young adulthood, and endurance reaches its peak potential soon after full physical maturation is achieved.

After maximum endurance is reached, it holds fairly constant of three to five years then begins to decline gradually because of several changes that occur in the circulatory and respiratory system with increased age. Men in their 70s or 80s have lost about one-half of their capacity for transforming energy aerobically.

The ability to supply blood to active tissues has decreased, and skeletal muscles are weak. Nevertheless, when working within the limits of their ability, many men well advanced in years can carry on work with a lower heart rate and less evidence of fatigue than that exhibited by certain younger men.

It should be noted that the loss of endurance at any stage in life can be reduced significantly as a result of training.

Overweight

Fat lacks the ability to contract; therefore, it does contribute to performance. In fact, it hinders performance in three ways: (i) fat within the muscles causes friction and contributes to inefficiency in muscle contractions; (ii) fat adds dead weight and thereby increases resistance against movement; (iii) fatty tissue place an overload on the circulatory system by one mike.

Pace

The most economical pace is an even rate over the entire distance. In walking, running, swimming, and other locomotive activities, stopping, starting accelerating, and decelerating are very costly in terms of energy. Theoretically a 4-minute mile should consist of four 60-second quarters; however, this is not feasible because the quarters are influenced by the start and finish of the race and by the necessity of gaining and holding position during the race.

The idea of an even pace also has strong application to long-duration games, such as basketball, soccer, tennis, or handball. Playing in "bursts" requires much additional energy and should be avoided when endurance is of prime concern.

Skill

During performance a certain amount of energy is in unnecessary and uncoordinated movements. A skilled individual wastes less energy than the unskilled. For example, an unskilled swimmer may use more than five times as much energy as a skilled person to swim the same distance.

Similar comparisons could be made between skilled and unskilled preferment in other activities. Repeated practice improves skill and efficiency, and thus influences endurance favourably.

Body Type

Physique studies by Cureton show that only swimmers with very high mesomorphic characteristics have held world records. A few slightly built ecto-mesomorphic swimmers have achieved high success at the long distance.

Cureton also learned that champion runners have slight frames with long and well-muscles legs. Distance runners are typically more slight and less heavily muscle than sprinters.

Morehouse and Miller claim that people of moderate build have the greatest ability to sustain prolonged muscular effort. Sills and Eeren, in a study of the relationship between extreme body types and performance, found that mesomorphs were only slightly better than ecto-morphs in endurance tests, and endomorphs were far inferior to the other two body types. Bookwalter produced evidence that generally supports Sills' findings.

In summary, it can be said that most people who find success in endurance activities have a high degree of mesomorphy,, and are also inclined towards ectomorph.

People of heavier body types are inclined to be more successful in activities requiring endurance, such as swimming the body weight is not carried by the muscles.

Sex Type

Studies show that upto the beginning of puberty, girls are about equal to boys in endurance. Women reach maximum endurance potential at about the age of 20, while men continue to increase until at a slight the mid-20s.

Comparing adults men and women, there is only a slightly difference in endurance in moderate exercise, but the endurance of women in strenuous activities is considerably less than that of men.

Morehouse and Miller point out that adult women, have only one-half the endurance of adult men in running. Limiting factors of endurance among women for vigorous activity are (i) a more rapid heart rate; (ii) a small heart with a resultant smaller capacity to deliver blood; (iii) smaller chest cavity, resulting in inferior ling capacity; and (iv) the blood of women is limited in its oxygen, carrying capacity due to fewer fed blood cells.

Joki has said this about girls: "Endurance training for girls ought to be initiated prior to the onset of puberty." Training seems to reverse the natural trend toward decline of endurance in untrained girls.

Once the effect of training upon performance is established, it can be stabilized over many years. And since sustained practice improves techniques, gains in efficiency may continue long after the establishment of optimal endurance.

Strength

Suppose a man has enough strength to move a particular amount of resistance through the range of motion one hundred times. If his strength were increased 50% he would be able to move the same resistance with greater ease; he could repeat the movement considerably more than one hundred times.

Vital Capacity

Vital capacity, the total amount of air than can be forcibly expired after a completed inspiration, has been used frequently as a measure of adequacy of the respiratory system.

Although it measures the approximate capacity of the lungs, recent information indicates it is of little use in predicting ability to perform tasks of endurance. Obviously other factors are more significant. For example, any limitation of the oxygen delivery system to the cells will reduce the effectiveness of the delivery, regardless of vital capacity.

Probably a large vital capacity is important in very intense exercise when the lack of oxygen may be fond in the alveoli, but it is of little value when the exercise is less demanding. The main advantage of time with fewer, but deeper, inspirations thus prolonging the onset of fatigue in the respiratory muscles.

Temperature

Grose found that endurance is adversely affected by immersion of the arm for 8 minutes in water at 120°F. Conversely, the effects of cold have proven to be advantageous, until a muscle temperature of 80°F. is reached.

According to Clark et. al. 80°F appears to be the optimal muscle temperature for endurance, and muscle temperatures below this level produce adverse effects on endurance.

Cross-Training

It has been demonstrated that by training one side of the body the counterparts on the other side may gain a limited amount of endurance and strength.

Hodgkins found that when a body limb undergoes endurance training, the opposite limb.

Hyperventilation

Hyperventilation may occur in an athlete either unintentionally or intentionally. It is brought on intentionally by forced deep beating which results in a greatly increased exchange of air to the lungs. Hyperventilation results in an appreciable build-up of CO_2 in the circulo-respiratory system, but it does not increase the amount of O_2 in the blood, as commonly believed.

The amount of oxygen transferred to the blood is not usually limited by the amount entering the lugs, but rather by the available are of contact between the alveoli and the capillary be and by the carrying capacity of the blood. If the blood is already fully saturated, the excess oxygen in the lungs will only be expelled in normal expiration, because oxygen cannot be stored.

DeVries found that hyperventilation can approximately double breath-holding time. Consequently, it will definitely improve performances where breath holding is important, such as underwater swimming, or crawl-stroke sprinting. But it is not established that hyperventilation is of any measurable value in performance where breath holding is not involved.

Significance of Endurance

Endurance is one of the basic components of general athletic ability, and it is usually considered to be the most important component of physiological fitness. Some of the activities in which endurance is of prime importance are running, swimming, cycling, wrestling, basketball, soccer, rugby, and football.

In all of these activities, endurance training

occupies and important place in preparation for performance. In less strenuous sports, such as baseball and golf, endurance is of less importance.

However, even in these spots a small amount of fatigue will have negative influence on performance. When endurance gives to fatigue as a result of muscular work, several elements important to good performance diminish: strength, timing, neuromuscular co-ordination, speed of movement, reaction time, and alertness.

How to Increase Endurance

Because endurance is factor in almost all vigorous performance, methods of increasing it are of primary concern. We have already discussed the need to apply the concept of progressive overload for the development of strength.

This concept must also be applied if endurance is to be increased. Overload for endurance simply means working the organism beyond previous endurance levels.

There are two forms of endurance that are of concern in athletic conditioning, muscle endurance and cardiovascular endurance. Development of the two forms requires different approaches.

Cardiovascular Endurance

Cardiovascular endurance refers to the ability of the circulatory system to provide oxygen to the cells to support the oxidative energy schemes of the body and to remove the waste products of metabolism. When many muscles are worked for long periods of time, these factors limit the amount of work which can be accomplished.

Therefore, the primary objective of cardiovascular endurance training is to improve the circulation to the working muscles.

Cardiovascular endurance training can be divided into two main categories: aerobic training and anaerobic training. Aerobic trainings involves training the systems which supply oxygen to the cells of the body, whereas anaerobic training involves the energy mechanisms which supply energy without the presence of oxygen.

Anaerobic processes are not actually involved in cardiovascular endurance except as they are called into play as a result of inadequacy of the aerobic process. Lack of ability by the cardiovascular system toe provide sufficient oxygen results in anaerobic work.

Aerobic Training

The ability of the body to supply the cells with oxygen is the key to cardiovascular endurance. When oxygen is not available in the cells in large enough quantities, the energy production shifts to the Anaerobic process.

This process produces ATP very inefficiently and it produces the fatigue toxin lactic acid. When large quantities of lactic acid are produced, activity must be lowered to a level below which no additional acid will accumulate.

This is fatigue. Because of the importance of oxygen in the production of energy for muscular work, the endurance level of an athlete can be evaluated in a laboratory by measuring the amount of oxygen he is able to use per kilogram of body weight.

Those with high oxygen uptake can generally work longer at a faster rate than those with low oxygen uptake. Of course the reason is that the greater oxygen uptake allows the body to use the more efficient energy-producing pathways and implies a larger circulation to the cells.

The purpose of aerobic endurance training then is to increase the ability of the oxygen transport system which results in more oxygen uptake, and in turn a better oxygen supply to the cells.

This type of endurance can be developed by working continuously for long periods of time such as in cross-country running, long-distance swimming, or cross-country skiing. However, perhaps the best method to develop cardiovascular endurance is known as interval training.

This technique consists of a series of work-outs with a short rest interval between bouts. Astrand and Rodahl found that a work load which could only be tolerated continuously for 9 minutes could be carried on for an hour when done intermittently. This means that much more total work can be accomplished before fatigue using interval training than continuous training.

In order for an interval-training program to continue to be effective over a period of time the intensity must be increased as endurance is gained so that overload may continue to be applied. On other words, as an athlete becomes better conditioned, he must do more work during each of the training periods to cause additional endurance gains.

Interval-training work-outs may be varied four different ways; (i) the number of work bouts can be increased; (ii) the length of each bout can be increased; (iii) the intensity of each bout can be increased; and (iv) the rest periods between bouts can be shorter. It is recommended that the work bouts be a 3 to 5 minutes in length, with light activity or rest periods between the bouts.

The number of bouts, intensity of each bout, and the amount of rest between bouts should be geared to the level of conditioning of the athlete. The athlete need not be fatigued at the end of each work period since there is no evidence that anaerobic processes help to develop aerobic endurance.

Heart rate should be used as the criterion for determining the optimal training load. It should be maintained at a rate within 10 beats of maximum heart rate during each of the 3 to 5 minute work bouts.

The rest periods between bouts should be equal to or less than the time of the work bouts. A training program of this type involving a sufficient number of bouts during each work-out will result in optimal changes in the effectiveness of the oxygen transport system.

It should be noted that if less than the optimal rate of increase in aerobic endurance is desired, the heart rate does not need to be maintained within 10 beats of maximum during each bout. Cooper for at least 5 minutes. In most athletes , 150 beats per m minute will produce against in aerobic endurance, but the gains will be less than optimal. Karvonen recommended that the heart rate during each bout be at least resting heart rate plus 60% of the difference between resting and maximum. It is very questionable whether karvonen's plan is vigorous enough to produce significant gains in trained athletes.

In summary, it should be said that aerobic endurance will develop at an optimal rate as a result of doing a sufficient number of successive bouts of work, 3 to 5 minutes in length with short rest periods in between, where the work bouts are intense enough to cause the heart rate to be maintained within 10 beats of maximal rate.

Further, aerobic endurance can be developed at less than optimal rather by doing bouts of work that are led intense, and therefore, do not maintain the heart rate within 10 beats of maximal rate. Also, aerobic endurance can be developed at a reasonable, but less than optimal, rate by doing continuous work over an extended period of time at considerably less than maximum intensity, such as cross-country running.

Anaerobic Training

Anaerobic endurance refers to the effectiveness of the processes of the body which provide energy for muscular contraction in the absence of oxygen, or in other words, when sufficient oxygen is not available to produce enough energy aerobically.

Anaerobic endurance is very important in activities requiring maximum effort for a short period, such as running a 220-or 440-yard spring, or in activities such as basketball and football, which require short bursts of vigorous activity.

Anaerobic endurance training is accomplished best by repeated short bouts of maximal effort, followed by brief rest period between bouts. Extremely high levels of lactic acid are found in the blood following four or five work bouts of this type, indicating great use of the anaerobic mechanisms in the cells. We-trained athletes are typically able to tolerate much higher lactate levels than untrained athletes. This indicates that anaerobic training would be of great value to athletes involved in vigorous short-duration activities.

It is important that work periods for anaerobic training not be too short. Research indicates that 10 to 15 seconds of vigorous work do not increase lactic acid levels a significant amount, and thus would have little, if any, effect on anaerobic endurance. Successive vigorous work bouts of about one minute in length are the most effective for his type of endurance.

Aerobic-Anaerobic Relationship

Training programs usually involve both aerobic and anaerobic training because most activities involve both aerobic and anaerobic processes. But it is important to know that for certain performance aerobic endurance should be emphasized, while anaerobic endurance should be emphasized for other performances.

Falls present valuable information which illustrates the relationship between different track event and the primary energy yielding components involved.

It becomes apparent that an athlete who is training to run the mile should devote 20% of the training program to development of speed, 25% to aerobic development, and 55% to anaerobic development. Notice that the time of the even has been included. Regardless of the kind of even, the time is related to the energy yielding systems involved.

Therefore, for a swimming event lasting 4 to 5 minutes, the athletes would use approximately the same training program as for the mile urn, which also lasts 4 to 5 minutes. The main difference would be the kind of activity used in the training program.

Repetitions of sprints involve the repetition of short sprints as a means of preparation for competitive running. Since sprinting means running at absolute maximum speed, there is not an "easy sprint." The effect of sprinting as a mans of training is the development of speed and muscular strength.

Continuous slow running refers to running long distances at relatively slow speeds. The distance covered, in this type of training should be related to the racing event. For example, a miller might run three to five times his racing distance or more.

The heart beats approximately 150 beats per minute during this type of training, and the speed depends upon the ability of the athlete.

Continuous fast running differs from continuous slow running in terms of speed. Because the pace is faster, fatigue is countered sooner. This training develops aerobic endurance.

It represents a form of effort that seeks gradually to condition the organism to tolerate the stresses encountered in running at faster and faster speeds.

Slow interval develops aerobic endurance. The speed is faster than in continuous fast-running training, thus adapting the athlete to running at a more intense effort. In this type of formal fast-slow running, the heart beats at the rate of approximately 180 beats per minute during the heavy work phase.

Fast interval develops anaerobic endurance or speed endurance. It is used after a background of aerobic or general endurance has been established. The heart should beat in excess of 180 beats per minute during the work phase. It develops the ability of the runner to withstand fatigue in the absence of an adequate oxygen supply.

Repetition running differs from interval training in term of the length of the fast run and the degree of recovery following each fast effort. It involves repetitions of comparatively longer distances with relatively complete recovery after each effort.

Repetition running is usually concerned with repetitions of distances such as 880 yards to two miles with relatively complete recovery between, during which time the heart rate falls below 120 beats per minute.

Conversely, interval training includes repetitions of shorter distances with less than complete recovery after each by jogging a distance equal to the fast run in a time period two to three times as long as required to complete the fast run.

Speed play is a form of training featuring informal fast-slow running, as opposed to the formal fast-slow running in interval training. It involves running preferably, but not necessarily, over natural surfaces such as golf courses, grass, or trails through woods, with emphasis on fast running. Fast and slow interval-running repetition running, sprinting, walking, and continuous fast-running training are informally combined in speed play. This type of training is also known as fartlek training.

Acceleration sprinting is the gradual acceleration from jogging to striding, following by sprinting. For example, an athlete may jog 25 yards, stride 50 yards and sprint 50 yards, followed by 50 yards of walking, then repeat the procedure several times.

This type of training emphasized both speed and

endurance, provided enough repetitions are performed to cause endurance overload.

Hollow sprints are two sprints joined by a "hollow" period of recovery jogging. Examples included sprint 50, jog 50, spring 50, and walk 50 yards for recovery prior to the next repetition; spring 110, jog 110, spring 110, and walk 110 yards before the next repetition; spring 220, jog 220, and walk 220 yards before repeating.

Other approaches have been taken to the problem of endurance training. One of the most interesting and helpful is the computerized running and training program developed by Gardner and Purdy. Through computer programming they have created thousands of individualized work-outs based upon the initial condition of the athlete.

These programs have been tested on hundreds of track athletes and appear to be extremely accurate and highly useful for improving cardiovascular endurance.

Muscle Endurance

Local muscle endurance is dependent upon the quality of the muscles, the extensiveness of their capillary beds, and the nerve mechanisms supplying them. Local muscle endurance is not limited greatly by the efficiency of the supporting body system.

It has been established that strength contributes to muscle endurance. In fact, there is a very high correlation between strength and absolute muscle endurance, which is the amount of time person can work against a certain resistance without regard to strength. Stronger subjects are usually able to continue exercise longer than weaker ones.

Coefficients of correlation ranging from. 75 to 97 have been found between strength and absolute muscle endurance. Conversely, there is very little relationship between strength and relative muscle endurance. If the resistance is adjusted to correspond with each person's strength, then the weaker persons display and much endurance as the stronger ones.

Since increasing strength is an effective method of increasing muscle endurance, the strength-building methods described earlier may be used for this purpose. However, if one desires to increase endurance as the stronger ones.

Since increasing strength is an effective method of increasing muscle endurance, the strength-building methods described earlier may be used for this purpose. However, if one desires to increase endurance without increasing strength, then the program must be altered to emphasized endurance without strength.

Research shows that 20 to 30 RMs with three sets will increase muscle endurance at a fast rate and will affect strength and muscle size very little. Hence, if only increased endurance is desired, many RMs with light weight should be employed.

Even though weight training has been used as an illustration, it should be recognized that muscle endurance can be increased by any form of exercise which results in overloading the muscles either in weight or repetitions. For example, calisthenic exercises, regular sports participation, manual labour, jogging, and walking are all effective for developing endurance in the muscles in which regular overloading is accomplished.

But, it should be remembered that muscle endurance is highly specific, and significant increases will be limited to the muscles which experience regular overloading.

Physiological Chances Which Accompany Endurance

Endurance training over a prolonged period results in the following changes in the organisation

Heart

The heart becomes larger and more effective as a pump. The muscle tissue which forms the wall of the heart responds to regular overload in much the same way as skeletal muscle; that is, it becomes larger and stronger.

However, growth of the heart is more gradual and less pronounced than in skeletal muscle. The increased size and strength of the heart causes a greater stroke volume and more cardiac output. In turning this results in a slower resting heart rate and smaller increase in rate for a given level of work.

Lungs

Consistent overloading of the respiratory system increases the strength and endurance of the respiratory muscles, and causes the interior volume of the lungs to increase. This allows a larger exchange of air per respiration.

The expansion results in the development of more alveoli, and in turn, more interior surface area where gases may be transferred to and from the circulatory system. This results in a slower breathing rate during rest and less increase in breathing rate during heavy work.

Blood

Blood volume increases approximately in proportion to the increase in capillaries. Carlsten and Grimby found that adult men who were well conditioned had about 20% more blood than those who were poorly conditioned.

Undoubtedly, highly trained athletes would show even a greater increase in blood volume. Additional blood volume increases the capacity of the circulatory system of transport substances to and from the working muscles. The composition of the blood changes as a result of training, and this increases the blood viscosity and its carrying capacity.

Blood Pressure

Little change in blood pressure while resign occurs even when great improvements in conditioning are achieved. In normal subjects, however, there is usually a slight increase in diastolic pressure.

A more pronounced result of training is the ability to maintain a near resting level of pressure under conditions of moderate work. The rapid return of resting pressure is a further indication of good condition.

Increased Efficiency

Extensive training brings about increased neuromuscular efficiency, meaning that less energy is expended to accomplish given amount of work. This is accounted for by (i) more efficient transmission of nerve impulses; (ii) less resistance from antagonistic muscles; (ii) less wasted motion; (iv) less fatty tissue in the muscles; and (v) more efficiency in the contractile processes of the muscle fibres.

Capillaries

As a result of extensive training, capillary beds in the lungs and in the trained muscles increase significantly. In turn, the increased capillaries provide opportunity for larger exchanges of gases between the interior of the lungs and the blood.

A similar effects takes place at the muscles. Also training causes the exchange between the blood and the cells to become more efficient, thus blood and the cells to become, thus allowing greater exchange of gases and other products between the muscle cells and the blood.

9

REACTION AND SPEED TIME

Even though and reaction time are somewhat related, they are distinct characteristics, and it is possible for people to be lacking in one of the traits and still have an abundance of the other.

Reaction Time

Reaction time relates to, but is different than, reflex time, movement time, and response time. It is interval between a stimulus and the initiation of movement. Teichner has divided reaction time into four phases: (i) the onset of the stimulus; (ii) the first latency period, during which the receptor process occurs; (iii) the second latency period, involving the central transmission of the sensory impulses to the motor fibres; (iv) the delay involved in the motor process preceding contraction of the muscles.

Tripp defines reaction time as being a human time lag consisting of (i) a sense time (ii) a decision time, and (ii) movement time.

Reflex time is a shortened reaction time wherein the thought or decision making phase is eliminated. In a relax the impulses travel through the sensory nerves, across the reflex arc, and through motor nerves to the muscle.

There are two types of reflexes, innate and conditioned. An innate reflex is a predictable response to a given stimulus which is accomplished below the level of conscious control. Such reflexes must originate in the afferent system, and the efferent response will usually occur before the organism is consciously aware of the stimulus.

If the organism is aware of the stimulus, the reflex response may occur without interference, or it may be consciously inhibited or intensified. Reflexes which are learned are called conditioned reflexes. If the performer learns to respond automatically in the same manner to the same stimulus, this is a conditioned reflex.

A conscious movement can be superimposed on a conditioned reflex the same as on an innate reflex..

Movement time starts where reaction time needs. It is the time that elapses between the beginning of a movement and its completion.

Response time is a combination of reaction time and movement time. It is the total time that elapses from the onset of the stimulus until the act is completed.

Factors which Influence Reaction Time

Several factors influences reaction time in different ways. Following are discussions of some of the more important factors.

Age and Sex Type

The correlation of age and reaction time has received considerable attention. Karpovich states that reaction time is slow in young children and gradually improves with age, reaching its maximum at the college age level.

Atwell and Elbel and Henry and Whitley found that maximum reaction time had not been fully reached at high school age. Teichner believes that reaction time improves up to about the age of 30, after which the latency period grows longer; but even at the age of 60 reaction time is faster than at the age of 10. This conclusion was supported by Tripp who indicates that recent studies who very little slowing of reaction time prior to the age of 60.

Regarding sex differences, Teichner and Tripp both agree that men react slightly faster than women. In a study of the reaction time of limb movements of men and women, Henry et al. found that reactions were slower in women, but the difference was slight.

The difference can probably be attributed to the fact that men practice activities requiring fast reactions more than women.

Readiness to Act

It is reasonable to assume that reaction time is influenced by the degree an individual is ready to react. Based on a study of track sprinters, Pierson concluded that imagining or anticipating an act prepares the muscles for movement before the stimulus triggers a response.

In a study concerning the effects of muscle stretch, tension, and relaxation upon reaction time, Smith found that subjects produced a reaction time 7% faster if the muscles were in a state of tension as opposed to being relaxed. Clarke and Glines studied the effects of preliminary muscular tension on reaction latency and found that the latency period is significantly shortened as result of tension.

Influence of Preparatory Signals

According to Teichner, reaction time is improved if a preparatory signal is given at 1.5 to 8 seconds prior to the stimulus. Such signal causes a performer to concentrate on the stimulus, and to prepare his muscles for a quick response once the stimulus is given. Practical experience also supports this claim.

Influence of Intensity of Stimulus

Teichner states that an increase in the intensity of visual, auditory, thermal, and pain stimuli produces improvements in reaction time. Baumesister et al., in a study involving both normal and mentally retarded subjects, found that both groups reacted quickly when the stimulus was intensified, with the retarded profiting more from increased intensity. Morehouse and Miller believe there is a limit or intensifying the stimuli, beyond which increased intensity will not speed up reaction time, and may even slow it down. The validity of this belief is questionable, and deserves additional research.

Influence of Numbers of Receptors Stimulated

Teichner claims that the greater the number of receptors stimulated, the shorter the latency period, and thus the shorter the reaction time. He also states that simultaneous combinations of light, sound, and shock, produce improved reaction times.

Morehouse and Miller believe that reaction time is slowed by stimuli that are too complicated, intermittent distraction noises, and by sound signals that vary in pitch and loudness. They believe that easily perceived stimuli produce faster reaction times. There is some evidence that the presentation of two stimuli close in succession causes a delayed response to the second stimulus.

Athletes vs. Non-Athletes

Karpovich and Morehouse and Miller claim that athletes have faster reactions than non-athletes, and sprinters have faster reactions than distance runners. Teichner indicates that faster reactions athletes are probable due mostly to the training they have received. This may be true, but it is reasonable to assume that training does not account for all the differences.

Diet

In a study of the effects of breakfast upon reaction time, Tuttle et al. discovered that a light breakfast resulted in a shorter reaction time than a breakfast consisting of coffee only, and that coffee only produced a shorter reaction time than a heavy breakfast. Subjects who went without breakfast were found to have slower reactions.

Information is lacking about the effects of the total diet on reaction time. It is doubtful that any relationship exists, provided the diet is conducive to good health. A survey of literature by Teichner showed that coffee and Benzedrine slow reactions in subjects who are awakened just prior to testing. Alcohol consistently slows reaction time under all circumstances. Smoking has been found to slow reaction time when the stimulus is in the form of a visual signal.

Effects of Fatigue on Reaction Time

Karpovich and Atwell and Elbel claim evidence that physiological fatigue lengthens reaction time. However, Keeler found that it takes a considerable amount of fatigue to slow reactions a measurable amount. Several experiments show that lack of sleep has little effect on reaction time when the subjects are concentrating on the stimulus.

Effects Weight Training

Bear and Gersten, in a study of the effects of various exercise programs on reaction time, found that high-resistance isotonic contractions produced a 13% improvement in reaction time, and that high-resistance isometric contractions produced improvement in reactions by 6% Low-resistance exercises produced no change in reaction time.

There is no substantial evidence which contradicts the results of this research. However, the topic deserves additional study.

Specificity of Reaction Time

An interesting question is whether reaction time is highly specific to a body part or a movement, or whether it tends to be general. Studies indicate a high degree of specificity by limb and by movement.

Thus an individual may be quick in reacting with the arms, but relatively slow with the legs. Also, he may be fast in reacting with certain arm movements and slower in other arm movements. Even though there is a high degree of specificity, there is still a general component that enables a person to be labelled either fast or slow in his reactions.

Relationship of Reaction Time to Movement Time

Another interesting question is whether movement time can be predicted from reaction time. The research fails to demonstrate a relationship between these two factors. Henry and Smith concluded that individual differences in ability to react quickly and ability to move fast are almost entirely unrelated.

Significance of Reaction Time

The speed with which an individual can react in a competitive situation is of great interest to those concerned with physical education and athletic performance. For example, this factor party determines how successful a basketball player can be on defence.

When the offensive player makes his move, the difference between a slow and a fast reaction by the defensive player can determine his success or failure. Both offensive and defensive players are often hindered by slow reaction because they are not able to demonstrate the quickness necessary to outmanoeuvred their opponents. Similar examples could be stated in connection with tennis, soccer, badminton, football, and several other court and field games.

How to Improve Reaction Time

Reaction time in specific movements will improve as a result of extensive practice of those movement. Tripp claims that practice reduces decision time by eliminating incorrect decisions and enables the correct decision to be made more efficiently.

If an act is practised enough, a conditioned reflex may develop. For example, a sprinter might develop a conditioned reflex to a pistol shot. A boxer might develop conditioned reflexes which cause him to automatically respond in specific ways to movement made by his opponent. Similar examples could be given in connection with the other performance. There is no evidence that a person's Improvements tend to be specific rather than general, meaning that improved reaction time in one act will not guarantee improved reactions in another act, or in body movements may improve reaction time, but this idea has not been substantiated by research.

Speed

There are different forms of speed: (i) speed of movement of body segment; (ii) running speed for a very short distance; and (iii) maximum running speed. Because of these different forms of speed it is difficult to label a person "fast" or "slow."

Speed of movement is highly specific to areas of the body. An individual with fast arm movement may have slow leg movements, for example. In fact, this specificity extends even to the type of task and the direction of movement.

Running speed can be discussed in terms of two factors: rate of acceleration and maximal velocity. The first factor is related to how fast a person can accelerate, such as the charge of a football runner or the acceleration of a sprinter. This factor is the most important consideration in speed for distances up to about 20 yards, and is very important in court and field games and short races.

On the other hand, for distances greater than 20 yards, maximal running speed is the more important factor. These two factors of running speed are not highly related. Therefore, an individual may be a slow starter with a fast maximal speed, or a fast starter with a slow maximal speed.

Indeed a person may be proficient in football, basketball, or tennis, where quick acceleration is important, but be a poor 220 yards sprinter , and vice versa.

Two other aspects of running speed are average speed and final speed. A runner who is attempting to cover a given distance in the shorter time possible, such as in the mile run, is concerned with the fastest average speed over the entire distance. Conversely, in jumping or throwing for maximum distance, average speed is of no concern, whereas final speed is of utmost concern.

Factors which Influence Speed

Several factors influence speed. Among them are the following:

Muscle Length

According to A.V. Hill and agreed upon by other physiologist, a muscle fibre that is ten times longer than another fibre can shorten ten times as fast, provided the intrinsic properties of the two fibres are the same. This means that muscles with long fibres have speed advantages over muscles with short fibres.

Force and Acceleration

According to Newton's second law of motion, acceleration of the body is proportional to the force causing it. This means that if the force is doubled, the rate of acceleration will also double.

Thus a sprinter increases acceleration by increasing the force he applies against the surface on which he runs, while a swimmer achieves increased acceleration by increasing the force of the kick and stroke against the water.

Regarding acceleration, it must be realized that muscle contractions provide the force, and more forceful contractions expend more energy. The energy cost of a contraction varies with the cube of the speed of contraction.

If muscle X contracts twice as fast as muscle Y, then its energy cost is 8 times as great as that of muscle Y. If muscle X contracts three times as fast as muscle Y, its energy cost is 27 times as great as that of muscle Y. This fact has much application in determining the rate at which a performer should accelerate, especially in endurance activities.

Effects of the Theoretical Square Law

This law has to do with the negative or retarding forces. The law states that air and water resistance vary approximately with the square of the velocity, meaning that if the velocity at which a body travels is increased by 2 the air or water resistance will increase by 16.

Thus, if swimmer pulls his arm through the water at the rate of 5 feet per second, he meets a given amount of water resistance, which he uses to propel him forward. If the rate of pull is increased to 10 feet per second, the resistance is increased 4 times, resulting in 5 times as much propulsive force from the stroke.

But, 4 times the propulsive force will not increase the swimmer's speed through the water by 4 times, because the water's resistance against him also increases with the square of his velocity, meaning that as he moves faster he meets proportionately more resistance.

Speed-Force Relationship

It has been shown through research that the force available from a muscle contraction decreases as the rate of shortening increases. A muscle can contract with is greatest force at zero speed. Likewise, a muscle can contract with its greatest speed when it applies zero force. As a muscle applies more force against resistance, it contract with proportionately less speed.

Age and Sex Type

Generally, men increase in all aspects of speed up to about the age of 20, after which speed tends to decrease at a very gradual but steady rate. Women reach maximum speed at a younger age, 16 to 17 years. Hodkins found that peak speed is maintained longer by males, whereas peak reaction time is maintained longer by females.

Records of sports events involving running and swimming speed indicate that women have about 85% as much speed as men. Limited research supports the claim that speed of body segments is also about 85% as fast in women as in men.

This difference between men and women might be accounted for differences in strength because strength influences speed, and men are stronger than women.

Temperature

Hill found that the contractile speed of muscles in animals is increased 20% by raising the temperature 2^0 C. He suggested that such changes might be brought about in humans by diathermy, or other deep-heat, treatment.

Somatotype

It is difficult to relate movement speed of specific body parts to body type, except to say that obese people tend to lack speed. Running speed favours people of medium stature with medium-light builds. They would be characterized as meso-extomorphs. However, there are many individual exceptions to this statement.

Strength

There is considerable evidence that strength and speed are only mildly related when light resistance is involved. A limited amount of information supports the idea that dynamic strength is more closely related to speed than is static strength.

Of course, as the resistance is increased, strength has a greater influence on speed because more strength is needed to overcome the heavier resistance at a fast rate.

The important question relative to this topic is not whether speed relates to absolute strength, but whether speed can be increased by improving strength. The answer is yes. Considerable evidence indicates a strong relationship between gain in strength and gain in speed of movement. The evidence also support the claim that there is some relationship between strength gains and running speed.

Flexibility

It is known that restricted dynamic flexibility, especially in the hip region, can retard running speed, because it increases the resistance provided by the antagonistic muscles toward the end of the range of motion. However, there is no evidence that speed will be increased by increasing flexibility beyond a reasonable amount.

Dominant Factors in Speed Under Various Conditions

There are several considerations under this topic; (i) IN lightly loaded and simple movements, intrinsic speed of the muscles, which depends on physicochemical and biochemical properties, is probably the main limitation on speed.

Neuromuscular coordination and strength are secondary. (ii) In lightly loaded movements which are very complex, it is likely that coordination of the various muscles and the different movements set the limits on speed. (iii) In heavily loaded and complex movements, coordination and strength are the dominant factors which influence speed.

Body Mechanics and Running Speed

Photographic analysis has shown that efficient spring running is characterized by a high knee lift, a long running stride, and placement of the feet on a line beneath the runner's centre of gravity.

It is important in running that the propelling forces be directed properly and efficiently. Specifically, the leg movements should be straight forward and backward, the arm and shoulder movements should be directed to pull the body in the desired direction, and the angle of projection should be optimum in order to achieve maximum speed.

An example of the negative effects of incorrect mechanics can be seen in turning the feet outward. If this is done, three undesired results occur: (i) Approximately 1 inch is lost on each stride because the foot covers less distance when turned outward.

In a 100-yard dash this would result in a loss of about 50 inches. (ii) Part of the propelling force is lost from the four smaller toes of each foot, thus reducing the total propelling force. (iii) The propelling force from the feet tend to be diagonal instead of straight forward. Other forms of incorrect running mechanics have different effect but similar results on running speed.

Significance of Speed

Running speed is an athletic event in itself and is also very important in numerous other sports. Speed and manoeuvrability are factors in almost all court and field games, and can make the difference in whether a performer is able to gain an advantage over his opponent.

Basketball provides good examples of the significance of speed. Fast hand arm movements are essential to good ball handling and can often enable a player to steal the ball from the opponents. Fast acceleration is important in both the offensive and defensive phases of the game, because it can enable a player to compete better against his opponent in floor play. Maximum speed, as well as acceleration, is important on fast break plays covering the length of the court.

Similar examples could be given of the significance of speed in other court games, such as games, such as football, soccer, rugby, and baseball. Often only a small increase in movement speed or running speed can improve an athlete's effectiveness a considerable amount.

How to Increase Speed

Speed is basically a result of applying force to a mass. In the case of human movements, body, or segments of it, represents the mass, and the muscle contractions represent the force. If the force is greater than the resistance, then movement will occur. As the force becomes greater, the speed at which the mass moves will increase proportionately.

In speed there are both positive and negative force acting. The positive forces are caused by muscle contractions, while the negative force are caused by friction, air resistance, gravity and inertia. Devries has calculated that in running, a person might have negative forces equal to 3.45 horsepower.

He determined the forces as coming from the following: (i) gravity, 0.1 hp; (ii) velocity changes, 0.5 hp; (iii) acceleration of limbs, 1.68 hp; (iv) deceleration of limbs, 6.67 hp; and (v) air resistance, 0.5 hp.

This means that in order to maintain a constant speed the runner would need to provide a propelling force of 3.45 hp. Of course, it must be recognized that this is only an illustration which does not accurately represent all cases. As the running speed is increased, the resisting forces are likewise increased, which means that more propelling force is needed to maintain a faster speed. Speed can be increased by either decreasing the negative force speed. Speed can be increased by either decreasing the negative forces or increasing the positive forces.

Reducing the Negative Forces

Some of the negative forces tend to be constant, while others are variable. Gravity is represented by the mass and is constant, except when weight is gained or lost. Velocity changes are variable and can be controlled rather easily. Velocity changes waste energy and influence overall speed in a negative way.

The negative effects of acceleration and deceleration of limbs can be only partially controlled. Unnecessary movements can be eliminated, and the efficiency of the necessary movements can often be improved. Air resistance can sometimes be reduced by altering the body's position. For example, cyclers, skiers, and skaters perform in a semi-flexed position to reduce the body surface in the direction of movement, and thus reduce the air resistance. Likewise, swimmers present the smallest surface area possible in the direction of movement in order to meet minimum water resistance.

Each kind of speed event offers slightly different possibilities for reducing the negative forces. The coach and athlete should analyse each case separately to determine what can be done to reduce negative effects.

Increasing Positive Forces

Under this topic we should consider (i) intrinsic speed of muscle contractions; (ii) the force which muscle can apply against the resistance; (iii) coordination; and (iv) the leverage involved in the movements. Each of factors will be discussed separately.

It is established that speed of contraction is inherent in the muscle tissue. Different muscle contract at different rates even when they are detached from the body and stimulated artificially. It is believed and supported by a limited amount of research that the rate of muscle contraction can be increased by repeated practice of fast movements. Such practice over an extended period will improve nerve innervations to the muscles and at the same time increase the efficiency of the muscle.

The speed of movement is directly proportional to the speed of contraction of the mover muscles. If the contractile rate were increased by 5%, the speed of movement would increase by the same percentage, if other factor remain constant.

Movement involves working against some resistance, even if the resistance is only the weight of the body segment. Because of this, contractile force can influence has less retarding effect on speed.

Where resistance is very light, it is doubtful that contractile force is a significant factor in speed, but as the resistance becomes greater, contractile force has a larger influence.

Increased coordination can increase the speed of specific movements. As the several mover muscles become better coordinated, they can cooperatively overcome the external resistance with greater speed. Also, as the agonists and antagonists become better coordinated, the antagonists furnish less resistance to the contractile efforts of the agonists. This is of utmost importance because, by reducing tension in the antagonists, speed is increased and the onset of fatigue is postponed.

Not only is it important to coordinate the muscles involved in a movement, but it is also important to coordinate the different movements which contribute to speed. This is demonstrated well in the baseball throw where each successive movement builds on previous movements. In speed swimming and running, the arms and legs all move simultaneously, and the movements must be well coordinated.

In motor performance the body functions as a system of levers, and often the leverage can be improved. It is known that if the angular velocity at the joint constant, then the speed at the end of the lever is directly proportional to the lever's length.

This means that if lever X is twice as long as lever Y

and if both levers rotate about their fulcrums at the same angular velocity, then the end of lever X will move twice as fast as lever Y, because it is twice as long. Thus speed can sometimes be influenced by voluntarily adjusting body levers to their optimal length. This is demonstrated in the overarm throw, where the hand passes high above the shoulder.

If the lever is purposely shortened, causing the hand to pass close to the shoulder, the speed the ball travels is reduced considerably. Other clear example of the influence of leverage on speed could be related to baseball batting, the discuss throw, or the hammer throw. To achieve the greatest speed, the best combination of angular velocity and lever length must be involved. Identically, the angular velocity is determined by how fast the muscles can overcome the external resistance.

In summary, the following has been pointed out: (i) Speed of muscle contraction can be increased a limited amount by training with repeated fast movements. (ii) Speed of movement against resistance can be increased by increasing the ability to apply force against the resistance. This method is ineffective against light resistance is increased. (iii) Speed can be increased by improving the coordination of the various muscles involved in each movement and by improving the coordination of the various movements involved in the skill. (iv) Speed can be increased by employing the optimum combination of regular velocity and length of the levers involved.

Special Considerations in Running Speed

Speed is determined by the length of stride and frequency of stride. In order to increased running speed, one or both of these factors must be increased. Length of stride is dependent primarily upon leg and leg power. Leg speed is mostly dependent upon speed of muscle contractions and neuromuscular coordination.

Sprinting is essentially a power performance. It depends on one's ability to project the body forcefully and rapidly from alternate feet. Developed relatively early in life, about the age of 20 for men and about 16 for women, running speed is a trait that can be improved only a limited amount.

Traditionally it has been thought that there are three possibilities for increasing speed: (i) increased the power (force × velocity) of the leg extensor muscles, thus causing more propelling force; (ii) practice running at top speed to improve the specific coordinations involved; and (iii) correct errors in running mechanics.

Slater-Hammel shed additional light on the subject when he demonstrated that the rate of leg alternation in sprinting ranges from 3.10 to 4.85 per second, while in cycling it ranges from 5.5 to 7.1 per second.

This illustrates that maximum leg alternation is not used in sprinting, and it indicates that the rate of alternation is probably not the limiting factors. Hubbard did research which demonstrated that the length of stride, rather than rate of leg alternation, is the main limitation in springing. It is known that length of stride can be increased by increasing leg power, which is the ability to apply more force rapidly.

10

AQUATIC ACTIVITIES

Aquatic activities are very different from other athletic sports because they are performed in the water. However, the characteristics required by an excellent swimmer are similar to those required by many other athletes, except the characteristics must be emphasized in different body parts.

For example, power is very important in court games and is equally important in swimming arm power is of paramount importance.

Swimming, like running, involves two general categories of events, sprint races and distance races. Obviously the sprint events depend primarily upon swimming speed over short distance, whereas distance races depend primarily upon swimming endurance.

As one progresses from very short races, such as the 50-yard sprint, to longer races, speed becomes progressively less important while endurance becomes more important.

Speed in swimming is dependent primarily upon a combination of two factors: (i) application of as much propelling force as possible by means of the stroke and kick, and (ii) the reduction of the resistive forces to a minimum. Correct technique will result in the correct body position and will also result in the correct movement of the arms and legs. However, in addition to correct technique, power is fundamental to fast swimming.

The swimmer must be able to apply great force rapidly with the arms and legs in order to propel the body through the water at high speed. This means that strong and fast muscle contractions are necessary. It can be said that in addition to correct technique, power and coordination are fundamental to success in speed swimming.

In the endurance events, speed is still a factor, because fast swimmer can swim at a given pace with greater ease than a slower swimmer. Thus, he will tend to fatigue less readily. In addition to speed, the distance swimmer must have a large amount of endurance and must learn to swim as efficiently as possible in order to conserve his energy.

Training Program for Swimming

Expert swimmers usually participate in tow competitive seasons—the winter season and the summer season. Even thought the winter season is considered the main one, most serious swimmers train rigorously during most of the year.

Competitive Season

During the competitive season, the stress-and-strain aspect related to endurance and general conditioning is more pronounced. During this season, many coaches prescribe double work-outs, and some even recommend three session per day.

Championship swimmers do a fantastic amount of work, with the world-class swimmers covering as much as 15,000 yards per day, while some college and high school swimmers do between 6000 and 9000 yards per day. This great volume of work seems to be the sky to excellence in swimming.

Because of the many hours devoted to training, it is important to vary the work-out as much as possible and still accomplish the objectives. This can be done by utilizing the various training methods such as sprint training, over distance, speed play, interval training, and time trails.

The training programs vary significantly between long-distance, middle-distance, and sprint swimming. However, the variation does not occur very much in terms of total work accomplished but more in the way the work is designed.

For example, if the training program calls for a total of 5000 yards in a given day, the sprinters might swim 1000 yards of easy swimming then fifteen 100-yards repetitions followed by thirty 50-yard repetitions, followed by 1000 by yards of easy swimming.

Middle-distance swimmer might swim three-500-yard repetitions, two 1000-yard repetitions, three 400-yard repetitions, and finish with three 100-yard repetitions. Physiologically, it is wise to taper off with a least 200 to 500 yards of easy swimming following a rigorous work-out. Long-distance swimmers usually do not of their work with middle-distance and sprint swimmers while doing some additional work separate from these groups.

Swimming endurance seems to be best developed by long swims with relatively short rest intervals. However, in addition to doing an extensive amount of this type of endurance work, all swimmers should do some speed work.

Sprint swimmers should spend considerable time on repetition short distances at 80 to 90% of maximum effort. This will help to increase their speed and will improve the anaerobic processes, which are very important in short maximum-effort events.

Even though swimmers need much high-pressure works at regular intervals, they also need relief from this pressure at certain times. Low-pressure gather themselves and once again prepare for high-pressure training. This helps to reduce the stress levels and tends to postpone the onset of staleness.

Because of the very heavy work load during the season, swimmers should taper off during the peaking-out process near the end of the season. The amount of tapering that should be done depends on the athlete's condition and whether there are any signs of staleness. However, some amount of tapering should be used with all swimmers. During the tapering period, start and turn work can be practised along with further perfection of swimming technique.

The Important thing during the tapering period is not to work the swimmer to fatigue, but at the same time not allow his state of conditioning to deteriorate. The purpose is to permit the athlete to become rested from the stress and strain of a long hard season and to permit him to concentrate on the fine points that results in better performance.

Pre-Season Training

The pre-season program should begin six to eight weeks prior to competition. During this time, lectures and movies can be used to improve skill and build enthusiasm. Dry-land exercises and weight training should receive increased emphasis in order to improve strength, flexibility, and muscle endurance to the desired levels. The intensity of the work done in the water should increase and should include work on stroke mechanics, starts, and turns.

Counsilman listed three purposes for pre-season training: (i) to improve the swimmer's strength and flexibility through dry-land exercises; (b) to improve the stroke mechanics, and turns, and for the swimmer; and (iii) to prepare or condition the body for the hard work that is to come in the next phase.

Care should be taken to be sure that the weight-training program does not develop the muscles to the point that their size becomes a handicaps to movement. Weight-training exercises should be designed specifically to improve and strength endurance of those muscles which are prime moves.

Any increase in the size of other muscles can slow the swimmer by creating additional drag. With regard to strength development, a practical question is whether an increase in strength will more than offset the disadvantage of the growth in size that may accompany the strength.

The object should be to attain a high level of strength with as little increase in muscle growth as possible.

There are five prime-mover muscle groups which should receive emphasis in the weight-training program. They are:–

(i) Arm rotators

(ii) Wrist and finger flexors

(iii) Arm adductors and extensors

(iv) Leg and ankle extensors

(v) Elbow extensors

Some attention should also given to the trunk muscles because of their role in streamlining and stabilizing the body.

The cardiovascular development activities used during this period should be mostly aerobic nature. Distance swimming, speed day, and long-interval swimming are recommended for endurance building. Sprint and short-repetition training are seldom used during pre-season.

Adequate attention should be given to flexibility exercises, because swimmers need great flexibility, mainly in two areas, the ankles and the shoulders. Ankle flexibility is very important in the free-style, butterfly, and backstroke events, because a large range of motion in the ankle results in more force against the water.

Adequate shoulder flexibility is necessary in the free style, backstroke, and butterfly, because these strokes require the arms to move long ranges of motion. To achieve the desired flexibility in the shoulder region, the interior deltoid and the pectoral muscles must be stretched.

Off-Season

During the off-season, the swimmer should work on activities which maintain a moderate level of fitness and are somewhat enjoyable to him. These activities should include dry-land exercises along with running, bicycling, tennis, and other sports which maintain cardiovascular and muscular fitness.

Training in the water during this season should concentrate mostly on skill development, with very little pressure placed on the athlete to increase speed. Continuous heavy work during this period may contribute to staleness during the competitive season; however a high level of general conditioning must be maintained.

11

TRACK AND FIELD ACTIVITIES

One of the unique features of track and field activities is that they are maximum effort events. In addition to competing against opponents, track and field athletes measure their achievements in terms of times and distances. In races, the athlete makes an all-out effort to cover the distance in the shortest time possible.

He taxes himself to his maximum in either speed or endurance or both. In throwing and jumping and jumping events, the athlete strives for maximum distance, and sometimes an inch can make the difference between success and failure.

The shorter races are tests of running speed. Such as acceleration speed, manoeuvrability speed, and top speed. Running manoeuvrability is not involved in track events since the athlete always runs a straight-line or curved-line course.

The relative importance of acceleration speed and top speed depends on the length of the race. In short sprints such as the 60-yards dash, acceleration speed is a major factor because it takes approximately half the distance of the race to race to reach top speed. As the race becomes less critical. Both acceleration speed and top running speed rate greatly dependent upon power and coordination, in addition to correct running technique.

Success is distance running is dependent primarily upon running stamina, where the main limitation is cardiovascular those who use less energy per given distance will place less load on the body systems. Speed also is a factor in stamina because a faster runner can coast and still keep ahead of the slower runner who may be working hard to keep up with his faster opponent.

The throwing events-shot put, discus, javelin, and hammer throw—are primarily power activities. They depend upon the athlete's ability to apply great force rapidly. Therefore, in addition to improving his technique, everything the athlete does is geared to increasing his ability to apply great force more rapidly in order that he can project the implement with greater speed.

The two components of power, strength and speed of contraction, have different relative importance in the throwing events, with strength being the dominant factor in throwing events, with strength being the dominant factor in throwing heavy objects such as the shot and hammer, and speed being proportionately more important with lighter objects, such as the discus and the javelin.

The four jumping events—high jump, long jump, triple jump, and pole vault–are also greatly dependent upon power, because they are tests of the ability to project the body through space. In these event, running speed, which in itself is greatly dependent upon power, will often make the difference between winning and losing because winning speed at the moment of take-off determines the horizontal component which carries the body over the given distance. In addition to running speed, a powerful vertical thrust at the moment of take-off is fundamental to success in jumping events.

The following information about training techniques for each of the four kinds of track and field events provides ideas and guidelines which will aid in establishing effective conditioning programs.

It is not possible to describe a conditioning program which would be acceptable under all circumstances, because of the difference in the state of conditioning and the maturity of athletes.

Jumping Events

Excellence in the jumping events depends primarily upon running speed and the ability to thrust the body into the air. The relative importance of these two factors, the vertical and horizontal component, depends on the nature of the jumping event, whether it is primarily vertical horizontal.

Competitive Season

During the competitive season, the jumper should continue with about the same routine as during the pre-season except he should place greater emphasis on running speed and on the fine points of jumping techniques. During this seasons, he should continue with conditioning exercise designed to develop power with emphasis on leg extension.

During the late part of the season, the athlete might want to increase the volume of work, depending on his state of conditioning and whether he shows any signs of staleness. Still the emphasis should be on (i) improving the fine points of his technique, (ii) increasing the speed of the approach run, and (c) increasing leg power which will aid him in his upward thrust.

Off-Season and Pre-Season Training

During off-season, the jumper should participate regular in vigorous activities which include a conspired amount of running and jumping. This will help to maintain a high level of general conditioning with emphasis on the development of the leg muscles.

This should be supplemented with a program of specific exercises selected to improve the power of the muscles involved in jumping with emphasis on the leg extensors.

During the pre-season, the athlete should participate extensively in wind sprints and running over low hurdles to improve his speed and consistency of his stride. Also during this period, he should increase the intensity of the conditioning exercises in order to improve power. He should spend a considerable amount of time perfecting the approach run and jumping technique.

Endurance Running

Distance races, including middle, distance, depend upon a combination of endurance and speed. The shorter the distance race, the more significant is speed; whereas the longer the race, the greater it depends upon significant is from spring speed.

It is speed at a relaxed pace and is usually called "coasting speed." A person who can run fast and efficiently at an easy pace has great advantage in distance running. The technique for developing this kind of speed is to do a large amount of running at nearly top speed and consciously relax while doing so in order to increase efficiency.

From the standpoint of endurance, it has been found that the main limiting factor is the oxygen supply to the working muscles. This supply, in turn, is directly dependent upon the efficiency of the cardiovascular system. Thus the distance runner must have great cardiovascular endurance.

The Competitive Season

During the competitive season, a combination of cross-country-running and interval training should continue with increased attention given to interval training, more particularly progress in such a way that it brings the athlete along at the most rapid rate possible, but not so rapidly that he peaks out prior to the end of the season.

During the season, the athletes would typically do some long-distance running at the beginning of his work-out; this would be followed by an optional amount of interval training followed by a tapering-off period of jogging and light exercises.

It is very important that the length and intensity of the work bouts be designed to fit the particular athlete's ability. Also it is important that the athlete be consistently improve throughout the season.

Again it should be mentioned that the emphasis should be on overloading the cardiovascular system in order to improve oxygen delivery to the tissues and to improve the aerobic processes.

During the late season, the athlete will continue with approximately the same training routine, except the amount of work will continue to increase as the athlete is ready to take more work. During this phase of the season, greater care must be taken to speak the athlete for the final races of the year without bringing on staleness, which may be caused by over-work or monotonous routines.

Endurance Running

Distance, races, including middle distance, depend upon a combination of endurance and speed. The shorter the distance race, the more significant is speed; whereas the longer the race, the greater it depends upon endurance alone.

The kind of speed that contributes to endurance running is different from sprint speed. It is speed at a relaxed pace and is usually called "coasting speed." A person who can run fast and efficiently at an easy pace has a great advantage in distance running. The technique for developing this kind of speed is to do a large amount of running at nearly top speed and consciously relax while doing so in order to increase efficiency.

From the standpoint of endurance, it has been found that the main limiting factor is the oxygen supply to the working muscles. This supply, in turn, is directly dependent upon the efficiency of the cardiovascular system. Thus the distance runner must have great cardiovascular endurance.

Off-Season and Pre-Season Training

During the off-season, the distance runner should engage extensively in vigorous activities which are enjoyable to him and which involved and extensive amount of running, such as soccer, basketball, and play-type running. In addition, some athletes choose to use conditioning exercises to maintained a high level of muscular endurance in the leg muscles with emphasis on the leg extensors. Conversely, many good distance runners do not become involved in such exercise during the off-season.

During the fall and early winter, the distance runner should be extensively involved in cross-country running. This is a competitive even by itself, but it is also an excellent off-season and pre-season conditioner for the distance runner in track.

During the pre-season, the athlete should continue with an extensive amount of cross-country running, but at the same time should move toward more systematic training schedules. The amount of work should increase, and the emphasis should shift more toward interval training, but should include some cross-country work.

The interval training should be of the type that emphasized aerobic development. Such a program should consist of a series of work bouts 3 to 5 minutes in length with short rest periods between bouts.

Sprint Races

Sprinting is primarily a power event because it is series of projections done alternately from the right and left legs. In order to increase sprint speed, an athlete must increase either the length of stride of the speed of leg movement or both.

Research has shown that the length of stride is the main limiting factor, while leg speed is usually not a serious limitation. Length of stride is dependent upon the ability to contract the muscles with great force rapidly. Leg speed is dependent upon coordination and contractile speed of the muscles.

The training program of the springer should consists primarily of three factors: (i) perfecting the techniques involved in starting and sprinting, (ii) doing a considerable amount of sprint running because this will help to improve leg speed and leg power, and (iii) weight-training exercise to improve power, with emphasis on the leg extensor muscles.

The Competitive Season

During this time the work-out will involve essentially the same techniques and procedures as during the pre-season, except the volume of work will gradually increase because the athlete will be better conditioning by this time and will be working toward peaking himself out by the end of the season.

Also during the competitive season, greater emphasis should be placed on the fine points of correct technique. In this respect, emphasis should be on three factors; (i) the start, (ii) the acceleration phase, and (iii) the top-speed phase of the race.

The increased amount of work during this season will result in greater anaerobic endurance, a contributing factor in sprint racing which become more significant as the race gets longer.

During the late season the sprinter will ordinarily do the same kind of training as during the earlier part of the competitive season, except the amount of work will normally increase at a gradual rate. How much the amount increases must be decided by the coach and athlete in the light of the condition of the athlete and whether he shows signs of staleness. During the last two or three weeks increased emphasis should be placed on the fine points of correct technique and form.

Off-Season and Pre-Season Training

Typically the off-season extends from June to December, and the pre-season includes January and February. During the off-season the athlete should maintain a relatively high level of general conditioning by participating regularly in vigorous activities which he enjoys.

Emphasis should be on activities involving short bursts of fast running, such as soccer, football, basketball, and play type running . This should be supplemented by an exercise program which emphasized the development of strength and speed in the muscle groups used the most in sprinting.

During the pre-season the sprinter should continue with the conditioning exercises, but with increased intensity in order to build a new maximum level of power in the key muscle groups.

Along with this, he should do a considerable amount of sprint running to develop power, and to improve his leg speed running mechanics and coordination. Also, he should practice starting and accelerating in order to prefect these phase of the race.

Throwing Events

Success in the throwing events depends primarily upon power and correct technique, with power being combination of strength and speed and correct technique depending primarily upon mechanics and coordination.

The competitive Season

It is important that athletes in throwing events develop the highest possible level of strength prior to the beginning of competitive season, because once this season begins the athlete can do little more than retain his strength level.

It is recommended that he do strength training only during the early part of the week, preferably on Monday, and that he concentrate on other forms of training between Tuesday and the competition on Friday or Saturday.

It is acceptable to do speed exercises on Tuesday or Wednesday because these exercises do not take as much out of the muscles, and they do not interfere as much with coordination exercises designed for strength and speed, the athlete should spend a great deal of time on per fetching his technique and on throwing less than maximum distance. At certain times during the early and middle portion of the week, he will want to make a few maximum effort throws.

He must spend much of his work-out time on drills selected to help improve weakness in his technique. Also he should do much repetitious throwing with emphasis on correct technique coordination.

During his training routine, the athlete should constantly keep in mind that is primary objective is to increase the final velocity of the implement as much as possible. This is what determines the distance the implement will travel provided it is projected at the correct angle. In order to achieve maximum final velocity, the athlete must apply as much force as possible as rapidly as possible and over the greatest distance possible so that he can accelerate the implement to a maximum velocity. Whatever he does towards improving technique and increasing his state of conditioning should be geared towards this end.

During the late season, the athlete should pay even grater attention to the fine points of his technique and to the development of movement speed. For some athletes, it might be wise to pay renewed attention to the development of strength during the few weeks prior to the final competitive events. Perhaps at this point in the season some strength will have been lost, or perhaps the athlete will have reached a plateau where he cannot increase any further without additional strength.

The amount of emphasis that should be placed on strength at this point in the season will need to be determined by the particular coach and athlete.

Off-Season and Pre-Season Training

During the off-season, the athlete should participate in a variety of activities which are vigorous and enjoyable. He should emphasize activities which tend to keep the total muscular system well conditioned. This should be supplemented by conditioning exercise which maintain a high level of strength in the muscle groups used in throwing. Also the athlete should do a considerable amount of throwing at less than maximum effort in order to improve his coordination and throwing mechanics.

During the pre-season, the intensity of the exercise program should increase to develop a high level of strength prior to the beginning of competition. During this season, the exercises should shift more towards power development which combines strength and speed training.

The relative emphasis placed on strength and speed will be influenced strongly by the particular throwing event for which the athlete is training, as the heavier implements require more strength and the lighter implements require proportionately more speed and less strength.

The particular muscles that should receive attention in a conditioning program can be easily determined by analysing the movements involved in the throwing event. Then exercises which involve those same movements or the muscle which cause those movements should be selected. For more detailed information on the correct approach for developing strength, power, and speed, refer to the correct approach for developing strength, power, and speed.

12

PSYCHOLOGICAL ASPECTS

The ability of a person to perform in any athletic event is obviously limited by his physical characteristics. But beyond these broad restrictions psychological factors play a decisive role. Many coaches and physiologists believe that future records will be broken primarily because of increased attention to the psychological features of the personality more than the physiological and mechanical aspects of performance.

Motivation

Motivation is probably the biggest word in athletics today, because it is well established that performances increase when athletes are properly motivated. They must be "up" for the game or "ready" for the competition. Bonder noted that the basic difference between ordinary and great athletes is mental attitude.

In order for a coach to motivate his athletes adequately he must (i) know how they think, feel, and respond to various circumstances; (ii) know about their backgrounds and experiences; and (iii) know the circumstances of the their homes and their relationships with their parents and friends.

The more the coach knows about each individual

athlete, the better equipped he will be to motivate the athlete properly for competition.

The word "motivate" means "to move, impel, induce, and stimulate." A highly motivate and motivating coach can stimulate athletes to the point where they can perform at nearly their maximum capabilities.

The coach may use any of the following methods to motivate his squad: group psychology, individual conferences, pep talks, a system of rewards, yells and battle cries, discipline, slogans, squad rules, peer-groups approval, special names for positions and groups, signs, point systems, grading, and seasonal goals.

Coaches may also use psychological controls to suppress situations or attitudes that might interfere with maximum performance. The coach may use a variety of approach to motivate, but they all point to an "adrenal explosion" at the time of performance.

Lawther states that, for the most part, sports possess, because of their very nature, intrinsic interest for young people; however, many persons are caused to work far beyond what would be considered mere love of the game.

They are further motivated by the desire for social approval and prestige and by economic and social rewards. The various motives and incentives which make sports participation so highly desired by so many youngsters are:

(i) Escape from anxiety related to adolescence, frustrations, worries, monotony, and boredom of the daily routine.

(ii) Greater attention from opposite sex.

(iii) Excess energy, play drive, and competitive urge.

(iv) Tendency to emulate admired adults and to excel in activities of which they approve.

(v) Desire to prove abilities to self and to others, to improve self confidence, self-respect, and self-realization.

(vi) Desire for prestige, approval of others, escape from inferiority feelings, and experience of success.

(vii) Attempt to release aggression and excess energy in socially approved ways.

Some athletes need very little "psychological prodding" in order to operate at maximum efficiency. These athletes are called "self-starters" and are highly sought after at recruiting time.

The self-starter has goals which seem to arise within himself. He seems to be able to find sufficient self-motivation to be psychologically prepared. He has good concentration and usually has a high degree of self-discipline and a mature attitude.

Research has produced the following information which relates to motivation and psychological preparation:–

(i) An emotional stimulus that is too strong has negative effects on both learning and performance.

(ii) Elimination of stress factors before competition is usually beneficial to performances.

(iii) Extreme emotional stimulus may produce tenseness or "buck-fever."

(iv) Noise tends to produce greater efforts.

(v) External stimuli such as "yells" help the athlete to overcome internal inhibitions.

(vi) Introverts generally respond to praise while extroverts often perform better under criticism.

(vii) Emotional excitement tends to be an aid in extending physical exertion bond normal levels.

(viii) Fans, bands, cheerleaders, crowds, and home courts have positive effect on performance.

(ix) An optimum amount of competitive tension is desirable.

(x) Too many emotional peaks in any one season may contribute toward staleness.

(xi) The fear of losing tends to contribute to motivation.

Emotions

Man is an emotional being. Emotions can be the causative factor in both victory and defeat. The intelligent coach is aware of this fact and conducts himself accordingly. He is ale to manipulate his players so their emotions act as an asset to them rather than a hindrance. There are times in sporting events when the performer must be calm and tranquil.

The presence of this feeling enables him to perform his assigned task in a successful manner. There are other times when the performer is better off if his emotions are at a fever pitch.

Having players "ready" at contest time is an important responsibility of the coach. It makes little difference how they feel on Friday or Monday when the contest is on Saturday. The idea is to have them ready when the contest starts. The coach must control the emotional climate of the team.

Some coaches control the emotional climate of the squad by explaining that if they play the way he was taught them to play, they will have the glory and credit if they win, while he will assume the blame if they should lose. This in effect, "takes the monkey off their back," and they can relax and play the game the way they have been taught.

Bryant feels strongly that emotion is one of the prime ingredients of a winner. He states, "From the time I played at Alabama until a few years ago, I believed that if you weren't winner, if the game didn't mean enough to you, you'd probably wind up quitting. So I've laid it on the line to lot of boys. I've shook'em, hugged'em, kicked'em, and embarrassed them in front of the squad. I've got down in the dirt with them, and if they didn't give as well as they took I'd tell them they were insults to their upbringing, and I've cleaned out their lockers for them and piled their clothes out in the hall, thinking, I'd make them prove what they had in their veins, blood or spit, one way or the other, and paying they would come through."

Bryant goes on to explain the importance of arousing players emotionally. He reflects about his college coach, Frank Thomas: "He knew what to say and when to say it, and that was his secret. I'll never what to say and when to say it, and that was his secret. I'll never forget, we were going out for the 1935 Rose Bowl Game. I went into the men's lounge on the train. Coach Thomas was sitting there with some of the coaches and Red Heard, the athletic director of LSU and two or three newspapermen. He said, Red, this is my best football player. This is the best player on my team'. Well, shoot, I could have gone right out the top. I mean, he didn't have to say anything else. I know now what he was doing, because I try to do it myself. He was getting me ready. And I was, too. I would have gone out there and killed myself for Alabama that day."

Some people try to say that morale is almost an accident; that either a team has morale or it hasn't and that's that! It is difficult to believe that something as important as team morale exists are found where the team is winning. Good morale can be thought of either as the reason for the team's success, or as a by-product of a team's success.

Once in a while, good morale exists in a losing situation. A group of young men and the coach can band together in a harmonious and closely knit unit if they believe in themselves and believe that their plan will work–that it might take a little while, but that eventually they will win and they work toward that desired goal.

Bobby Dodd, the legendary coach of Georgia Tech, tributes much of his success to the fact that his teams were always characterized by outstanding morale. The following are guidelines he used to achieve exceptional team morale:

(i) The coach must be loyal to his team at all times.

(ii) The must feel friendly and kindly toward every boy on his squad.

(iii) The coach should prevent inferiority complexes on the part of young second-string players.

(iv) When the team is losing, it needs encouragement and not destructive criticism and sarcasm.

(v) Require group loyalty. Prohibit criticism, wrangling, ad jealousy within the squad at any cost.

(vi) He should try to treat all players fairly.

(vii) He should be friendly with all of his players, but not too familiar.

(viii) In dealing with each disciplinary situation, the following procedure is suggested: do not speak until there is absolute silence; then talk with a low tone of voice; do not say too much; be; sure a penalty can be enforced before it is announced; and do not hold any malice afterward—treat the incident as closed.

Stress

Selye claims evidence that stress is an important psychological factors which can influence a person's adaptability and his ability to function normally. Generally as stress increases beyond a minimal level, reasoning, problem-solving ability, and efficiency progressively decrease. It appears that as an individual adapts to one kind of stress he loses by his ability to tolerate other stresses.

The organism is apparently limited by its defensive resources, so that if the resources are mobilized against one stress they are not able to cope with other stresses as effectively. This helps to explain how sustained psychological stress can lower resistance to biological stress.

Many people believe that after undergoing severe stress, rest can completely restore the person. Generally, this has been an assumption among coaches and athletes. Selye presents evidence that this is not true of irreversible wear and tear. Experiments with laboratory animal have shown that such stress leaves incurable scars, in that it uses up reserves of adaptability that cannot be replaced.

Since we continually go through periods of stress and rest during life, just a little deficit of adaptation every day adds up to what we call aging. An ever-increasing proportion of the human population die from the so-called "wear-and-tear" diseases, or degenerative diseases, which are primarily due to stress.

According to Sely, as the stress level in athletic competition increases, intelligence goes down, and so do the biological adaptations of the body. Coaches and athletes must be aware of these factors and help to equalize stress, or in some cases eliminate it so that competition does not leave an inedible scar. Obviously, stress will not affect all individuals to the same degree. Each athlete will react to stressful situations in his own way, according to his past experiences and his emotional stability.

Inspiration

A popular song for all who are interested in the battle and preparation for battle is entitled "Stout-Hearted Men." The more popular lines read:

"Give me some men who are stout-hearted, men,

And I'll soon give you ten thousand more."

But there are others lines in the song that more correctly describe the importance of inspiration:

"Hearts can inspire other hearts with their fire,

And the strong obey when a strong man shows them the way."

Throughout the ages men have inspired other men by the example of their own lives. In coaching, this fact is especially importance. Someone once said, "A champion is a person whose heart can educated." It is important when working with young men to get them to a fever pitch—to get them hot in the heart. The best and most effective way to teach and coach is by example.

Personality of the Athlete

Even though there are numerous theories concerning the personalities of athletes, only a limited amount of research has been done to gain information to support the theories. Neuman and Seist both suggest that participation in high-level athletic competition provides an important addition to one's personality.

They claim that harmonious development comes about through sports participation. In their research they found that athletes were more sociable, more aggressive in their approach to problems, more self-confident, more critical of themselves, and more extroverted than non-athletes.

In his study of a group of Austria's best athletes, Seist found that male athletes were less neurotic than male non-athletes. Male athletes were more stable under stress than female athletes, and females tend to be more susceptible to depression.

Research and practical experience indicate that only certain personality types have the ability to undergo the social and physical stress of participation it high-level competitive sports. As an athlete continues participation, he experience both negative and positive personality changes as a result of his athletic involvement.

Athletes as a group cannot be labelled as either more or less intelligent than the population as a whole. Like other young people of today, contemporary athletes tend to be well informed, and they expect to be treated accordingly. Thus, it has been found helpful to prepare contemporary athletes intellectually as well as physically and emotionally for the demands of competition.

This preparation takes the from of discussions, lectures, reading about the psychological, physiological, and biochemical demands of the sport, viewing of films of opponents and other performers, and analysing their own performances on film.

Personality of the Coach

The history of sports is replete with the names of unsuccessful coaches who taught fundamentals very well but mishandled their players. Because of this, it becomes apparent that coaches must have personality and character traits which inspire respect and confidence by their athletes.

The young athletes looks up to the coach who knows his field well—so well that to work with him is to learn. But the young athlete also wants a teacher whom he can admire as a man.

The mature coach with a pleasant personality, wholesome outlook on life, and a good measure of idealism has a great appeal to young people. Many coaches occupy a higher station in the minds of their athletes than do the fathers of the athletes. The coach's life and character must justify this trust.

Coach Paul Bryant of the University of Alabama is a master of the art of handling men. Bryant tells of when he was coaching football at Texas A & M and held a particularly hard scrimmage which was to act as a "gut check."

He was trying to "separate the men from the boys," and one of his targets was young sophomore named John David Crow. After the scrimmage Bryant asked Crow why he didn't quit. The player looked the coach straight in the eye and said, "Because I'd killed you before I'd let you make me quit." Needless to say, John David Crow went on to become an All-American and later an All-Pro running back.

One of the most important aspects of coaching is the ability of the coach to recognize a winner and to get him in the game. Through the years, sports pages have been filled with the exploits of great players who were not outstanding athletes but were winners.

It's easy to recognize winners who have great ability, but some winners do not have unusual ability and are much more difficult to identify. Paul Brayant says, "Once I'm convinced that a boy is not a winner, I don't care if he runs 9.3 and is eight feet tall, I'm forgetting him. He's not a winner and I'm not interested in all that other stuff."

The successful coach must be a practical psychologist as well as a sound technician. He must study his men to know how their minds work and to understand their dispositions and personalities in order to get the best results from them.

There is no foolproof method or standard approach. What works in the case of one athlete may be poor approach to another. A coach who endeavours to treat all of his players alike and handles all of them in the same manner is destined to encounter many needless problems.

Ogilive and Tutko researched the personalities of successful coaches and found that they consistently possessed the following positive and negative traits:

Positive Traits:

(i) Highly orderly and well organized.

(ii) Unusually well equipped to handle emotion and stress problems.

(iii) Exhibiting a high degree of psychological endurance.

(iv) Exhibiting an abundance of leadership qualities.

(v) Success-driven with an outstanding need to be on top.

(vi) Outgoing and warm.

(vii) Having developed consciences and very much in tune with the appropriate values of the culture.

(viii) Open and trusting and not excessively defensive in their relationships with others.

(ix) Showing dominant, "take-charge" attitudes and actively seeking roles of leadership.

(x) Emotionally mature and tending to face reality in a direct manner.

(xi) More prone to blame themselves than others when things go wrong.

Negative Traits:

(i) Inflexibility or rigidity in terms of new learning techniques to increase performance. This is indicative of egocentric individuals.

(ii) Exhibition a low tendency to be interested in the dependency needs of the athlete, such as listening to personal problems, protection when in trouble, emotional support, etc. Their typical response was I "I'm no social worker. My job is teaching them how to win."

Staleness

Staleness implies general fatigue as a result of over-training or sustained emotional stress. This problem, which is apt to occur in the latter part of the season, must be perceived in the initial stages if a quick curies to occur.

Frequent symptoms of staleness are slowness of reflexes, lack of enthusiasm, lack of interest, gradual loss of weight over an extended period, tiredness, a lack of staying power in a fast contest, and irritability.

Contributors to staleness include inadequate sleep and lack of rest after hard work, too much routine and too little diversion, academic loads that require irregular and excessive emotional tension is believed to the major factor contributing to staleness.

The state athletes tries to improve but seems to get worse. He seems unable to drive himself to do better, and often the harder he tries the poorer are the results. The best cure for staleness is a combination of rest and diversion. If the state athlete is even allowed to attend practice, his work outs should be kept to a minimum until his energy and enthusiasm return to normal.

It appears that the athletes is state because of too much hard physical exertion, the antidote is rest or rest combined with exercise done ion a playful manner. If the staleness seems to be associated with emotional stress, then the emphasis should be placed upon freeing the athlete from his worries and anxieties.

Some athletes must be taught to worry less about

losing. They need to be taught to emphasize the positive aspects of self-improvement and enjoyment of the game, and worry less about winning and losing.

According to Ogilive and Tutko, J. H. Schultz has devised a methods of alleviating pre-competition stress, known as Das Autogenne Training. He recommends the method for individuals whose pre-competition tension is too high or too low. Either to raise or to lower levels of activation, the following procedure is recommended by Schultz: After assuming a comfortable position, usually on the back, the athlete breathes deeply several times and concentrates on his breathing.

He then tightens all of his muscles maximal for several seconds and then relaxes as completely as possible. He pretends that the body is extremely heavy and concentrates on each segment until he is completely relaxed. After complete relaxation, he trends that the body is becoming warm as if submerged in warm water.

Then the athlete tries to sleep. At this point the athlete repeats the procedure one or more times. It is hypothesized that after successive relaxation and reactivation the athlete will return with more positive mind and ready for effective performance. Schultz estimates that 40 to 45% of all athletes can profit from this procedure, while the remainder may find the procedure of little or no value.

Macback, a professor of psychology at Charles University in Prague, has developed a variation of the Schultz method: Each individuals imagines himself in an environment which will create relaxation; for example, the seashore ora forest. Activation is accomplished by combing short breaths with application of muscle tension. Otherwise, the procedure is the same is in the Schultz method. Macback's method is supported by limited experimentation and its value is still questionable.

Hypnosis has been found to be generally ineffective in helping athletes overcome stress. Experience shows that specific hypnotic suggestions are likely to be disruptive and may lead to rigid kinds of movements that may detract from performance.

The Will to Win

Take an athlete of the often labelled a "real winner," one who has an intense will to excel; analyse him; throw the psychology book at him; study the boy. Notice that when he goes forth do something he has a clear, vivid picture in his mind of the thing he is fighting for, and at the same time he has a burning desire to fight for it.

When he is successful, when he wins, he wins graciously—When he is successful, when he wins, he wins graciously—he doesn't crow about it. And when he loses, and sometimes a real winner does lose, he loses gracefully—he does not complain and criticize.

If he does lose, and if you say to him, "Why did you lose? You are supposed to be a real winner," he would likely look you squarely in the eye, put his hands on his hips, glare at the scoreboard, and say, "I don't know why we lost. We didn't plan to lose. We didn't practice to lose we didn't play to lose. We used every ounce of our energy and every spark of our sprint all the way from the opening whistle until the final gun.

The scoreboard says we got beat. Let me tall you something. We got beat on the scoreboard, but we didn't get great in the heart. We are still undefeated where it really counts, and we'll bouncing back on that scoreboard very soon."

Well, you can bet on it, because very fibre of this athlete vibrates with a powerful, positive punch which pounds toward victory. It is natural for him to win. He was brought up that way.

You might ask, "How can a coach make an athlete into a winner?" It isn't easy, because your are dealing with the forming and reforming of the personality. Personality traits are not easily influenced, but they can be changed as a result of effective teaching and exposure to the right kind of experience.

It is within the ability of a good coach to inspire and motivate an athlete to want to be a winner, and the coach teach courage, initiative, and good conduct, all of which are characteristics of a winner. Through his efforts, the coach will be able to make winners out of some athletes who otherwise would never achieved such distinction.

Psychological Aids

Psychological aids, or "crutches," can alter performance in very direct and specific ways. Certain crutches such as drugs, alcohol, cigarettes, and extreme dietary alternations usually hinder an individual's performance, according to how frequently and excessively he leans on the crutches.

The most important consideration is whether or not the athlete's feelings of inadequacies, frustration, or anxiety are so great that is crutches become addictive. In some cases, an athlete will use another person as a psychological aid.

He might be directly dependent upon his coach, his father, or some other individual to prepare him psychologically for competition. In the absence of this person, the athlete will tend to falter. Every athlete should be encouraged to avoid too much dependency on any kind of psychological crutch and should be encouraged to find psychological strength within himself.

13

NEUROMUSCULAR SKILL

Skills is the ability to perform a combination of specific movements smoothly and effectively. It is the coordination of all the different muscles involved, whether they are agonists, antagonists, neutralizers, or stabilizers. In other words, skill is the ability to use the correct muscles at the correct time, with the exact force necessary to perform the desire movement an the proper sequence and timing.

Co-ordinated movement occur as a result of muscle contractions, and muscles contract only in response to nerve impulses. Therefore, coordinated movement occurs if nerve impulses reach the proper muscles at the correct time.

Even though skill is a result of the teamwork of the nervous and muscular systems, it is primarily a function of the nervous system, since the muscular contract at specified times and with certain amounts of force as dictated by the nervous system.

Of course, there are some conditions of the muscles themselves, such as strength and speed of contraction, which influence skill. But even these factors are partially determined by the functioning of the nervous system.

Factors which Influence Skill

Several factors relate to skill and influence its development. Among the factors are the following:

Endurance

Endurance makes a contribution to skill in performances where fatigue is a consideration. It is known that refined coordinations are adversely golfer make more mistakes and basketball players shoot lower percentages when fatigue becomes excessive. Thus, endurance contributes to skill in long-duration performances.

Strength

The exhibition of strength is a skill in itself because it requires correct muscle involvement and coordination of a number of muscles in different roles: agonists, antagonists, stabilizers, and neutralizers. Dynamic strength requires more coordination than static strength, and total body strength movements require more coordination than strength movements of specific body segments.

It is question than strength movement of strength has any direct influence on specific skills. However, research by Berger and Blaschke and Larson supports the idea that strength contributes to general motor ability and that dynamic strength contributes more than static strength.

Mental Practice

Research results support the idea that skill can be increased through mental practice. In the strict sense, mental practice means concentrated thought about the movement patterns involved. However, some researchers have included in the definition of mental practice the viewing of films and demonstrations and other non-manual activities which clarify the mental image of the performance.

Stebbins, Egstrom, Oxendine, and Phipps and Morehouse all produced evidence that skill can be increased within certain limits by mental practice, either in the form of mental concentration or other non-manual techniques.

Reciprocal Inhibition

The inhibition or blocking of nerve impulses to those muscles in opposition to a desired movement is of utmost importance to the efficiency of that movement. It appears that the antagonistic muscles are automatically inhibited. Thus, one may wonder whey it should even be discussed.

It must be recognized that with the practice of a movement, the inhibition of the antagonistic muscles becomes quicker and more complete. Obviously, antagonistic tension interferes with the effectiveness of a performance, and by reducing tension, effectiveness is increased, and the onset of fatigue is postponed.

Anxiety or other emotional involvement can limit the effectiveness of reciprocal inhibition. Thus, such heightened emotions tend to hinder performances where fine muscle coordinations are required. Golf is an activity that is adversely affected by anxiety.

Another example is a basketball player who misses free throw when the pressure is on. Conversely, activities not requiring a high degree of the muscle control may benefit from heightened emotions.

For example, the performance of a football lineman or a shot-putter may be enhanced by anxiety. But if the football player must handle the ball, his performance is likely to suffer. Many-so-called "sophomore mistakes" are attributable to the inability to contend with emotional stress because it has a detrimental effect on refined neuromuscular coordinations.

Proprioception

Awareness of body position is determined by a variety of sensory inputs to the central nervous system. The organs of balance in the inner ear, vision, and pressure applied to the surface of the body all help to provide information about position about position of the body and its segments.

The muscles and joints are provided with special organs to sense position and tension within the muscles and in the joints. All of this sensory information about body movement and position is termed "proprioception," and can be classified into two general areas: vestibular and kinaesthetic.

Vestibular Reception

Vestibular receptor are found in the non-auditory area of the inner ear. The most important system involves three small fluid-filled canals called the "semicircular canals." These canals are especially sensitive to acceleration, deceleration, and rotation, which cause the fluid in the canals to displace small hair-like organs called cristae. The movement of the cristae is transmitted to the brain causing the awareness of the movement.

Two other system in the inner ear are the utricle, which provides the body with information concerning the sense of body position, and the saccule, which is involved in sensory perception of vibrations.

Kinaesthetic Reception

Kinaesthetic sense is an important factor of body segments or limbs. Because of this sense, a person can touch his fingers together in front of his face with his eyes closed, or can place a spoon to his mouth while looking out the window. Likewise, a golfer is able to swing a club correctly without taking his eyes off the ball, and a basketball player can concentrate his sight on the basket and perform a jump shot with awareness of the positions and movements of all his body parts.

A baseball player can concentrate on the baseball, and still be aware of the position of the bat. This "muscle sense" or kinaesthetic sense involves mainly the following receptors: (i) the muscle spindles, (ii) the Golgi tendon organs, (iii) the Pacinian corpuscles, and (iv) free nerve endings.

The muscle spindle is sensitive to changes in length and tension of muscle fibres. When the fibres are stretched, the muscle spindle is also stretched, and an impulse is generated which carries this information to the spinal cord.

This incoming impulse causes a motor neuron with which it synapses to "fire," resulting in contraction of muscle fibres to oppose the muscle stretch. At the same time, impulses travel through a separate motor neuron which causes contraction in the intrafusal muscle fibre to reset the spindle at a new length coinciding with the new contracted length of the surrounding skeletal muscle fibres.

It can also be used as a "servomechanism" to allow the body to contract a muscle to a predetermined length in a coordinated movement. For a more complete discussion of muscle spindles.

The Golgi tendon organ functions somewhat different from the muscle spindle. Although it is also sensitive to stretch, it operates as a sensor of high tension on the muscle tendon. When there is a possibility that the muscle tendon will become overload as a result of strong muscle contractions, the Golgi tendon organs causes an antimyotatic reflex which inhibits contraction in the muscles most involved and often in the contralateral muscles also. This reflex acts as a protective mechanism for the involved joints and muscles.

Pancinian corpuscles, found outside of muscle tissue in the sheaths of tendons and receptors may be as important as spindles in detecting passive movement or body part position in space.

Free nerve endings are located widely throughout the body in muscles, tendons, joints, ligaments, and so forth, but their function with regard to kinaesthetic sense is largely unknown.

How to Increase Skill

An athletic performance consists of several specific skills, and each skill involves a combination of movement. An effective and systematic approach to improving performance requires analysis of the performance to determine what skills are involved, and then a program designed to improve those skills.

For example, basketball is composed of such skills as running, rebounding, jumping, dodging, dribbling, passing, and catching. Basketball performance may be improved by improving one or more of these skills. The problem, then, is to identify the specific skills in a performance and to employ effective techniques to improve them.

Essentially, skill improvement involves (i) determining the correct mechanics and (ii) practising the skill repeatedly. The skill must be practised correctly until the movement patterns become effective and efficient. As a result of such practice, the performer will also increase his skill by improving judgment of speed, distance, and time, and by developing insight into the various circumstances of the performance.

There are several categories of basic skills which require different emphasis. Skills are logically divided into (i) accuracy skills, (ii) power skills, and (iii) manoeuvrability skills.

Examples of accuracy skills are putting in golf often do not involve fast or vigorous movements, but require great concentration and much practice of fine muscle coordinations. Under competitive conditions, some accuracy skills are performed with high speed.

Slowing down the performance during practice will aid in analysing the mechanics of the skill and improving the movement patterns. But for best, accuracy skills should be practised extensively at the same speed and intensity as they will be performed in competition.

In addition to being dependent upon neuromuscular coordination, accuracy skills are also dependent upon judgement of speed, distance, and time. For example, such judgments are important to a football player when he throws downfield to a running receiver.

The passer must be able to judge the distance to the receiver and the speed at which he is moving, then throw the ball so it will meet the receiver. In shooting a basketball, the player must correctly judge it should go. If the post man passes to a guard cutting in for a lay-up, the passer must correctly judge the speed of the guard. When the guard lays up the shot, he must correctly judge his speed and the rebound angle of the ball.

Many other examples could be given of activities in which judgements of speed, distance, and time must be frequently made in order to enhance accuracy skills. Among the power skills are football blocking, shot putting, long jumping, sprint swimming, and sprint running. These skills are performed with great speed and force.

In developing power skills, the emphasis is on neuromuscular coordinations which result in fast and forceful movements. There are some skills which combine accuracy and power. Examples are baseball pitching, baseball batting football field-goal kicking, and boxing.

Manoeuvrability skills include gymnastic performances, skiing, court games such as tennis, basketball, and badminton, and field games such as soccer, football, and rugby. In developing these skills, the emphasis is on agility.

In some cases mobility skills are best improved by practising the specific movement patterns over and at increasingly faster speeds and with more precision. In other cases mobility skills can be increased a limited amount by increasing some of the contributing elements such as strength, speed of movement, and reaction time of the specific movement.

Instructional Techniques

In theory, skills development is a simple matter, but in actually it is very difficult. The key is repetition. But, it is necessary to repeat the skill pattern correctly. Otherwise, lack of skill or incorrect technique will result. In order to insure correct practice, the learner must know what is correct. This means his practice must be preceded by information about the correct. Technique.

The information may be obtained from instruction by one who knows correct technique, from reading, watching film, or observing a skilled performer. One the learner understands the elements of correct technique and has had some opportunity to practice that skill, error detection and correction become an effective tool fort the instructor.

As the learner practice the skill over and over, the instructor detects imperfections and prescribes methods for correcting them. But by bit, as result of practice and correction, the skills is perfected.

A key role of the teacher or coach is to recognize incorrect techniques and prescribe drills which will cause improvement. The younger the performer, the easier, quicker, and more precise will be his development, assuming his nervous system has matured adequately to develop the skill in question.

Nervous System Involvement

In general, the lower the involvement is in the central nervous system, the more gross, primitive, and stereotyped the movement will be. For example, a walking or running stride can probably be repeated over and over with the involvement of only the cerebellum, brain stem, and spinal cord. But if an abrupt change of direction or speed is required, the more involved coordinations and judgements would probably require the higher involvement of the cerebral cortex and/or the thalamus.

It has been postulated that, as skill develops, the innovation is relegated to lower centres of the CNS. The pathways of impulses within the cerebrum develop ruts by repeatedly travelling the same paths, and these ruts allow faster impulse travel with fewer detours. The performance of the act then requires less conscious consideration to keep the impulses on the proper course.

It is generally agreed that skilful acts are accomplished without conscious thought, except for the thought needed to begin the act. Consequently, highly skilful acts are mostly conditioned reflexes. For example, we can perform the skill of walking while we occupied in deep thought or conversation. Actually, we may walk more skilfully under these conditions than if we concentrate on the movement.

The movements involved in walking result from conditioned reflexes. During active contests, it is often necessary for the performer to concentrate on external cause, and any preoccupation with specific body movements will destroy his effectiveness. In such cases, while the general idea of the desired response is conveyed by the cerebrum, lower centres of the central nervous system work out the details.

In the final analysis, the resulting movements are dependent upon three factors: (i) which neurons conduct impulse volleys, (ii) the frequencies of the impulses, and (iii) exactly when these impulses reach the muscle fibres. Another important factor is which muscles are prevented from contracting because of neural inhibition.

As a certain skill is developed, its specific movement tend to become less variable and more exact, because the selected patterns of impulses become more easily duplicated. This is because the impulse volleys tend to follow previously established pathway within the nervous system. As stated earlier, the impulses are conducted along the paths of least resistance.

Nerve pathway possibilities re inherited, but it is use that determines the development of the pathways. As certain synapses are used repeatedly, their thresholds are lowered, and the chance of repeating that pattern under like conditions is increased. Conversely, it is difficult to blaze new pathways for the same act once the pathways have been established.

As in walking through deep grass, the more often a certain path is taken, the deeper the pathway becomes. Paths to repeated tend to become obscure, but they are not completely eliminated.

When one begin to learn a skills, many pathways are possible. But gradually, pathways are selected which have resulted in successful performances, and the other pathways are rejected. The more often a pathway is repeated, the more firmly ingrained the pattern becomes and the more difficult it is to avoid. Gradually the path is used with greater ease and smoothness, and superfluous movements are eliminated. Unproductive paths are rejected, and the act becomes "skilful."

Certain obstacles exist such as the following: (i) Conditions, both of the internal and external environments are never exactly the same from one time to the next. (ii) Most skills are complex enough to involved several joints and many muscles, and even though the skill may appear correct, variations in only a few movements may detract from success. (iii) The performer may incorrectly judge his performance as successful and continue to perform incorrectly.

For instance, he may throw with the wrong foot forward and assume this is the correct procedure since he achieves a degree of success. Or a young basketball player who is a head taller than his opposition may use and undesirable shooting technique with much success until he meets an opponent of equal height.

From Basic to Refined Skills

The acquisition of refined skills necessitates prior learning of gross skill patterns. Highly refined skills are usually only slight modifications of basic pattern. For example, if a child learns a basic throwing pattern by throwing objects of all sorts under a variety of conditions, the addition of a forearm rotation and a wrist snap in the direction of the little finger can result in a curve ball. Similarly, once a tennis player has learned the basic tennis strokes, he can add slight modifications which results in spin on the ball.

In golf, the basic stroke patterns are learned rather quickly, but the refinement of them and the learning of stroke variations require much time and practice. In every athletic activity there is a set of basic skills, and there are refinements and variations of the basic skills which make the difference between mediocrity and excellence.

Significance of Skill

Effective performance requirements amounts of several physiological traits, such as strength, speed, endurance, agility, and flexibility, but athletes possessing lesser amounts of these traits often outperform their stronger and faster opponents because of well-coordinated neuromuscular patterns .

The excellent athlete has an abundance of all the mentioned physiological traits combined with the exact neuromuscular control needed to assure success. Some performance experts claim that control needed to assure success. Some performance experts claim that skills is the most important single factor in performance.

Each activity requires certain specific skills. For example, performance in basketball requires skill in humping, shooting, running, throwing, catching, and dribbling. A soccer player must be able to dribble, pass, screen, dodge, and kick effectively.

Each of the other sports has its own set of specific skills. Regardless of the other traits a person might possess, he will not be an effective tennis player until he learns the skills which are specific to tennis, and he will not swim well until he develops the specific skills of swimming. The development of specific skills is one of the greatest concerns of the coach and teacher.

14

FLEXIBILITY AND RANGE OF MOTION

Flexibility is expressed by the range of the motion in a given joint or combination of joints. It is influence by three factors: (i) the bone structure of the joint; (ii) the amount of bulk surrounding the joint; and (iii) the extensibility of ligaments, tendons, muscles, and skin crossover the joint. The third factor is of greatest concern to those seeking to increase flexibility.

The first factor is well illustrated in elbow and knee joints. Because of their bone structure, these joints are unable to extend beyond the 180^0 position. Nearly every joint has limitations due to its bone structure. An example of the second factors is the restrictions due to its to the mass of the biceps muscles. If the biceps were doubled in size, the range of motion would be reduced considerably.

The third factor is best illustrated by attempting to flex at the hips and lower back to place the hands flat on the floor. In order to do this, the muscles and connective tissues located in the backs of the legs and lower back must possess sufficient extensibility.

Inactivity causes muscles and connective tissues to lose their normal extensibility, and thus reduces flexibility. Inactivity may also contribute to accumulation of body fat which further restricts flexibility.

There are tow types of flexibility, passive and dynamic. Passive flexibility is demonstrated by the range of movement that occurs in a joint when the muscles are relaxed and the body part is moved by another person. Dynamic flexibility is demonstrated by the range of movement that occurs in a joint as a result of contractions of the muscles which control the joint. Obviously, dynamic flexibility is of greater concern in performance.

How to Increase Flexibility

Flexibility can be improved on an immediate or a long-range basis. For immediate improvement, flexibility can be increased a limited amount by preparatory stretching exercises. DeVries found that prior to warm-up antagonistic muscles relax slowly and incompletely when the agonists contract, and thus retard free movement and accurate coordination.

Warm-up exercise cause the antagonists to relax more completely, and the movements become smoother and better coordinated. Slow-stretch exercises where the antagonistic muscles are stretched and consciously relaxed for several seconds are the most effective for immediate improvement in flexibility.

To consider long-range improvement in flexibility, recall the previous statement that flexibility is limited by three factors: (i) bone structure; (ii) amount of bulk surrounding the joints; and (iii) the extensibility of the ligaments, tendons, muscles, and skin which cross over the joint.

The first factor is constant. The second factor offers some potential for flexibility improvement in the case of some individuals. Overweight persons can increase flexibility throughout the body by losing weight. Take, for example, the person who is unable to touch his hands to the floor because of too much in the abdominal region. For nearly all athletic performers, however, the third factor is the one that offers significant potential for improvement.

Two forms of exercises have been used to stretch muscle and connective tissues, ballistic and slow-tension. Flexibility can be increased effectively with either method. But the slow-tension method is recommenced because it has these advantages: (i) there is less danger of exceeding the limits of extensibility of the tissues, which would cause injury and soreness; (ii) this method does not activities the stretch reflex; and (c) it provides the opportunity to relax the antagonistic muscles consciously and allow them to stretch.

Logan and Egstrom and DeVries conducted separate studies which support the claim that flexibility at the hip and lower back can be increased significantly with either ballistic or slow-tension exercises.

The subjects who performed ballistic exercises experienced soreness, while those who did slow-tension stretching suffered no soreness. Hansen studies the effectiveness of only ballistic stretching and received favourable results.

Slow-tension exercises can be done either passively or actively. Passive exercise are useful in therapy, but are less desirable than active exercises in athletic conditioning.

The specific recommended procedure for improving flexibility is as follows: Go through the movement slowly until muscles and connective tissues stretch far enough to experience the "stretch pain." Hold the position for 8 to 10 seconds; while doing so, consciously relax the antagonistic muscles, allowing them to stretch as freely as possible. Repeat this procedure five or six times for each movement in which greater flexibility is desired.

The best results are accomplished when stretching is done daily. Dynamic stretching is preferred over passive stretching because flexibility from dynamic stretching is to increase the range through which the body part can move by its own force.

Dynamic stretching involves difficult coordinations because the agonistic muscles must contract while the antagonists experience almost complete relaxation. Change brought about by stretching exercises persists for a considerable period of time after stretching is discontinued. A sizable percentage of the increased flexibility will be retained for as long as 8 or 10 weeks.

Factor which Influence Flexibility

There are several factors which influence the amount of flexibility that exists and the rate at which it can be developed.

Body Type and Proportion

Research has shown a low relationship between flexibility and somatotype. Neck, hip, and trunk flexion show the highest relationship, with flexibility steady decreasing in these movements with increased endomorphic characteristics. Body fat, as measured by skinfold callipers, shows a negative correlation with flexibility.

The amount of muscle tissue is apparently unrelated to flexibility unless muscles bulk actually interferes with completion of the movement.

No consistent relationship has been shown between flexibility and length of the arms, trunk, and legs. Those who have extremely long arm and trunk measurements in relation to their legs have an advantage in the toe-touching tests, but such extreme body builds are rare, and seldom need to be considered.

Age and Sex Type

The grater flexibility is usually achieved during the early elementary school years, and it never again reaches that level. Numerous test results indicate that elementary school children gradually become less flexible until they are 11 or 12 years old.

Then they tend to increase slowly in flexibility until young adulthood. From that point on, flexibility gradually decreases with difference continues to exist throughout life.

Weight Training

Numerous research have produced evidence that weight training does not have harmful effects on flexibility when done properly. Massey and Chaudet point out that weight training tends to increase flexibility in the body regions that are exercised through the range of motion, but it may reduce flexibility in the unexercised regions or in regions where the exercise is done through short-ranges. Gardner studied the effects of both isotonic and isometric strength training and found that neither program had detrimental effect on flexibility. Judgment and observation tend to support these findings.

Stretch Reflex

When a muscle is stretched suddenly, it automatically responds, due to the stretch reflex, with a contraction which varies with the suddenness and intensity of the stretch.

The stretch reflex is primarily a postural reflex, and it is essential in maintaining an erect position. An obvious example of it occurs when one falls asleep while sitting and the head nods, causing the neck extensor muscles to be suddenly stretched. The stretch reflex responds, returning the had to the erect position with a jerk.

The stretch reflex also aids in contractions during voluntary movements. Example are the dip just prior to the thrust in the vertical jump, or the backward movement of the arms and shoulders just prior to the forward action in baseball batting.

The reflex results from a volley of impulses which are automatically discharged from within the muscle spindles when the muscle is stretched suddenly. Conversely, slow stretching does not activate the stretch reflex, and this is one of the arguments for using slow-tension exercises for increasing flexibility. Walker found that the amount of tension for a given amount of stretch is more than doubled by a quick stretch as compared to slow stretch, when the degree of the stretch is the same.

Temperature

Wright and Johns found that by warming a body region to 113^0 F dynamic flexibility increased about 20%, while cooling to 65^0 F resulted in decreases of 10 to 20%.

It is believed that increasing body temperature through exercise increases the extensibility of muscles and connective tissues, thus increasing flexibility temporarily. Further, it is believed that this increased extensibility will reduce the chances of injury to the tissues.

Activity Level

Excessive inactivity causes muscles and connective tissues to lose their normal extensibility. Complete inactivity, as when, a broken limb is in a cast, results in great loss of flexibility. Inactivity may also contribute to accumulation of body fat which may further restrict flexibility.

Conversely, regular activity tends to maintain normal flexibility, and unusual amounts of flexibility can be developed with specific exercises.

Specificity of Flexibility

Research results have established that flexibility tends to be highly specific to particular movement, meaning that a person might have large ranges of motion some movements and rank below normal in other movements. This is determined primarily by the extensibility of the muscles and connective tissues surrounding the particular joint.

Significance of Flexibility

Therapist and movement experts claim that lack of flexibility is one of the frequent causes of improper movement. When ungainly movement is observed, especially in walking and running, flexibility should be one of the first things to check.

Flexibility is involved in many motor patterns, and its inadequate development may be regarded as another possible deterrent to achievement in certain spots. There is no set standard as to the amount of flexibility a person should possess.

This depends on the activities in which he desires to participate. Most activities require no more than normal flexibility. But, a few activities are directly dependent upon an unusual degree of flexibility in certain joints. Gymnastics, diving, hurdling, modern dance and ballet all require great flexibility in certain body evidence that more than average flexibility will improve performance in such activities as basketball, tennis, volleyball, and gold.

Some experts claim that in games like football, soccer, and rugby, better-than-average flexibility will reduce likeliness of injury. But this idea is based only on observation and judgement and is not supported by research. Conversely, other experts claim that too much flexibility may make a joint injury-prone, because it reduces the stability of the joint.

Cureton found that competitive swimmers have a large amount of flexibility in the ankle joint and in trunk flexion and extension. Other studies support the idea that ankle flexibility is important in swimming. Cureton also reported that the 1949 Danish Exhibition Gymnastics Team scored higher than any group ever measured by him in trunk flexion and extension.

Research has shown little or no relationship between flexibility of the body appendages and performance in sports. Conversely, significant relationships have been shown between the flexibility of the trunk and hips and performance in several activities.

Based on research and practical experience. It can be concluded that a normal amount of flexibility throughout the body is desirable in all athletic performances, and some activities demand large degrees of flexibility in specific body regions. By seriously analysing the task to be accomplished, the coach or athlete can determine which body regions need additional flexibility.

15

FITNESS AND HEALTH

Fitness and health are not necessarily the same thing. A person can be perfectly health without being able to urn a mile in under four and a half minutes, play five sets of tournament tennis or survive an afternoon's football.

Fitness for an athlete is very specific. It implies training, though it can and does include health: no sportsman can train effectively for his sport if he is not completely sound.

It incorporates postural training, the elementary knowledge of body mechanics, sound nutrition, general training, preparation for solo sports, group practice for team sports, readiness for special events and the retraining needed after an injury before the sportsman should be allowed to return to full activity.

Nutrition

Nobody is going to excel in sport unless his body is in good repair. He should have neither too much weight nor too little. The body should also respond instantly and accurately to all commands of the brain. For this, good posture is important; but the right amount of the right foods is equally important.

All foods are used for heating, energy, repair of existing tissues and the creation of new ones where necessary. An athlete's daily intake is often upwards of 4,000 to 5,000 calories—about thirty or forty per cent of which is efficiently used. If this seems a small proportion, it is still four times as efficient as the average motor car.

A certain amount is stored, as fat, against a hungry day. Our early ancestors in caveman days had no corner shop and had to depend on their luck out hunting.

During exercise, more heat than usual is provided by the body. It is not exercise itself that warms the body but the waste heat which results from the system providing a little more of everything than is actually needed. When, in those primitive, times, fear made the heart, lungs and sweat glands work overtime it was to provide the instant means of 'flight or fight.'

This was accomplished by releasing adrenaline into the blood stream. The mechanism still exists today and can be useful in providing an athlete with that extra spark which he needed to win an important event.

There are three categories of food. Proteins are needed to build and repair; fats and oils for lubricating and for the production of heat and energy; and stored as fat if not used up in activity.

The protein group is the most important of the food categories. With almost any reasonably balanced diet the body can borrow a sparking-plug from some other food. What it can't do is to manufacture some of the vital ingredients of protein; these must be provides from outside sources.

The bio-chemists know there are twenty-three essential factors, known as amino acids, which can be strung together in a wide variety of combinations and permutations to form proteins, There is a certain element in protein, however, which cannot be produced synthetically in the test tube.

Some nutritionists have even called this the germ of lite. This is why, they say, protein foods are of first importance and why, in the under-developed countries, people die because they cannot get enough protein.

At one time it was thought that all athletes required their essential protein in the form of vast quantities of meat. But protein can just as well be obtained from dairy produce—eggs, milk, cheese–and from many vegetable materials–nuts, legumes, root vegetables, and from whole grains.

The best protein of all may well be fish, for the Japanese and Hawaüans and other big fish-eating nations can produce just as great athletes as the meat-eating countries. Athletes should eat three servings a day of protein food but are advised not to rely on meat as the sole source.

As well as 'oiling the works' fats and oils provide some of the body's energy, from a protective layer round the nerves and act as a medium for carrying the fat-soluble Vitamins A, D and E round the body. Some fats oils, preferably vegetable and also preferably unsaturated, should be eaten every day.

Vitamin A is needed for eye-sight, healthy skin; Vitamin D for strong bones. Vitamin E, for which nutritionists are continually discovering new important uses, has long been known as necessary for the heart and circulation.

Foods containing Vitamin A are plentiful. It comes in leafy vegetables, in the yellow vegetable in the form of carotenes which the body changes, into Vitamin A. It is also found in butter, margarine, cream, whole milk, eggs and liver.

Vitamin D comes from sunshine, fish livers or irradiated vegetable oils. Vitamin E is obtainable from whole grains, wheat germ and wheat germ oil and pressed vegetable oils, especially soya, peanut or sunflower.

Carbohydrates are chiefly sugars and starches. Sugar in fruits, milk and honey is better for you can that white sugar has been depleted, in processing, of is vitamins and minerals. Starches are mostly derived from flour. Whole grains: whole wheat, steel-cut oats, brown rice and whole rye are the best ways to eat carbohydrates because they have not had the goodness taken our of them.

White bread is, of course, 'enriched' by the addition of some of the vitamins and minerals that were removed from it. 'Enriched' is rather a misleading word. In their natural state foods are put together in a very cleaver fashion so that each food is complete with everything in it that the body needs to metabolise it. M an has been very unwise in disturbing the pattern by slitting the foods up, often taking out the very factor without which the remainder is almost valueless. It is as if the sparking-plug of a motor car was removed and the petrol expected to burn anyway.

The chief group of petrol vitamins removed from white flour is the B complex. A great deal is known about this group of twenty or more integrated vitamins and it is said that if the knowledge were universally applied, the improvement in world health would be beyond imagination.

Among the group, all of which are found in liver and yeast as well as in whole grains, is an anti-fatigue, anti-stress, anti-anaemia factual sugar is also the best source of Vitamin C. One of this vitamin's many functions is to maintain collagen, a strong, cement-like material which binds every cell in the body. Strong connective tissues are important to the athlete who probably receives more minor injuries than the unathletic type.

The ability to met broken bones is helped by Vitamin C. One well-known American orthopaedic surgeon, whose practice was largely among footballers and water skiers, advocated a 'cocktail' of citrus fruit, eggs and powdered milk whenever he had to treat broken bones.

An excellent carbohydrate food is the Swiss cereal muesli, which is made from several whole grains—wheat, rye, oats—various nuts, honey or Babados sugar and dried fruits, and which is especially valuable nutritionally when eaten with cheese, live yogurt and/or whole milk.

A balanced diet consists of a wide selection from each of these categories daily. From the protein group at least three servings of meat, fish or eggs; two from the dairy—milk or cheese. From the fat section, margarine or butter, in energy of 4,000 to 5,000 calories a day is not likely to go short of vitamins on a balanced eating plan. Nor should he need anabolic steroids: these were once advocated to strength muscle power and favoured by weight lifters, among others, until their use was stopped as part of the movement against drugs.

The human body is very flexible and can break down any food into its essential ingredients for growth, maintenance and repair, but it needs a selection from which to choose everything it needs.

If the components are not adequate—if straw' is provided instead of 'bricks'—the repair work will still be done but it will not be as lasting or as satisfactory.

Yet different peoples survive on very different selections, from blubber, to rice, to fruit and nuts—as long as they get some protein they can live, if not always healthily. Healthy, adequate diets can vary widely also.

The Japanese like raw fish and rice, the Italians spaghetti and veal, the British meat and two veg. and plenty of bread. As a result of air travel and occupying armies, however, diets have become more standardised on a world-wide basis, though this is not always to the best advantage.

There is still, however, a certain problem for the catering departments during international sports gatherings. In fact the caterers have more of a problem than the human body with its infinitely complicated engineering process of conversion.

Fitness and the Mechanics of Movement

It may be easier to acquire Active Alerted Posture if your understand, to a certain extent, the mechanisms of body movement and how these can be used to achieve or enhance certain skills.

The skeletal framework—bones—gives the requisite rigidity to enable the body to resist gravity and maintain an upright stance. Six levels comprise the skeleton: the head on the spinal column; the arms on the shoulder girdle, attached to the neck and trunk, the spinal column on the pelvis; the pelvis on the hips; the top of the body on the knees; the whole body on the ankles and feet. These are the levels where the most strain occurs in the upright position.

The central and perhaps most important of these bony laments is the spinal column, which consists of twenty-four movable vertebrae, five immovable vertebrae fused into the sacrum, and four into the coccyx. Between each two movable vertebrae is a cartilagious disc starting between the second and third cervical vertebrae and finishing at the bottom lumber vertebra and the first sacral vertebra.

Bones are covered with a fibrous membrane called the periosteum by means of which muscle and tendons and blood vessels are attached to them. These bones are fastened to each other at the joints: without them the skeleton would be stiff.

There are a number of different types of joint, and the degree of movement possible is dependent on the type. Some joints, in fact, are fixed; some have limited movement; while others, like the ball-and-socket joints of the shoulder and hip, have considerable freedom of motion in all directions. Capsules strengthened by ligaments bind the bones together forming the individual joints so that dislocation is rare.

There ligaments combine with the contour of the bones as well as the overlying muscles and are an important limiting factors in joint movements. The joints are kept firm and flexible by the muscles, which are elastic.

Although there are other types of muscles in the walls of the blood vessels and the alimentary canal, as well as the pumping muscles of the heart, those of interest in regard to posture are the skeletal muscles, without which the bones and joints cannot move.

You have probably seem, in medical books, pictures

of a person peeled of his skin so you can visualise the way the muscles are arranged in groups according to their action. Each muscles consists of millions of fibres woven on to the outside of the skeleton.

Muscle tissue needs a more rapid turnover of food material than any other part of the body; the arteries bring the materials to the blood stream. The waste products left over from the combustion of foodstuffs must also be removed, and this is accomplished by the venous and lymphatic circulations.

As well as the arteriole, venous and lymphatic circulations, fifty percent of body find consists of the fluid within the cells which make up the various tissues. Fifteen percent is in the spaces between them. We call the two latter ones the fourth circulation.

This circulation is propelled by the pumping action of the skeletal muscles. If, through injury, or inactivity caused by lengthy bed rest, the fourth circulation is diminished and there is the possibility of oedema–the accumulation of excess fluids and metabolities, in the tissues. The latter tend to cause tissue tenderness, feelings of fatigue and pain.

A similar conditions results following strenuous exercise when the removal of waste products has lagged behind their rapid production, or it may be due to slumping posture when the anti-gravity muscles become fatigued through working at a mechanical disadvantage.

The muscle group primarily concerned with producing any particular movement is called the prime mover or activator. These muscles are assisted by muscles called synergist, but both sets must work on a firm base held steady by the muscles called the prime fixers, as when hitting a tennis ball and kicking a football.

For example, if a door were opened before it was firmly attached to the door frame by hinges and screws it would fall away from the frame.

The muscles which restrain or control the given action are called the antagonists. For example, when one group of muscles pulls the forearm upward—flexion—another set of muscles is available to pull it downward again. When your get a contraction of the activating group, the opposite group elongates.

Every movement of which the body is capable is effected by means of this balanced system of opposing muscle groups. When the muscles are in harmony and synchronise perfectly, the movements will be graceful and smooth.

Imperfect synchronisation produces awkward, jerky movements. In order to achieve harmony, all muscles must be able to contract strongly and quickly and to relax and lengthen just as quickly.

Muscle tissue is also supplied with nerves: sensory nerves for sensation and motor telephone switchboard. The part of the brain which is the switchboard or control tower receives messages from all the body senses, coordinates the information and ten orders changes of position where and when desirable.

Where the body is trained to react correctly–as, for instance, in that of an Olympic sportsman–its movements are co-ordinated at a high level of integration. The control tower in the brain is constantly monitoring and relaying information from various sensory sources and the result may be perfect motion.

But even in a less-than-perfect action—a movement, say, performed by a cricketer on the village green rather than one in a Test match at Lord's—a system of action, integration and reaction almost impossible to visualise is involved.

The movements of an athlete, even of the village-green variety, are seldom simple. They twist and curve and, even in running or walking, flexion and extension of the hip joint are combined with some degree of rotation. Similar mechanisms are at work in the joints of the feet, knees, spine and arms.

The athlete, pole-vaulting, running or jumping, has not time to think of all the component parts of a perfect movement; his years of training have made these almost automatic. Almost but not quite. When things go wrong—when Jackin goes off his game or Bille Jean King is beaten by an unseeded newcomer—someone has to know enough to recognise the cause of it and put it right.

This is why their coach or trainer has to have a working knowledge of the mechanics of joint movement that he is able to spot where things have gone wrong.

There was the case of a famous bowler at cricket who had experienced recurrent attacks of pain in the under surface of h is left foot. The pain disappeared in the winner when he was not playing but returned each year as soon as spring practice began.

It became progressively worse during the season and was diagnosed as a strain of the spring ligament and the short muscles of the longitudinal arch caused by planting his left foot flat on the ground as he finished the action of bowling—he was right-hander-so that the foot and the ankle were twisted outward.

He was shown how to correct his ankle and foot posture. As he was taking the final step with the left foot he was told to plant the foot firmly on the ground with his weight on the outer side, and at the same time to grip with his toes and turn his foot slightly inward.

This had the effect of fixing the foot firmly on the ground so that there was no more pain but his bowling improved. It took him a little time to learn the new pattern of distributing his weight on the correct weight-bearing part of his foot, so that his right arm and body had a firm platform from which to work, but once he learned to activate on a firm base he had no more trouble.

A baseball pitcher, who is over-ambitious and under-trained, can suffer from a strain of the muscles on the inner side of the elbow with swelling and pain or, in Little Leauge pitchers, possibly inflammation of the growing part of the humerus bone at the elbow. If he continues pitching incorrectly this may result in serious irrevocable damage to the still undeveloped bone.

In both cases it is the expert trainer who sports the faulty mechanisms in his trainer and shows him how to put these right, or, if symptoms of pain and swelling appear, stops him pitching at once.

The Avoidance and Prevention of Injury

Some injuries are impossible to avoid, of course, and the injured person cannot be held responsible. If a player gets a direct hit from a hard ball he is accountable only if he saw it coming and made an unsuccessful attempt to avoid it.

Some injuries can be circumvented by the use of special skill. If a horse slips, refuses, or bricks, he may throw the rider out of the saddle, but a skilful enough horseman can often retain his seat or, at the worst, know how to fall so that his injury is minimised.

Other injuries are inherent in the sport itself. A football player—any type—cannot evade physical contact which could, and often does, damage him. In American football the players, by wearing protective clothing, do a good deal to lessen contact injuries.

On the other hand, part of the protective apparel can actually be used as a weapon, especially the helmet which-in some cases illegally—can butt an opponent in the stomach or other parts of the body very painfully.

In soccer a collision of two players humping to head the ball can result in an injury to foreheads, eyes, noses, or in a pulled hamstring, calf, groin or back muscle. It is apparently unavoidable and is much more likely to occur in player who either are not warmed up, not fully fit, fatigued, or are using incorrect posture.

If a perfect action is analysed it is found to be executed in two distinct and separate phases. The muscles which fix the action must be alerted and then the muscles which activate the action assisted by their companion muscles which or joints. A good simile is a gun which must be loaded and then, with the safety cock off, can be fired instantly.

If the action is performed before this fixing takes place, there is a danger of muscle strain and strains on joints and eventually perhaps stress fracture. An example of an accidental, un-fixed movement is coming down steps in the dark and missing the last step, jarring the whole system.

Other accident-provoking affections, such as muscle cramps, stitch, foot blisters, sun or heat stroke, can usually be avoided with simple methods.

Muscle cramps in the leges during play may due to dehydration carrying salt out of the system. Tennis tournament player can often be seen taking salt pills during the crossover. Tight garters obstructing circulation may also be the cause of muscle cramps which are relieved by removing the constricting garter.

A stitch is usually caused by eating too larger a meal immediately before taking strong sunlight may avert trouble. Covering the whole body with a track suit or other suitable garments is important in cold weather and may make all the difference to efficiency of performance.

Many pulled muscles are caused by activating in cold weather before the body is warmed up and the athlete should keep his track suit on until his body is really well warmed. Even in the summer, tournament tennis players wear a sleeveless sweater until they are thoroughly warmed up.

Jim Peters, once holder of the word's best marathon time, had a way of preventing tendon trouble not only for marathon and road running but also for distance running. He cut the inner sorbose out of an old pair of plimsolls and put them into the ones he was wearing. By absorbing the shock, this took much of the strain off the tendons.

To avoid personal injury, the sportsman himself should be as fit as possible before the start of the game or event, learn to fix his movements on a firm base, obey the rules of the sport and hope that others will do the same. An umpire or referee can help here by penalising a dangerous act but he may not be able to prevent it happening in the first place.

Postural Training

Sportsmen are possibly aware that correct posture is necessary for coordinated movement but very few, except perhaps a gymnast, a tightrope walker or a ballet dancer, realise how essential to their athletic prowess it is to maintain a balanced upright posture. Good posture can also do a great deal to help avoid accidents.

Poor, slumping posture contributes not only to indifferent performance but also to the passibility of injury. There are two kinds of upright posture: Active Alerted, which some adopt naturally but most have to be taught, and Inactive Slumping, which is the stance of most people.

That these postures are connected with mind and mood is obvious when you think of a depressed person, eyes cast down, shoulders hunched, and compare him with someone whose moods is confident, who swings along, head up, shoulders back, moving with grace and control. Active Alerted Posture, which is an attitude not only of the body but of the mind, is a complete way of living and moving, promoting both mental and physical equilibrium and poise.

Since man stood upright instead of on all fours, he has had to contend with a greater force of gravity pulling at his joints and internal organs. Gravity is, of course, necessary. Without its force we would be floating around in space like balloons filled with gas.

The straighter the line of gravity, and with a reasonable width of base, the more stable we are. As soon as the line of gravity passes outside the area enclosed by the supporting base—for instance if your stand on one foot-the line of gravity will waver outside the base and it is easy to lose your balance.

In order to visualise how the pulls of gravity can affect your body, think of a child's tower made of varying sized bricks. If the bricks are placed securely one above the other so that the line of gravity passes through the centre of each of them, the tower can be made quite tall without tumbling; if, however, each brick juts out to one side or the other, or goes too far over in one direction like the Tower of Pisa, it will soon collapse.

One of the great benefits of Active Alerted Posture is that is aligns the 'bricks' one above the other so that the line of gravity is centralised above a firm base. This lessens, to a considerable extent, gravity's downward tug on various part of the body, such as internal organs and joints. For this reason, it is a posture which makes immediate dynamic action possible.

It helps to avert accidents due to slow co-ordination of mind and body action.

This is how it is achieved. You stand with the weight evenly distributed on the heels, the outer side of the feet, gripping the ground with the toes. The knees are slightly flexed and act as shock absorbers.

The buttocks are tucked under, the pelvis tilted so that it is at right angles to the ground. The shoulders are lifted and relaxed, shrugged slightly forward. The head is held so that the contraction of one group of muscles at the back of the neck balances the ones in front. The chin is tucked in and the back of the neck held straight and lifted so that the top of the head is as if tied to the ceiling.

By making the feet a firm base you will lessen the chance of foot troubles, such as fallen arches, both longitudinal and transverse. You will be able to activate with a spring.

In addition, your internal organs will be well supported in the pelvic basin by the balanced contraction of the abdominal, back and buttock muscles.

This posture encourages the full expansion of the lungs by ensuring balanced action between the muscles of the abdominal wall and the diaphragm. The whole process is like a bellows. This means that all the waste products from the bottom as well as the top of the lungs are removed regularly.

The flexible, lifted shoulders will neutralise gravity's pull on the upper limbs, the shoulder girdle and neck muscles. The blood flows more freely to the brain, carrying the oxygen needed to counteract fatigue, poor memory and headaches.

The ability of the body to perform many and complex patterns of motion makes possible the great variety of movements demanded of a sportsman and it is the brain which commands these movements. An ape, for instance, the animal nearest to man, has the physical capacity to perform certain inherited skills and it might possible be taught to perform certain inherited skills and it might possibly be taught to use these to play golf, for example. But it would never achieve the brain power to win an Open Championship.

General Training

For almost all sports a period of general training at the beginning of the season, after a rest period, is necessary. The athlete has to work at raising the level of his achievement to within sight of his ultimate goal. Unless he has ben sensible enough to cut down on his intake of food during the rest period, when his output of energy was lesser, he may be overweight.

The only efficient way to reduce is to cut down on the amount of food and step up the output of energy by exercise. Most doctors and coaches advise a period of graduated exercise to work up to full activity.

Weight lifting, walking, jogging, interval running can all be part of a useful programme at the start of training. In addition, most people interested in their own fitness do a daily dozen and there are great many systems which exercise muscles not usually reached in everyday living: Isometrics, Mensendieck, Yoga, the Alexander Method, the Canadian Air Force Method, and others.

Most people have their favourite routine. Breathing exercises are also of value of all sports. Jogging on the spot is very much favoured by Americans and can easily be included in the daily routine. Skipping with a rope can also be done in a limited space.

Weight lifting or training produces good conditioning of the body and increases the working efficiency of the muscles. Basic weight-resisting exercises are nowadays considered an important part of modern training—not in order to become a weight lifter but to increase muscle power, stamina and cardio-vascular fitness.

Athletes who move quickly—such as short-distance runners, footballers and tennis players—should confine their amount of weight lifting to about 20 lb. Discus throwers and shot putters should gradually work up to as much as lb.

Both the Swedes and the Germans developed interval

running just before the Second World War. The Swedish idea was the more aesthetic. They believed that by training in picturesque settings with varying terrains they could combine fast bursts of speed with relaxing slow periods to suit the contours of the land.

The German method was more precise: short bursts of running at speed with recovery periods. Circuit training is a form of interval training nowadays popular in the United States, although it has been with success in England for years. It consists of a series of exercises done at various stages. There are about ten different routines according to the equipment available.

The circuit is performed as fast as possible doing each routine a given number of times before passing on to the next. When the athlete has mastered one circuit, the number of circuits is increased and all rounds are against time.

As he improves, his time is reduced until he reaches a maximum speed at which point the degree of fitness possible for him is said to have been achieved.

These methods have been standardised and included in most plans of general training so that there are specific length of time of time for speed, and recovery. Most sports require the athlete to be able to run effectively. If, however, a miller is being trained, he will run a quarter of a mile at speed, a slow quarter, a fast quarter and a slow, gradually increasing the fast quarters until he is approximating four minutes for his mile.

Alford, the athletic trainer who was the famous pre-war miller, has said that present-day athletes train at least five times harder than their counterparts before the war. For top athletes there is no such thing as a complete season of rest; they train almost all the year round even during the off season. This concentrated training is probably the reason for the breaking of records each year.

Training Exercises

Bertie Mee, who guided Arsenal to many triumphs, devised a set of exercises for his players which would be good preparation for any sport though 'Soccer is the most popular game in the word', he declares firmly. 'Soccer never stands still.' He also has certain tests for fitness.

Soccer is game which takes a heavy toll of weak muscles. If you think of a muscles as a piece of elastic strength it out to full length and let it snap together and it will return to its original length. If your stretch it to its full length many times, each time releasing it gradually, it will eventually lengthen.

That is what we try to do with our stretch exercises. It the beginning these exercise were devised for rehabilitation. Sometimes a player, eager to return to the game, would claim full recovery, but when tested him we found that he still favoured the injured side.

We then put him on a full course of exercises which would build up the injured muscle. Then it seemed possible that if these muscles were stretched and strengthened before play the injuries might not occur and this has proved to be the case.

We reduced the injuries on the field by fifty percent. These injuries were mostly soft tissue injuries to hamstrings, calves, quadriceps and adductors. You must have full extensibility before soft tissue injuries can be considered recovered or they will break down again.

In testing the hip, if the injured hip is not one-hundred-percent fit the weight is not fully taken on the injured foot, the hip coming up slightly. Again, when sitting on the heels and leaning back on the hands, if the hip is not completely fit the exercise will not be done equally on both sides and the trunk will tend to lean towards the good side.

When testing hamstrings in a forward bend with stiff knees, the players is apt to touch the toe only on the uninjured side, favouring the injured hamstrings.

Here are the fitness exercises:–

Exercises for the rectus femoris—Exercise for the rectus femoris, which is the kicking muscle. Feet wide apart, make a slight lunge, bending the knee outward. Then lunge on the opposite side.

Exercise for the groin—Put one foot on a chair with the leg at right angles to the body. Bend towards the chair feeling the stretch on the inside of the things from groin to knee. Changes legs and repeat.

Exercise for the calf—Without shoes, heels flat, knees straight, stand about a foot from a wall, hands supporting the body at shoulder height, then lean forward, feeling the stretch of the muscles all up the back of the calf and thigh. Push upright again and repeal. Knees must be straight.

Mental Preparation

Mental and psychological fitness are necessary to reach the pinnacle of any sport. When an athlete, capable of reaching the heights, has an off day he will usually excuse it by saying, 'I was simply not able to concentrate.'

This maybe due to some personal worry or to the fact that his morale had somehow been lowered; sometimes it is caused by a belief that he will fail, or by a boredom caused by over-training, sometimes even by economic worries. On the other hand, concentration comes from many sources and some professional sportsmen are said to be able to concentrate more effort into winning when the prize is bigger. Dedication to the sport, the will to win and even fear of losing can all play their part.

Preparation for Specific Skills

Towards the end of the second week those who are training for special sports—golf, tennis, boxing, sculling, show jumping, swimming, athletics, football, cricket and a great many others–start doing specific activities connected with their sport. By this time any early stiffness should have worn off.

Hot baths and rubbing with a coarse towel should ease any pain but in the case of excessive stiffness the level of exercise should not be increased until the stiffness has worn off.

Preparation for Special Events

By the end of the sixth week of training the athlete has already taken part actively in his sport but he probably has some special future event in mind. He may be close to one-hundred-percent fitness but still needs just that extra impetus.

He should try to keep himself at the level he has reached until the time comes to raise himself to the very summit of training.

Obviously, with every sport, the final toughening up period will be different. Each athlete and his trainer will know best how to reach maximum fitness without going over the top into over-training and staleness.

However, while at one time it was considered that the only way to overcome staleness was to rest, it is now believed to be better to work through the barren period and get over it, and that there is no such thing as over-training.

16

REHABILITATION BEFORE RETRAINING

Even though an injury has been successfully treated and the athlete pronounced fit to return to his sport, some weakness in the damaged part may remain. The aim of treatment is to get one-hundred-percent complete recovery. This means a full range of movement and muscle control.

The joint must be as stable as it was before the injury: any residual weakness may result in a repetition of the accident and not necessarily under the same conditions.

For example, an ankle which has been damaged at football may, if not completely stable and rehabilitated, rick in a game of tennis or golf, in ski or even walking along the street. Or again, a collarbone broken in a riding accident may be associated with stiffness in the shoulder and neck muscles with limitation of movement, and these can be aggravated and give rise to painful symptoms in other sports like shooting, or any sport in which the shoulder and neck are used.

After the injury the muscles and soft tissues may become contracted and shortened and lose their resilience and elasticity. If this is not successfully counteracted, the joints may also undergo deterioration, and eventually degeneration, leading later in life to osteo-arthritis—though this is a situation that the young sportsman may feel is too far off to worry about.

His successful return to his sport, however, is something that matters to him. Home treatment when done regularly and conscientiously after an accident can do more than prevent deterioration in the future. It can ensure that the sportman goes back into his sport in perfect condition.

He should learn always to stand in the Active Alerted Posture as this not only distributes the body weight evenly over the joints, and especially the joint which is recovering, but also prepares it for action and helps prevent future injury.

Home treatment can be started, with the doctor's permission, even while the limb is in plaster of Paris or immobilised in some other way. Isometric exercises, elevation and hanging the limb can each be done for fifteen minutes daily, as can surging faradism if a faradic battery is available. Contrast baths can be used to bring extra blood-flow to the injured part. Products of injury are thereby carried away more rapidly.

Contrast bathing can be done in several ways, depending on the region of the injured part, beginning and ending with very hot water, as hot as it can be borne, and then alternating with ice-cold water. Two basins and tow sponges can be used or a hot and then a cold shower taken.

The sponge-and-basin method has the advantage that ice can be placed in the water. Two minutes of hot followed by two minutes of cold is the correct procedure. Always start and finish with hot.

Self-physiotherapy is a useful adjunct to the

physiotherapy that may be given in the clinic or clinic or hospital. The recovering athlete can use talcum powder or a lubricating ointment, such as Vaseline or Nivea, and gently rub the injured part, learning to dig the fingers into the tender points. He may also have a heat lamp.

Exercises in the bath are easy to do and additions to the water will help to give a special spa treatment. For instance, if coarse sea salt is added it gives the same effect as a dip in the ocean.

The salt is good for the skin, containing, as it does, all the minerals of the sea. A seaweed preparation can be added which also contains valuable sea minerals, especially iodine, a powerful disinfectant. Liquid seaweed added to hot water helps the body to get rid of impurities through additional sweating.

The bath is a good place to do some rehabilitating and general exercises.

1. For the Hip Joints, Pelvis and Lower Back

Resting against the back of the bath put the legs straight out in front of you. Rest one foot on the instep of the other. Press the top foot against the resistance of the lower foot. Reverse foot. Repeat five times.

2. For the Hips and Pelvis, and also to Strengthen the Lower Spine

Lean against the back of the bath with feet pressing against the tap end. Push the feet alternately against the bath end like a cat pressing its paws on a blanket. Do this twelve times.

3. For the Feet and Ankles

Sitting upright in the bath, feet at a right angle to

the legs, turn toes in. Pull the foot up towards the insides of the ankles. Turn the toes out and pull up to the outside of the ankles. Do six times on each side and then repeat, but this curling the toes and keeping them curled as you pull up. The exercises can also be done in bed.

4. For the Lower Back

Sit upright in the bath, pull in the muscles of the abdomen slowly, starting at the pit of the stomach. Roll the muscles as if to tuck them under the ribs. Hold for a count of six and then very slowly relax. Repeat six times.

5. For the Shoulder Girdle

Sitting upright and with extended arms, clasp the hands in front. Keeping the arms straight, swing them overhead, then bend arms at the elbow, swing them over clasp the back of the head, elbows forward slowly. Relax and repeat five times.

Home Treatment and Exercise for the Neck

The cause of injury may be a fall in polo or any other equestrian sport; a motor racing or motor cycle racing accident could result in a break or dislocation or a whiplash injury, as could a head-on blow in rugby. A sudden whipping accident to the head in boxing may cause an injury.

A collar may have been prescribed while the injury was recovering. It is a good thing to continue to wear this at night or even intermittently during the day.

A woollen muffler worm while sleeping or an electric hot pad wrapped round the neck when first in beg may help relax the muscles.

Contrast baths and self-physiotherapy also strengthen weakened muscles and help to relieve tension.

The following exercises may be done at odd moments during the day, though six times for each one is enough at any session.

Neck Exercise (A)

Sitting upright, chin tucked in, back of the neck straight, bend the head very slowly forward to a count of six, then very slowly backward to a count of six, times each way.

Neck Exercise (B)

Still with fixed shoulders, rotate the head slowly clockwise then anticlockwise, ending the head over as far as possible.

Neck Exercise (C)

In the same position turn the head as far as possible to the left to a slow count of six, then slowly to the right, keeping the back of the neck straight. Do this six times each way.

Neck Exercise (D)

Sitting upright, chin tucked in, back of the neck straight, bend the head very slowly forward to a count of six, then very slowly backward to a count of six, six times each way.

Neck Exercise (E)

Grip the sides of the chair so as to fix the shoulders and then bend the head slowly to the left side, trying to touch the shoulder with the ear. Do this to a slow count of six and similarly go over to the right. Do the double movement six times.

Swimming

This is one of the best possible rehabilitation exercise because it is non-weight-bearing. Even if the pool is small there are exercises that can be valuable because they are done against a natural resistance of the water. Swimming uses every muscle in the body.

Pool Exercise (A): for the Waist and Top Half of the Spin

Stand in water up to the neck with feet wide apart, arms outstretched, and tucked in. Twist at the waist, swinging the whole torso sideways, pressing slowly but firmly against the resistance the whole torso sideways, pressing slowly but firmly against the resistance of the water.

Swing slowly and purposefully round, pushing the resisting water away from you. Keep head still and eyes looking straight ahead, which gives extra resistance. Six times each side.

Pool Exercise (B): for the Feet

Run on the spot, raising knees as high as possible, this can be done at several depths for as long as you want.

Pool Exercise (C): for the Hips and Legs

Using a corner of the pool at the shallow end, rest your arms on the pool's ledge and support your weight on them–the water bears most of this burden. Spread your legs out behind you and swing the left leg over the right, then the right over the left in a scissors movement. Legs should be straight out at about waist height. Repeat six times.

Pool Exercise (D): for the Insides of the Thighs

Stand in the shallow end, holding on to the side of the pool. Allow the left leg to float slowly sideways to the surface until it is an near as possible at right niggles to the surface until it is an near as possible at right angles to the body.

Then press it down again hard, against the resistance of the water. Repeat with the right leg. Do this exercise six times with each leg.

Pool Exercise (E): for the Feet

Rise on the tips of the toes ballet-style. Although this is not feasible on dry land, except, of course, for the ballet dancer, the water makes it easy by supporting the weight of the body. Walk on your "points, at neck depth, holding the body very straight and with the head held highly.

Pool Exercise (F) for the Knees and Hips

At a depth of three feet do a Russian sword dance, shooting feet vigorously out in front of you.

Underwater Massage

Rub, squeeze and knead the part that was injured and do those of the 'land' exercise that particularly apply to the injured part. Most of them can be adapted to water.

Home treatment and Exercise for Fingers, Hands and Wrists

Hands, wrists and fingers can be damaged at almost any sport. Fingers can receive a direct blow from a ball, be trodden on in football, snapped or dislocated when they take the brunt of a fall.

The complications which can occur with broken, sprained or dislocated fingers or thumbs are usually due to disturbed blood circulation: traumatic effusions of blood and lymph not being readily or fully absorbed. When this happens, adhesions and thickening result with stiffness and limitation of movement and chronic stiffness of joints and even, eventually, deformity.

Fractures, dislocations or subluxations of the wrist are more common than anywhere else in the body as one or other of these may happen if the hand is put down to avert a fall.

Until the condition is one-hundred-percent symptom-free contrast paths should be given twice daily to helps disperse the effusions. For a broken wrist without displacement a protective wrist gauntlet may be used fastened with Velcro for easy removal.

Sprains and Strain of the wrist occur in sports where a racquet, club or other tool is used incorrectly over a period without the wrist being properly fixed with the balanced action of the surrounding tendons.

The following wrist exercises are designed to put the joint through a full range of movement.

Finger Exercise (A)

Spread hands flat on a table top, spread fingers apart and bring them together again. Do this six times, both hands simultaneously.

Finger Exercise (B)

Palms flat on the table, lift all the fingers together, extending the tips backward six times.

Finger Exercise (C)

Hands together in front of you, palms and fingers together, fingers pointing upward as in prayer. Press the finger only over to the left keeping the palms upright and without giving way in the wrist. Press the fingers on the left hand backward with the fingers of the right. Do this twelve times and then reverse.

Finger Exercise (D)

In the same position, pull the palms away from the fingers, keeping the insides of the knuckles together, especially the little finger. The wrists should come up at right angles. Do this twelve times.

Finger Exercise (E)

Keeping fingers flat on the table top, lift the palms six times.

Finger Exercise (F)

Same position, then twist the palms upward and then downward, six times.

Finger Exercise (G)

'Play the piano' on the table, raising the fingers high.

Wrist Exercise (A)

Rest the forearm on a table with the wrist and hand extended over the edge, palms facing down. Bend the wrist down and up six times.

Wrist Exercise (B)

Same position but make a fist and rotate the wrist clockwise six times, then anti-clockwise six times.

Wrist Exercise (C)

Same position but swing the hands from side to side from the wrist six times.

Wrist Exercise (D)

Same position, then twist the palms upward and then downward, six times.

Home Treatment and Exercise for Hips and Thighs

When athletes fracture their thighs it is usually in the middle or lower end of the femur—the main bone that runs through the thigh. Pulled hamstring muscles and other strains and sprains of the upper leg muscles usually occur after a fast sprint.

Fractures can happening ski, football, all equestrian sports, and in various types of athletics. Strain may e due to insufficient warm-up before running.

Dislocation of the hip is rare in athletics. It is a vulnerable area for contusions in sports where hitting a hard ground is likely: rugby football, ice hockey, falls in equestrian sports. Strains of the hip muscles are common and often associated with bursitis.

It is most important to make sure there is a full range of movement after recovery before returning to active sport. This can be accomplished by graduated exercises. Kneading and massage are also useful.

Exercise (A)

Standing upright, holding on to the back of a chair for support; start by putting all the weight on the left foot. Then raise the hip and the hell of the right foot, swing the toes in and the heel out.

Do not point the foot down. With an upright posture raise the leg sideways and go on pulling the leg back and out. Repeat on the other leg. Do this twelve times, alternating legs.

Exercise (B)

Sitting on the floor, bend forward and grasp the toes if possible. Don't strain if by can only reach the ankles or calves. Draw the top of the body toward the feet, with the head as far as possible towards the knees. Hold for a count of six and repeat six times.

Exercise (C)

Lying on the back, legs out straight, feet a few inches apart, turn the toes inwards as far as they will go, then outwards as far as they will go. This rotates the hip. Repeat six times.

Exercise (D)

Lying on the back, bringing one knee to the chest and circle it first clockwise, then anti-clockwise. Change legs and repeat, six times each side. Keep the back flat on the floor at the waist.

Exercise (E)

The second movement is carried out in the same position holding to the back of a chair. Standing on both feet, transfer all the weight to the left foot, raise the hip and the heel on the right side and put the leg diagonally back with the foot turned out, not pointed down. Raise the leg from the hip, and go on pulling the leg up in small further movements. Do this twelve times then change legs.

Exercise (F)

The third of this series is performed in the same position. Raise the hip and the heel on the right side and go back with the left, upright posture-twelve times each leg.

Home Treatment and Exercise for the Knee

The knee joint, thought it is surrounded by powerful muscles and strong ligaments, is, nevertheless, very vulnerable to both direct and indirect injuries. Torn ligaments are common in many sports; ligaments are there to stabilise the joint by preventing undue movement.

The severity of the injury often depends on how badly the ligaments are strained, torn or ruptured. Dislocations are uncommon although in some cases the patella—knee cap—dislocates.

Subluxations occur from lax ligaments and lead to joint instability.

After a knee injury, especially a dislocation or subluxation, the knee should be strapped with a stretch bandage, or an elastic half-stocking when a return to sport takes place.

Even after full movement has been restored, either by operative procedure or conservative treatment, and the athlete discharged from medical care, it may take a further tow or three weeks before strenuous exercise should be undertaken. During this period, home treatment by the sportsman himself is important.

The aim is to avoid a recurring injury or weakness which could happen if the damaged structures were not returned to full and complete stability.

The home treatment exercise should be continued even after the return to sport to ensure that the muscles and ligaments are kept at their peak condition.

In order to test that the knee has full extension and full flexion, sit back on the heels. This should be easy and painless. If it is, do a further test. While sitting back on the heels put hands on the floor , fingers pointing away from the body and land back with straight back, head dropping backwards.

The main thing, before returning to full activity, is to get full power in the medial quadriceps muscles down the inner side of the thighs.

Exercise (A)

Sit upright on a couch with the legs supported and straight out in front of you, knees relaxed. Tighten the thigh muscles by pressing the knee down on the couch. Exercise both legs though only one has been injured. Dot this six times.

Exercise (B)

Lie flat on the floor on a blanket. Bring the feet up along the floor toward the chest, raise the legs in the air and do a bicycling movement with the legs, gently at first and then more vigorously if no pain is felt. Legs together, knees bent, feet on the floor, straighten legs.

Exercise (C)

With the injured knee braced, raise the leg upwards then swing it out and across to the other side, back and then down. Repeat the movement on the other side. Do each leg alternately, six times.

Exercise (D)

Sit on the edge of the couch with a cushion under the knees and the legs hanging down. Straighten the injured knee firmly. AT the same time bend the other knee, pulling the calf hard against the resistance of the coach. Slowly and deliberately change position so that the knee becomes straight, and vice versa. Do this six times.

Home Treatment and exercise for the Feet and Ankles

Feet can suffer many direct injuries in a variety of sports. They can be hit by hard balls, mallets, hockey sticks and os on; they can be kicked by a horse and they can receive bruises or breakages from being stepped on by cleated shoes. Toes can be broken by stubbing; stress fractures can occur. Strains of the foot are common in many athletic activities.

The metatarsal bones at the base of the toes can be fractured by being heavily stepped on, and fallen arches are common to both metatarsal arch and longitudinal structures.

Ankles sprains are common to many sports. The ankle may rick over while running. Broken ankles occur in snow skiing but in deep, soft snow. A ruptured tendo-Achilles can also result from a similar fall.

Tennis and hurdling may produce tendo-Achilles injuries as well.

In rugby football a direct blow, or people falling over an extended leg in a pile-up, can cause fracture of the ankle bone. The tendo-Achilles' and its component muscles in the calf can best strained, torn or ruptured. Muscles can be torn from the shock strain of flat-footed so that the muscles, not being prepared, tear. This can happen in tennis, golf, cricket, volleyball, netball and similar sports.

Before and after returning to a sport following ankle injury, ankle strapping may be advisable. The heel or the arch may need to be raised with a rubber pad fitted into the shoe.

If there is any sign of swelling when activity again takes place, until the swelling has gone down. A group of exercises have been devised to put the joints through their full range of movement and strength all related muscles.

Toe Exercise (A)

In the same position, feet apart and parallel, knees apart and bent, bring the feet upwards and hold. Grip the balls of the feet with the toes and go on gripping to a count of twelve.

Toe Exercise (B)

Stand upright, feet parallel and a few inches apart, raise straight toes off the ground as far as possible. Hold, then curl them under, balancing on the heel. You may hold on to back of a chair if necessary. Hold fora slow count of six.

Toe Exercise (C)

Rest the forefoot so that the base of the toes is resting against something hard, then the toes from the ball of the foot, keeping the toe joints straight. Splay the toes and draw them upward, still keeping the toe joints bet. Do this twelve times.

Ankle Exercise (A)

In the same position, bend the feet backwards so that the toes point upward, then down so that they point downwards. Repeat six times.

Ankle Exercise (B)

Sitting on a couch with the knees straight, feet out

in front, circle the feet from the ankle, first clockwise, then anti-clockwise: six times each foot.

Ankle Exercise (C)

In the same position, turn the toes out and pull them up towards the outer sides of the ankles, feeling the pull as your stretch the inside of the ankles and contract the outside. Doe this twelve times, then reverse by turning the toes in and pulling the insides of the feet up towards the insides of the ankles: twelve times again.

Ankle Exercise (D)

In the same position, turn the soles inward to fact each other, then outward, keeping the knees together. Do this times.

Home Treatment for the Arms and Elbow

As is the case for all injuries, the muscles of the arm which has been involved tend to waste and must be returned to normal before the sport is resumed. The whole arm must be treated as an entity.

In tennis or golf the elbow joint and its surrounding muscle are prone to recurrent strain, secondary to a sprain or progressive strain of the lifting muscles of the forearm. If this is not corrected the shoulder and neck muscles may become involved.

Anyone who has once had any symptoms of a 'tennis elbow' should continue home treatment as long he continues the game itself and even after, since, in an older person, the chronic 'tennis elbow' may become osteo-arthritic.

The original cause may have been a continuous and prolonged incorrect use of the forearm muscles and this should be corrected before returning to play. For instance, in a backhand tennis, shot the activator muscles should be aided by the synergist at wrist, elbow and shoulder, but firmly controlled by the flexors at the shoulder girdle and neck, and the whole arm, from shoulder to fingers, moved as a controlled entity.

It there has been a fracture or a dislocation of the elbow or shoulder very gentle exercise should be performed. Too-vigorous exercises or physiotherapy may cause calcification to occur in the ligaments and near the joints.

There should be no lifting or carrying of heavy articles and deep massages around the elbow should never be given within the first four months after the injury.

The following four exercises are designed to put the elbow joint through its full range of movement and at the same time strengthen the associated muscles.

Exercise (A)

This exercise is beneficial to the wrist and shoulder joints but particularly to the elbow. Sitting upright, let the arms hang at the side. Make a fist and rotate the fist and the entire arm outwards as far as possible and then right round inwards as possible. Rotate right out and down and then right in and down six times.

Exercise (B)

With wrists facing forward and at shoulder height, drop the fists, still clenching the bandage. Squeeze the bandage on straightening, relax on bending six times.

Exercise (C)

Holding a small plastic sponge or an unrolled

Elastoplast bandage, and with the arms at the sides, squeeze the bandage as you raise the arms to touch the shoulders. Return to starting position.

Do this six times, squeezing the bandage on bending, relaxing when straightening, fists facing forward.

Exercise (D)

Reverse the wrists so that fists face backward and repeat the exercise. Do this six times.

Exercise (E)

With wrists facing backward repeat Exercise 3 six times.

Exercise (F)

Do an imaginary tennis backward shot, holding the upper arm with the other hand so that the movement is restricted to the elbow. Do this six times.

Home Treatment and Exercise for Shoulder Girdle and Collarbone

Dislocations and subluxations are among the commonest injuries in many sports and in athletes. A broken clavicle— Collarbone—can often happen to steeplechase jockeys, show jumpers, three-day events, or in any sport in which the athlete falls on the shoulder or outstretched hand.

It can also happen if a gun kicks back while game shooting. There is sometimes a subluxation of the outer or inner end of the collarbone.

On returning to active sport the injured shoulder should be well protected as otherwise the injury might be reactivated. It should be well strapped or a shoulder harness worn if allowed, or the joint protected or supported with a felt pad or strapping.

Steeplechase jockeys often choose to ride at an early stage in recovery wearing clavicle rings, even running the risk of damaging their injured shoulder further rather than give up riding in an important race.

Anyone who has dislocated shoulder, or has had a clavicle injury, should continue his home treatment and exercises until he feels completely recovered. In addition, Active Alerted Posture should always be practised because the position in which the shoulder is held in this posture is important in preventing the weight of gravity causing degenerative changes in the shoulder and cervical spinal joints.

The shoulders should always be lifted and relaxed, held slightly forward, so that the arms are not a dead weight on the shoulder girdle.

The following exercises should be done with both arms, even if only one has been injured.

Exercise (A)

Bring the right had to the shoulder. Cut the right elbow with the left hand and gently press upwards to a count of six. Repeat on the other side even if only one shoulder is painful.

Exercise (B)

With the tops of the arms close to the body, swing the arms from elbow forward, down, sideways, down, backwards, down; repeat six times.

Exercise (C)

Bending forward from the waist with the arm hanging down in front, fists facing frontwards, make six forward circles, then reverse the wrists with the fists facing backward; make six backward circles.

17

STRENGTH TRAINING

Strength Training

Principle of Overload

The principle of overload indicates that physiological systems improve in function when challenged to work at supra-normal levels. Muscle hypertrophies only when forced to operate beyond customary intensities. The stimulus threshold represents the work intensity below which no effect accrues. The ability to train muscle is greatest when strength training begins though some muscles may be in poorer condition than others and respond more readily. The load must be progressively increased to elicit further adaptive reactions as training develops and the training stimulus gradually raised. Gains become increasingly difficult to obtain as the muscle approaches its theoretical potential. Overload is accomplished by emphasising the duration or intensity of exercise. Many repetitions of low intensity work improve muscular endurance while few repetitions at high intensity develop strength. High intensity work at speed promotes muscular power as well as strength.

Many sportsmen wish to develop strength without accompanying hypertrophy. Boxers, wrestlers and oarsmen want to avoid excessive increases in muscle bulk which necessitate moving to a higher competitive weight category. Belated attempts to shed weight by dehydration are counter-productive since strength abates with fluid loss. Hurdlers and jumpers whose extra muscle constitutes an additional load to be lifted against gravity similarly seek to avoid undue weight gains. Alternatively throwers and rugby forwards can utilise beneficially the extra mass acquired. Though the demarcation line for non-hypertrophy is unclear, speed of contraction appears important in reducing the extent of hypertrophy.

Experience suggests that repeated sets of four to six repetitions at maximal intensity invokes hypertrophy while fewer sets of six to ten repetitions short of maximal effort promotes strength without concomitant muscle growth. Maximum can be conveniently determined by De Lorme's repetition maximum criterion which indicates the maximum load that can be lifted a given number of repetitions and varies with the number attempted. Mac Queen reported that when body builders employed less than RM intensity for considerably more than 10 repetitions and more than four or five sets hypertrophy did not result. Hypertrophy is regulated largely by testosterone which explains why pronounced muscle growth is not found when female athletes undertake severe strength training regimes.

Hypertrophy is observed when training is supplemented by synthetic sex hormones or anabolic steroids. Bouts of progressive exercise overload should be interspersed by regular rest periods to allow recovery. The common practice of weight training three or four times a week seems reasonable to avoid overuse but a minimum of twice-weekly strength sessions is recommended to provide adequate training stimulus.

Ryan acknowledged insufficient rest as a factor contributing to injury and intermittent illness. De Lorme and Watkins found that five days per week was usually the heaviest schedule that could be employed without developing serious signs of delayed recovery. Clarke concluded that training at 6 RM for three sets, three times a week seemed an optimal combination. Progression involves an evolving upward spiral of overload-fatigue-recovery, with recovery improving as the individual gets fitter. Frequency and intensity may be reduced during the peak of the competitive season when the objective is to maintain the strength level already acquired and concentrate on speed and skill.

Evaluation and Measurement

Regular strength testing provides an objective basis for rescheduling regimes to apply progressive resistance. It serves also to evaluate the conditioning programme and give valuable feedback on the athlete's progress. It helps to identify weaknesses and devise individual schedules. Performance tests provide convenient criteria for strength measurement. Selected weight lifts can be used for 1RM, 6RM or 10RM. Tests involving moving a heavy load to exhaustion are also employed since muscular strength and absolute endurance are highly correlated. Strength measurement has typically employed instruments capable of recording the maximum force of an isometric contraction. These include cable tensiometers, dynamometers, spring balances and electrical strain gauges and administration is hardly feasible outside a sports science laboratory.

Peak force during dynamic movements may be recorded using isokinetic machinery. Static and dynamic measurement of rotational movements can be achieved by a dynamometer based on a rotary torque activator. The vertical and standing broad jumps conveniently indicate explosive strength and leg power. The softball throw or shot putt for distance have been used as indicants of muscle power in arm work. As power is a function of the rate of the rate of force application, strength is a major component. A power lever, based on wheel and axle lever system, permits direct measurement of the horsepower in a single explosive movement.

The stair run test of Margaria et al was designed to indicate the horsepower output of the phosphagens or maximum alactic anaerobic power. A comparable test for the bicycle ergometer has also been designed. Though these tests may be used for monitoring conditioning progress, the ultimate test of the validity of the training is the competitive performance.

The Principle of Reversibility

Reversibility indicates that a training effect subsides if training is discontinued. Strength gains are lost at about one-third their rate of acquisition. Athletes who abruptly terminate a crash course of pre-season strength training are likely to lose form in mid-season due to the relatively rapid strength loss. Isotonic training leads to greater retention than isometric. Strength loss after daily isometric training equalled the rate at which it was acquired in Muller's investigation. Hettinger and Morehouse claimed that strength gained can be retained with one high intensity session every two weeks.

At least a weekly work-out seems preferable for retention in top athletes through the competitive period through fortnightly sessions probably serve to retard strength loss. Strength gained is not entirely lost, a portion of it remaining indefinitely. Retraining, when commenced, is also considerably easier than initially. Special care is needed during the early weeks of retaining to avoid muscle pulls as athletes are often reluctant to accept their diminished function through inactivity.

Law of use and disuse

The organism habituates to the load placed on it indicating that structure is modified by function. Connective tissue and bone adapt as well as skeletal muscle. The muscle fibre and its surrounding sarcolemma thicken and the connective tissue of the muscle broadens and toughens. Primary cellular multiplication occurs in ligaments and tendons which grow and increase in tensile strength. Bones adapt to suit stresses and strains within their tolerance by forming new supportive trabeculae. Calcium phosphate and calcium carbonate in bone increase in response to training providing greater sturdiness. Severe repetitive strain may result in inflammation and osteoporosis as occurs in stress fractures. With prolonged rest, bones demineralise and weaken and muscles atrophy. The trainer's quandary is the recognition of the thin line separating harmful overload form the maximal stimulant for physiological accommodation. The triple principles of overload, reversibility and specificity contain a framework for regulating training regimes to permit continuous adaptation.

The Principle of Specificity

Specificity suggests that strength training effects may be limited to the pattern of muscular involvement in the conditioning exercise. Different types of motor units exist within muscle so that a give type of exercise units exist within muscle so that a given type of exercise recruits a specific combination of motor units best adapted to that demand. It is desirable that strength training routines should simulate closely the motor programme of the event and employ the specific muscle groups involved. This invites preliminary analysis of competitive skills. Specificity is also shown is isometric exercise in the strength gains may be restricted to the angle at which training occurred, so that isometrics should be undertaken at a series of joint angles.

Where great strength in needed only at the beginning of the movement, as in ballistic actions, exercises in that range may suffice. Specificity is further corroborated in that isometric programmes increase isometric strength more than they do isotonic strength, the reverse being also true. A strength training schedule should evidently be planned to suit individual needs. This must vary with the sport and be adjusted for age and sex. The curves showing average strength values in relation to age and sex can be altered by training which not only arrests the normal gradual decline after mid-20s but brings further improvement for another 10 to 15 years.

Though the difference between the sexes varies with muscle groups, it is common after adolescence to expect two-thirds of male strength in females. The difference is largely attributable to men's greater muscle mass though on average their bones, tendons and ligaments are also more robustly constructed. Female athletes are often unwilling to undertake strength regimes for social reasons and in consequence suffer more injuries in sports requiring explosive efforts.

Strength

Strength reflects the ability to apply force and overcome resistance. It is a function of the neuromusculo-skeletal system and closely related to muscle cross-sectional area. Its development is indispensable for success in sports performed against high power demands as shown by the muscular physique in top throwers, jumpers, sprinters and gymnasts. Muscularity and strength also favour performance in contact sports where the rigours of competition are more easily endured without injury. Manifestation of strength is found under various conditions.

Explosive strength

Explosive strength as defined by Fleishman denotes the ability to expend energy in one explosive act, as in jumping or projecting some object as far as possible. The force generated may be sub-maximal since force and velocity are interrelated. Muscle shortening velocity is greatest when externally unloaded while force is maximal at zero velocity or isometric conditions. In rapid contractions there is limited time for liberation of chemical energy and interconnections of myofibrilar filaments. Forces developed in eccentric contractions are greater at all velocities than those of concentric work.

Power output and mechanical efficiency are improved if muscle is pre-stretched allowing storage of elastic energy for immediate utilisation in concentric action. This is achieved in appropriate leg musculature by sinking the hips prior to jumping and in arm muscles by winding up before bowling. As explosive strength is applied rapidly under dynamic conditions it is imperative that technique is perfected to avoid injury. Absolute strength provides inadequate compensation for poor coordination when muscle or articulo-skeletal damage is promoted. In team games explosive strength must be allied to good timing. The rugby forward must strive to out jump his line-out opponent, win ball possession and avoid collisions at the same time.

Isometric Strength

Maximum isometric strength is defined operationally as the force of reaction achieved when the greatest possible effort is intentionally brought to bear in a static muscle contraction from two to six seconds duration. The muscle length stays constant and no movement occurs. Isometric strength is important when allied to the requisite sport skills where performance is periodically under static conditions or movement initiated by overcoming large resistance. This applies in rugby scrimmaging, tug-of-war, weightlifting and wrestling, for example. The hammer thrower needs to counter great centrifugal forces as he rotates and the soccer player balances statically on leg while place-kicking

Dynamic Strength

The strength of the limb muscles applied to moving or supporting body mass repeatedly over a given period of time was known as dynamic strength by Fleishman. It reflects the strength endurance of the organism or its ability to withstand fatigue under sustained strength expenditure exemplified in performing press-ups. Dynamic strength is especially important in maximal efforts of half-minute to three minutes duration. It is distinct from muscle endurance which indicates the ability of a muscle group to contract continually against a light load and which depends on the circulation. When muscle repeatedly contracts in a vigorous fashion fatigue is shown by its inability to continue delivering the same mechanical work. Maximal power output declines more rapidly due to a shift in the substrate subserving contraction.

Highest power is produced in the first few seconds of activity, values up to six horse power being found. Fuel here is furnished by intramuscular phosphagens. When all-out effort is extended beyond these first seconds energy is supplied from glycogen within muscle anaerobically. This store increases the work capacity at a reduced power production. Eventually maximal effort is limited within a minute or so of onset by accumulation of metabolities and lowered pH within muscle, or lack of metabolic substrate due to retarded adenosine triphosphate synthesis. Under such fatigued conditions skill may become disjoined, judgement impaired and injury promoted.

Even in sustained activities where the organism operates with almost limitless though subdued power supply through oxidative phosphorylation, added strength facilitates both performance and individual safety since the relative strain on working muscles imposed by a fixed work load is now reduced. The poor strength and muscularity of endurance competitors leaves them vulnerable when responding to spurts from opponents or encountering steep uphill gradients.

Strength and muscle size

In general the larger the muscle the greater its strength, though the relationship has qualifications. Differences between muscles in strength capability arise from their pennation or manner of tendonous attachment. Muscles with parallel fibres, e.g. sartorius, have poor force production but great mobility compared to muscles whose fibres converge obliquely on the tendon. Surface area of contact is increased where muscle fibres approach the tendon from one side, e.g. soleus, both sides, e.g. rectus femoris, or multi-pennately, e.g. deltoid, rather than the end. Distributions of fibre types similarly account for variability between muscles and between individuals.

Thigh and calf muscles of top sprinters are endowed with high proportions of white or fast-twitch fibres compared with the abundance of red or slow-twitch fibres in endurance athletes. Responses of muscles and individuals to work-induced hypertrophy may very because of differences in fibre-type distributions. Finally, endurance training may reduce muscle size by decreasing intramuscular lipids or temporarily increase muscle diameter by combining exhaustive training and diet to boost muscular glycogen stores as done by marathon runners the week before racing.

Strength Training Methods

Mechanical and Physical Resistances

Weight training presents a convenient method of overloading muscle and is commonly employed in conditioning for competition. Loads are provided by dumb-bells or weights barbells and are easily adjustable for progressive resistance. Eccentric work can be incorporated by weight lowering in addition to the more usual lifting exercises so elastic as well as contractile elements in muscle are trained. Spring loaded devices allow eccentric arm work though they do not have inherent progressive resistance. Pulley systems permit alteration of the direction of force application and re frequently employed in land conditioning of swimmers. Hydraulics have been effectively incorporated in the design of rowing machines.

Isokinetic equipment allows constant speed of contraction and maximal force exertion throughout the complete range of movement. Multi-station apparatus affords an opportunity of training various muscle groups and engaging a squad of players on a single machine. Strength training can employ partner work if equipment is unavailable. Routines may involve pushing against an opponent's shoulder who reciprocates or performing half-squats with partner supported supine on the back. A whole team can be occupied in relay races, each member carrying a colleague on his back during his effort, adding variety to training. Resistance work using a partner is useful in sports where a partner or opponent is actually supported during performance as in ice-skating or wrestling.

Where facilities are improvised, a bench, box or chair is still easily obtained for step-ups. This can be useful where different strength requirements are juxtaposed. The long jumper, for instance, who needs great leg strength for take off and isometric back strength to stabilise his upper body in flight, can train both simultaneously by holding a medicine ball while stepping-up. Bench stepping has long been used for fitness testing as well as training as it permits calculation of mechanical work done. Other ergometric modes present suitable strength training methods under precisely controlled conditions. Cyclists might use friction braked bicycles which are also valuable in rehabilitation since bodyweight is not supported. Whole body and rowing ergometers are useful in conditioning oarsmen while motor driven treadmills can be modified for skiers. Flumes could be used for preparation of swimmers, canoeists and rowers under exact control. These facilities are expensive and could reasonably be made available only to the elite at centres of sporting excellence.

Isometrics

Isometrics implicate muscular tension without corresponding limb movement. Body segments or external objects may provide the resistance. Special isometric racks have been designed for use in diverse fashions in gymnasia. The scrummaging rack used by rugby forwards in training outdoors affords another example. Isometric programmes gained widespread appeal from the pioneer studies of Muller. The magnitude of the training effects reported initially were not replicated in later studies of fitter subjects. For these the work load had to be substantially elevated beyond the advocated daily contraction held for six seconds at 66 per cent of maximal isometric capacity to get similar results. Consequently the claims attributed earlier to isometrics were considerably qualified. Furthermore improvement may be restricted to the angle at which the contraction is held and this may not appreciably assist dynamic performance.

Thirdly, the concomitant compression of the vascular bed with occlusion of blood supply to the muscles under tension and the rise in blood pressure this precipitates make isometrics unsuitable for sedentary individuals undergoing exercise for prevention of coronary heart disease, particularly if they already possess predisposing factors. Isometric training is recommended where competition places specific demands for isometric strength It may be especially valuable to athletes desiring increased muscle strength without corresponding hypertrophy since isometrics do not provoke muscle growth. For the majority, isometrics can be judiciously incorporated into a broader conditioning programme.

Functional Overload

Strength can be improved by overloading the individual in practices closely related to competition requirements. Running in heavy boots, jumping with ankle weights or jackets weighted with lead are examples. The obvious advantage of this approach is the high likelihood of strength transfer to the event trained for. Functional overload can be applied to runners either by attachment of a harness held by a trainer at its ends, or drawing as led. The vigorous running action needed should not be greatly modified from normal for optimal effects. Wrist weights used by gymnasts are another example while weight throwers use excessively heavy implements or attempt explosive release of medicine balls. Various forms of rebounding and plyometric drills fall within this category.

These emphasise elasticproperties of muscle in their execution and tend to develop explosive strength. Drills include repetitive hopping on both legs together or separately, jumping decathlons or exaggerated bounding strides. In hopping, the hips should not sink below the level where the femur is parallel to the floor to safeguard the knee joint. Elevation onto or over a bench or box top on descent from a greater height. The quadriceps are stretched in lowering bodyweight prior to contracting powerfully and by storing elastic energy in the process increase the tension developed in positive work. Since the shock on landing is absorbed largely by the knee joints the complete drill must be smoothly controlled to avoid injury.

Strength training is considered an indispensable part of preparation for athletic competition and injury prevention. The programme should be geared to the individual's specific needs and be based on progressive resistance. General and specific conditioning should be developed and uneven strength gains avoided. Retraining during rehabilitation is important before returning to competition.

Natural Resistance

Muscles may be overloaded in working against supernormal resistance by carefully exploiting natural conditions. Running up sand dunes was vindicated in the performances of Australian middle-distance runners in the early 1960s. Flat soled shoes are recommended as barefoot athletes may tread on broken glass concealed in the sand. Weekly sessions are sufficient in incorporating sandhill training into the overall schedule in the early phase to avoid Achilles tendon trouble. Running along a flat beach or soft sand is another form of resistance training. In inland areas grassy hills provide a satisfactory alternative to sand dunes. Running on soft ground is also recommended provided conditions are not so slippery that hamstring tears are possible.

All these methods are eminently suitable for training dynamic strength. Other variations depending on climate and location include running on snow or ankle deep in water, as long as the normal running motion is not severely altered. Work in water may be especially useful for rehabilitation of leg muscles as the strain from lifting bodyweight against gravity is absent. Cyclists may take advantage of otherwise inclement windy conditions by repetitive short sprints against the wind. Man built environments may similarly be exploited. If conditions are too difficult for outdoor work, suitable indoor staircases can substitute for uphill gradients. Stadium terrace steps are frequently used by football coaches in the training of players.

Strength for Injury Prevention

Muscles act as agonists, antagonists and synergists to cause, permit and assist movement. Unwanted actions are prevented by muscles acting as stabilisers. The orderliness of patterned muscular involvement is regulated by the nervous system. Greater strength in stabilising musculature improves individual tolerance to those external exigencies promoting imbalance in various sports. The gymnast needs great leg strength to control landing from a vault as well as for the more explosive operations. In field-invasive games, greater leg strength assists the manifold manoeuvres such as turning, accelerating, decelerating, tackling and avoiding tackles without injury. In contact games great arborisation is needed and players with poor strength have greater difficulty in surviving prolonged competitive periods without being injured. Cahill and Griffith showed that pre-season total body conditioning significantly reduces the frequency and severity of knee injuries in American university footballers. Imperfect strength development in particular muscle groups may predispose to local injury.

This is because muscles may secure the integrity of joints by crossing the joint or having their tendons inserted around the capsule. Knee stability, for example, is considerably enhanced by strengthening the quadriceps which safeguard the joint in conjunction with the cruciate and collateral ligaments. Quadriceps exercises are especially recommended in rehabilitation of knee injuries as the joint is further unstable if their strength subsides. Return to contact games should be delayed until adequate knee strength is restored. Quadriceps development can allow professional athletes to make ligament or meniscus damage and osteoarthrosis. Similarly, shoulder stability is enhanced by training surrounding musculature and many back problems are avoided by developing the erector spinae. Improving the strength of abdominal and back muscles not only helps prevent lumbar pain but serves also to remedy low back pain conditions. Bodnar reported a relationship between the incidence of shoulder and neck injuries and weakness of the cervical muscles in American college footballers and recommended strengthening cervical and trunk muscles as protective measures. Uneven distribution of strength is likely to predispose to injury.

This may be manifested in disproportionate development in one of the agonist/antagonist pair. The hamstrings, antagonists to the quadriceps during the first 160 to 165° of leg extension, must equally be considered when devising training programmes for quadriceps. A greater susceptibility to hamstring strains is found when individuals have an inappropriate flexor-extensor strength ratio. The hamstring/quadriceps strength ratio recommended by Klein and Allman is 0.60. Uneven distribution is also evident in contralateral differences in strength acquisition. This inequality is seen in the girth of the serving arm in top tennis players compared with the non-playing limb and is a logical outcome of repetitive practice in throwing events and racket sports which impose unilateral demands. Imbalance can have serious consequences in the lower extremities as it is then likely to prompt asymmetrical locomotion. Liemohn found that all hamstring injuries in a group of track and field athletes were to the non-moniment leg, substantiating that the weaker side is the more susceptible.

Though specific unilateral demands are imposed in certain athletic performances, preparation should still involve bilateral strength training to avoid uneven gains. Some contra-lateral effects do occur in the non-exercised limb but are of insufficient magnitude to excuse not training both. Cross-training effects can however be exploited to reduce muscle atrophy and for reconditioning after immobilisation. Isotonic exercise has been found preferable to isometric for producing cross-training though both methods have shown equal effectiveness when equated for load and duration. Action potentials occur in contralateral musculature, demonstrating the irradiation of nerve impulses to extremities other than those directly engaged in activity. Seemingly, innervation of descending pyramidal fibres that cross sides before supplying muscles overflows to the smaller number of uncrossed fibres, so that movement occurs in an activated muscle and isometric contractions in its symmetrical partner.

Sufficient overflow occurs only under strong volition so high intensity is desirable for cross-education. The effect is supported by historilogical findings and underlines nervous system involvement in force application. Neural control of maximal voluntary effort results in a strength reserve not normally expressed. This reservoir may amount to 25 per cent and is released in exceptional circumstances and emergencies. It serves normally to protect the muscle, its tendon and bony attachment from over-exertion. This inhibition is eliminated under extreme motivational conditions. The effect is attributed to adrenaline release and reduced nervous inhibition which permit greater motor unit recruitment. This safety reserve is harnessed under strong motivation by athletes prior to strength events. It may also be tapped in training muscle by electrical stimulation though attendant risks make it inadvisable. Electrotherapy is valuable in rehabilitation to stimulate muscle which has temporarily lost its effective innervation since the motor pathways are minimally involved in electrical training.

Strength training reduces the effect of the inhibitory mechanism and permits greater tension to occur. This may be due to greater antagonist relaxation as the movement proceeds or to increased shielding of Golgi sensory organs by muscle connective tissue thickened from training, allowing innervation of the muscles to progress further uninhibited. A basic programme of general muscle conditioning is advocated to avoid leaving local weaknesses in the athlete' make-up.

A broad basis of general strength sets a foundation on which specific strength can be safely developed. Improved arm and back strength allows the legs to be overloaded in power cleans and half-squats when leg strength in being specifically developed. An outstanding single benefit to a strengthened muscle is that greater stresses can be borne without training. Developed muscle also provides a fleshy shield to cushion the effect of blows on bone or abdominal organs, thereby affording some protection in combat sports.

The common definition of strength is the ability to exert a force against a resistance. The strength needed for a sprinter to explode from the blocks is different to the strength needed by a weight lifter to lift a 200kg barbell. This therefore implies that there are different types of strength.

What are the classifications of strength?

The classifications of strength are:

1. Elastic strength – the ability to overcome a resistance with a fast contraction

2. Maximum strength – the greatest force that is possible in a single maximum contraction

3. Strength endurance – the ability to express force many times over.

How do we develop each strength?

1. Elastic strength can be developed with:
- medicine ball exercises
- conditioning exercises
- complex training sessions
- weight training
- plyometric exercises

2. Strength endurance can be developed with:
- dumbbell exercises
- hill and harness running
- circuit training
- weight training

3. Maximum strength can be developed with:
- weight training

How do we get strong?

A muscle will only strengthen when it is worked beyond its normal operation, it is overloaded. Overload can be progressed by increasing the:

1. number of sets of the exercise

2. intensity reduced recover time
3. number of repetitions of an exercise

Medicine Ball

The ability to generate strength and power is a very important component for success in many sports, particularly in those involving explosive movements. Medicine ball training, in conjunction with a programme of weight training and circuit training, can be used to develop strength and power. Certain medicine ball exercises can also be used as part of a plyometric training programme to develop explosive movements. Medicine ball training is appropriate to all levels of ability, age, development and sport. To be most effective the programme should contain exercises that match the pattern of movements of the sport.

Technique and Safety

To ensure personal safety and good technique while doing medicine ball exercises the following points should be remembered:

1. On standing exercises plant feet before beginning to throw the ball
2. Maintain technique do not sacrifice control for distance
3. Inexperienced athletes should not take the ball too far back behind the head when carrying out overhead throws
4. Complete throws with full extension of the arms
5. When picking a ball, ensure the knees are bent and the back is kept straight
6. Always use the full joint range in the correct sequence in carrying out each exercise
7. When carrying out exercises lying on your back,

ensure the lower back always remains in contact with the surface

8. Prior to a catch, ensure you:

- keep hands together
- keep arms extended
- keep eyes on the ball
- do not attempt to catch balls thrown wildly
- reach out to meet the ball prior to making contact

Planning a programme

The following are some guidelines in planning and running a medicine ball session:-

1. Before starting a session, explain the procedures for each exercise with your athletes
2. Medicine ball exercises must precede high intensity work
3. The programme should have exercises that match the pattern of movements of the sport
4. You will need to have a number of different weights of ball available-heavy, medium and light
5. Check there is sufficient space and that the structure of the walls are safe if any rebounding exercises are used
6. An effective work-out with medicine balls can be achieved in about 30 to 40 minutes, if the athlete works efficiently
7. Initial, athletes should use a light weight ball and gradually progress to heavier ones
8. Quality of movement is more beneficial than quantity of exercise repetitions or sets
9. Maintain good discipline as medicine balls can be dangerous if used incorrectly
10. Plan the programme to exercise alternate body parts

11. Always ensure the athletes carry out a thorough warm up and warm down

12. Partners who feed the medicine ball on certain exercises should be well drilled on what is required

13. Start sessions with lighter less dynamic exercises, then progress to heavier exercises

Example the following is an example of a programme of general medicine ball exercises.

Standing torso twist

1. Stand back to back 1 metre apart
2. Keep your hips facing forward and legs slightly relaxed
3. Keep your hips facing forward and legs slightly relaxed

How many – Two sets of ten reps

Chest push

1. Step forward and push ball upwards and towards your partner
2. Feet together
3. Hands behind ball and elbows out

Hamstring curls

1. Roll the ball along the back of legs
2. On reaching the heels the ball is filched up
3. Lie flat on the ground

Double leg kicks

1. Soles of feet facing partner
2. Partner throws ball in a looping path onto your feet
3. Lie on your back
4. Partner stands 3 metres away
5. Do not lower you legs to the ground
6. Bending your knees back to your chest the ball is

then kicked back to your partner

Vertical extensions

1. Ball is returned between the knees
2. Stand back to back approx. 60cm apart
3. Ball is passed overhead

Straight arm standing throw

1. Place one foot 50 cm behind the other
2. Step forward and throw the ball to your partner, keeping the arms straight
3. Take the ball back, ensure hands are high, shoulders stretched and chest out

Lay back double arm throw

1. Throw another medicine ball to your partner
2. Partner returns ball to an overhead position
3. Support your back with a large medicine ball

Abdominal curl

1. knees bent
2. Draw knees up to the chest
3. Sitting up slightly, resting on your hands
4. Return to the starting position
5. Ball is held by the knees

Conditioning

One of the misconceptions in the sports world is that a sportsperson gets in shape by just playing or taking part in his/her chosen sport. If a stationary level of performance, consistent ability in executing a few limited skills, is your goal then engaging only in your sport will keep you there. However, if you want the utmost efficiency, consistent improvement, and balanced abilities sportsmen and women must participate in your round conditioning programs. The bottom line in sports conditioning and fitness training is stress. Not mental stress, but adaptive body stress. Sportsmen and women must put their bodies under a certain amount of stress to increase physical capabilities.

Physical Fitness

Physical fitness refers to the capacity of an athlete to meet the varied physical demands of their sport without reducing the athlete to a fatigued state. The components of physical fitness are: Strength, Endurance, Speed, Flexibility and Body Composition.

Complex Training

The two benefits from traditional strength work are:

1. increased muscle mass
2. increased neural activity

Strength work has been shown to improve sports performance particularly for sprinters, jumpers and throwers but it is not beneficial in developing rate of force the speed with which force is achieved in a movement. For example it takes around 400 msec to develop maximum force during a squat exercise, but the foot-ground contact time in sprinting is around 90 msec so there is not enough time to produce maximum force in sprinting. Therefore for speed strength events, like sprinting, it is the rate of force development that becomes more important than absolute strength. To develop the rate of force the Type IIb muscle fibres need to be targeted as these are ones that produce force most explosively allowing for maximum power. The sort of exercises that develop the Type IIb fibres are:

1. Plyometric exercises e.g. bounding.

2. Speed strength exercises e.g. weighted squats jumps

Many athletes include plyometric exercises in their training programs and are were aware of their benefits. However, it is slightly less well known that the combination of traditional strength with power and plyometric exercises together results in greater Type IIb recruitment and consequently greater improvements in power and rate of force development.

Definition of Fitness

Exercise scientists have identified nine elements that comprise the definition of fitness. The following lists each of the nine elements and an example of how they are used:–

1. Power — the ability to exert maximum muscular contraction instantly in an explosive burst of movements

2. Strength — the extent to which muscles can exert force by contracting against resistance

3. Agility — the ability to perform a series of explosive power movements in rapid succession in opposing directions

4. Flexibility — the ability to achieve an extended range of motion without being impeded by excess tissue, i.e. fat or muscle

5. Cardiovascular Endurance — The heart's ability to deliver blood to working muscles and their ability to use it

6. Coordination — the ability to integrate the above listed components so that effective movements are achieved.

7. Balance — the ability to control the body's position, either stationary or while moving

8. Local Muscle Endurance —a single muscle's ability to perform sustained work

Of all the nine elements of fitness cardiac respiratory qualities are the most important to develop as they enhance all the other components of the conditioning equation.

Quality not Quantity

To get the best from these training workouts you need to be physically fresh and motivated. Type IIb fibres are not magically recruited by just doing the workout, you have to be focused on the exercises and perform them as explosively as possible. Try to avoid hard aerobic or anaerobic sessions for at least 48 hours before a complex session. Once a complex session has started do not perform any static stretching exercises as this will relax the muscles and reduce force production potential. It is the quality of execution o f each exercise that is important, not the quantity. To ensure quality is maintained have the correct rest periods.

What is complex training?

Complex training is a workout comprising of a resistance exercise followed by a matched plyometric exercise e.g:

1. bench press followed by plyometric press up

2. squats followed by squat jumps

The logic behind these matched pair of exercises is that the resistance work gets the nervous system in to full action so that more Type IIb fibres are available for the explosive exercise, hence a better training benefit.

Plyometrics

Speed and strength are integral components of fitness found in varying degrees in virtually all athletic movements. Simply put the combination of speed and strength is power. For many years coaches and athletes have ought to improve power in order to enhance performance. Throughout this century and no doubt long before, jumping, bounding and hopping exercises have been used in various ways to enhance athletic performance. In recent years this distinct method of training for power or explosiveness has been termed plyometrics. Whatever the origins of the word the term is used to describe the method of training which seeks to enhance to explosive reaction of the individual through powerful muscular contractions as a result of rapid eccentric contractions.

Choose the method to fit the sport

The golden rule of any conditioning programme is specificity. This mans that the movement you perform in training should match, as closely as possible, the movements encountered during competition. If you are rugby player practising for the line-out or a volleyball player interested in increasing vertical jump height, then hop jumping or box jumping may be the right exercise. However if you are a javelin thrower aiming for a more explosive launch, then upper body plyometrics is far more appropriate.

Muscle Mechanism

The maximum force that a muscle can develop is attained during a rapid eccentric contraction. However, it should be realised that muscles seldom perform one type of contraction is isolation during athletic movements. When a concentric contraction occurs immediately following an eccentric contraction than the force generated can be dramatically increased. If a muscle is stretched, much of the energy required to stretch it is lost as heat, but some of this energy can be stored by the elastic components of the muscle. This stored energy is available to the muscle only during a subsequent contraction. It is important to realise that this energy boost is lost if the eccentric contraction is not followed immediately by a concentric effort. To express this greater force the muscle must contract within the shortest time possible. This whole process is frequently called the stretch shortening cycle and is the underlying mechanism of plyometric training.

Plyometric Exercises

The following are examples of lower body and upper body plyometric exercises.

Upper body

A variety of drills can be used to make the upper body more explosive:

Medicine Ball

Another means of increasing upper body strength popular with throwers is to lie on the ground face up. A partner then drops a medicine ball down towards the chest of the athlete, who catches the ball and immediately throws it back. This is another high-intensity exercise and should only be used after some basic conditioning.

Press ups and hand clap

Press-ups with a hand clap in between is a

particularly vigorous way to condition the arms and chest. The pre-stretch takes place as the hands arrive back on the ground and the chest sinks, and this is followed quickly by the explosive upwards action. Once again, to get the best training effect keep the time in contact with the ground to a minimum.

Lower Body

Bounding and hurdling

If forward motion is more the name of your game, try some bounding. This is a form of plyometric training, where over sized strides are used in the running action and extra time spent in the air. Two-legged bounds reduces the impact to be endured, but to increase the intensity one legged bounding, or hopping, can be used. Bounding upstairs is a usefulway to work on both the vertical and horizontal aspects of the running action. Multiple jumps over a series of obstacles like hurdles is a valuable drill for athletes training for sprinting or jumping events. Examples of lower body plyometric exercises with intensity level:

1. Jumps from standing –Standing long jump, Standing hop, standing jump for height

2. Multiple jumps with run in – 11 stride run +2 hops and a jump into sandpit, 2 stride run in + bounds

3. Eccentric drop and hold drills – hop and hold, bound/hop/bound/hop over 30m, drop and hold from a height > one metre

4. Standing based jumps performed on the spot – Tuck Jumps, Split Jumps

5. Depth jumping – jumps down and up off box, bounding up hill

6. Multiple jumps from standing – bounds, bunny hops, double footed jumps over how hurdle, double footed jumps up steps

Drop Jumping

This exercise involves the athlete dropping to the ground from a raised platform or box, and then immediately jumping up. The drop down gives the pre-stretch to the leg muscles and the vigorous drive upwards the secondary concentric contraction The exercise will be more effective the shorter the time the feet are in contact with the ground. The loading in this exercise is governed by the height of the drop which should be in the region of 30–80 cm. Drop jumping is a relatively high impact form of plyometric training and would normally be introduced after the athlete had become accustomed to lower impact alternatives, such as two-footed jumping on the spot.

Planning a Plyometric Session

The choice of exercises within a session and their order should be planned. A session could:

1. work through exercises that develop concentric strength
2. begin with exercises that are fast, explosive and designed for developing elastic strength
3. finish with training for eccentric strength.

An alternative session could be:

1. progress to bounding and hopping,
2. finish with medicine ball work out for abdominals and upper body.
3. begin with low hurdle jumps
4. continue with steps or box work

Example plyometric sessions for the arms and legs are detailed on the Leg Plyometric page and the Arm

Plyometric page.

Conditioning for Polymetrics

Higher than normal forces are put on the musculoskeletal system during polymetric exercises so it is important for the athlete to have a good sound base of general strength and endurance. Most experts state that a thorough grounding in weight-training is essential before you start polymetrics. It has been suggested that an athlete be able to squat twice his body weight before attempting depth jumps. However, less intensive plyometric exercises can be incorporated into general circuit and weight training during the early stages of training so as to progressively condition the athlete. Simple plyometric drills such as skipping hopping and bounding should be introduced first. More demanding exercises such as flying start single-leg hops and depth jumps should be limited to thoroughly conditioned athletes. Conditioning programmes to develop leg strength are detailed on the Lower Leg Conditioning page and the Leg Conditioning page.

Warm up

A though warm up is essential prior to plyometric training. Attention should be given to jogging, stretching, striding and general mobility especially about the joints involved in the planned plyometric session. A cool down should follow each session.

How many?

It is wise not to perform too many repetitions in any one session and since it is a quality session, with the emphasis on speed and power rather than endurance, split the work into sets with ample recovery in between.

Young athletes

Some authors suggest that moderate jumps can be included in the athletic training of very young children. However, great care needs to be exerted when prescribing any training procedures for pre-adolescent children. Because of the relatively immature bone structure in pre-adolescent and adolescent children the very great forces exerted during intensive depth jumps should be avoided.

Where to do it and what to wear

For bounding exercises use surfaces such as grass or resilient surfaces. Avoid cement floors because there is no cushioning. Choose well-cushioned shoes that are stable and can absorb some of the inevitable impact. All athletes should undergo general orthopedic screening before engaging in plyometric training. Particular attention should be given to structural or postural problems that are likely to predispose the athlete to injury.

Arm Plyometrics

This page contains a selection of plyometric exercises designed to develop the elastic strength of the arms.

How to perform the drill

1. Stand facing each other with your feet shoulder width apart and your knees slightly bent

2. Pass the ball to your partner, pushing it off your chest and ending with your arms straight

3. This drill requires a partner

4. Try to anticipate the catch and return the ball as

quickly as you can

5. Begin by holding the medicine ball with both hands at chest level, elbows pointing out

6. Keep the catch time to the shortest time possible

7. Your partner catches the ball, allows the ball to come to the chest before passing it back to you

Incline Push up depth jump

1. Face the floor as if you were going to do a push-up, with your feet on the box and your hands between the mats

2. Two mats, three to four inches high, placed shoulder width apart

3. Push off the mats with both hands and catch yourself in the starting position

4. A box high enough to elevate your feet above your shoulders when in a push-up position

5. Push off from the ground with your hands and land with one hand on each mat

How to perform the drill

1. Lie supine on the ground with your arms outstretched

2. Your partner drops the medicine ball into your hands.

3. This drill requires a partner

4. Your partner stands on the box holding the medicine ball at arm's length

5. Catch the ball with elbows bent

6. Extend the arms to propel the ball back to the partner on the box

7. Keep the catch time to the shortest time possible

8. Allow the ball to come towards your chest

How to perform the drill

1. Lean back at a 45 degree angle, keeping your abdominals tight

2. Work with a partner and sit facing each other

3. Pass the ball to your partner, pushing it of your chest and ending with your arms straight

4. Try to anticipate the catch and return the ball as quickly as you can

5. Being by holding the medicine ball with both hands at chest level, elbows pointing out

6. Your partner catches the ball, allows the ball to come to the chest before passing it back to you

7. Keep the catch time to the shortest time possible

Young athletes

Some authors suggest that moderate jumps can be included in the athletic training of very young children. However, great care needs to be exerted when prescribing any training programmes for pre-adolescent children. Because of the relatively immature bone structure in pre-adolescent and adolescent children the very great forces exerted during intensive depth jumps should be avoided.

Where to do it and what to wear

For bounding exercises use surfaces such as grass

or resilient surfaces. Avoid cement floors because there is no cushioning. Choose well-cushioned shoes that are stable and can absorb some of the inevitable impact. All athletes should undergo general orthopaedic screening before engaging in plyometric training. Particular attention should be given to structural or postural problems that are likely to predispose the athlete to injury.

Bounds

1. Push off with your left foot and bring the leg forward, with the knee bent and the thigh parallel to the ground

2. Hold this extended stride for a brief time, then land on your left foot

3. Make each stride long, and try to cover as much distance as possible

4. Jog into the start of the exercise

5. At the same time, reach forward with your right arm. As the left leg comes through, the right leg extends back and remains extended for the duration of the push-off

6. The right leg then drives through to a forward bent position, the left arm reaches forward, and the left leg extends backward

7. You should land on the sole of the foot, allowing energy to be stored by the elastic components of the leg muscles, and immediately take off again.

Hurdle Hopping

How to perform the drill

1. The movement should come from your hips and

knees

2. Tuck both knees to your chest

3. Keep your body vertical and straight, and do not let your knees move apart or to either side.

4. You should land on the balls of the feet, allowing energy to be stored by the elastic components of the leg muscles, and immediately take off again

How much

1. Allow a full recovery between each set

2. One to three sets using 6 to 8 hurdles

3. Hurdles should set up in a row, spaced according to ability

4. Quality of hurdle hopping is far more important than quantity

5. The height of the hurdles should be in the region of 12 and 36 inches high

Single Leg Hopping

How to perform the drill

1. Push off with the leg you are standing on the jump forward, landing on the same leg

2. You should land on the ball of the foot, allowing energy to be stored by the elastic components of the leg muscles, and immediately take off again

3. Try to keep your body vertical and straight

4. Beginners will use a straighter leg action where as advanced athletes should try to pull the heel toward the buttocks during the jump

5. Stand on one leg

6. Use a forceful swing of the opposite leg to increase the length of the jump but aim primarily for height off

each jump.

7. Keep the foot touch down time to the shortest time possible

8. Perform this drill on both legs

How much

1. One to three sets over 30 to 40 metres

2. Quality of bounding is far more important than quantity

3. Allow a full recovery between each set

Depth Jumps

How to perform the drill

1. Stand on the box with your toes close to the front edge

2. Try to anticipate the landing and spring up as quickly as you can

3. Step from the box and drop to land on then balls of both feet

Keep the feet touch down time on the ground to the shortest time possible

How much

1. Allow a full recovery between each set

2. The height of the box should be in the region of 30 80 cm

3. One to three sets using 6 to 8 boxes

Box Jumps

How to perform the drill

1. Keep your hands on your hips or behind your head

2. Assume a deep squat position with your feet shoulder width apart at the end of the row of boxes

3. Maintaining the squat position, jump off the box

onto the ground, landing softly in a squat position on the balls of the foot

4. Jump onto the box, landing softly in a squat position on the balls of the feet

5. Keep the feet touch down time on the ground to the shortest time possible

6. Jump onto the next box and so on

How much

1. Allow a full recovery between each set

2. One to three sets using 6 to 8 boxes

3. Quality of box jumping is far more important than quantity

4. The height of the box should be in the region of 30-80cm

Where to do it and what to wear

For bounding exercises use surfaces such as grass or resilient surfaces. Avoid cement floors because there is no cushioning. Choose well-cushioned shoes that are stable and can absorb some of the inevitable impact. All athletes should undergo general orthopaedic screening before engaging in plyometric training. Particular attention should be given to structural or postural problems that are likely to predispose the athlete to injury.

Warm up

A thorough warm-up is essential prior to plyometric training. Attention should be given to jogging, stretching, striding and general mobility especially about the joints involved in the planned plyometric session. A warm-down should follow each session.

Young athletes

Some authors suggest that moderate jumps can be included in the athletic training of very young children. However, great care needs to be exerted when prescribing any training procedures for pre-adolescent children. Because of the relatively immature bone structure in pre-adolescent and adolescent children the very great forces exerted during intensive depth jumps should be avoided.

Plyometric Exercises

Emphasis on these exercises is a high knee action and height–except for speed bounding where the emphasis is speed across the ground. The upper leg should be parallel with the ground, lower leg vertical and the foot dorsi flexed.

Weight Training

Better performances can be the product of a number of factors. This product is primarily the outcome of efficient technique, the progression of speed and the maturing competitive attitude on a sound basis of general endurance, all round strength and general mobility. The development of all round strength is best achieved via circuit training and then progressing this through strength training. Weight training is the most widely used and popular method of increasing strength.

Complex Training

Specific phase of training – example 2 sets

1. Weight Exercise - 4 reps with 8 RM
2. Plyometric exercise
3. 3 min recovery

4. Weight Exercise - 4 reps with 8 RM
5. Plyometric exercise
6. 3 min recover

Repeat for next exercise

General phase of training–example 2 sets

1. Weight exercise – 6 reps with 12 RM
2. 1 min recover
3. weight exercise – 6 reps with 12 RM
4. 1 min recover
5. Plyometric exercise
6. 3 min recover
7. Repeat for next exercise

How do we get stronger?

A muscle will only strengthen when forced to operate beyond its customary intensity. Overload can be progressed by increasing the:

1. resistance e.g. adding 10 kg to the barbell
2. number of sets of the exercise
3. number of repetitions with a particular weight

Which weight training exercises?

The exercise must be specific to the type of strength required, and is therefore related to the particular demands of the event. The coach should have knowledge of the predominant types of muscular activity associated with the particular event, the movement pattern involved and the type of strength required. Exercises should be identified that will produce the desired development. Although specificity is important, it is necessary is every schedule to include exercises of a general nature – e.g.

Power Snatch
Power Clean

Back Squats
Bench Press
Sit Ups
Chest Press
Shoulder Press
Lat Pull downs
Lower Back Extensions
Calf Raise
Tricep Press
Bicep Curls
Leg Extension
Leg Curls
Leg Press

These general exercises give a balanced development, and provide a strong base upon which highly specific exercise can be built.

Muscle Fibre Hypertrophy

Resistance training will increase the muscle size. Muscle growth depends on the muscle fibre type activated and the pattern of recruitment. Muscle growth is due to one or more of the following adaptions:

1. Increased number of and size of myofibrils per muscle fibre

2. Increased enzymes and stored nutrients

3. Increased contractile proteins

4. Increased amounts of connective, tendinous and ligamentous tissues

Olympic Lifts

The Olympic Lifts are recommend exercises for inclusion in power and speed training programs. The objective of these exercises is to develop the large muscles of the body in an explosive action which requires the use of many joints and muscle groups in a coordinated movement. The Olympic Lifts comprise of the Clean and Jerk and the Snatch. The Power Snatch and Power Clean are auxiliary lifts that aid in the training of the Clean and Jerk and the Snatch.

1. Jerk
2. Power Snatch
3. Power Clean

How Much?

The amount of weight to be used should be based on a percentage of the maximum amount of weight that can be lifted one time, generally referred to as one repetition maximum. The maximum number of repetitions performed before fatigue prohibits the completion of an additional repetition is a function of the weight used, referred to as repetition maximum, and reflects the intensity of the exercise. A weight load that produces fatigue on the third repetition is termed a three repetition maximum and corresponds to approximately 95% of the weight the could be lifted for 1 RM. For maximum results athletes should train according to their genetic predisposition.

An athlete with a greater proportion of slow twitch muscles would adapt better to an endurance training and a muscular endurance program using more repetitions of a lighter weight. An athlete with a greater proportion of fast twitch muscles would benefit from sprint training and a muscular strength program using fewer repetitions of a heavier weight.

Rest Interval between sets

The aim of the recovery period between sets is to replenish the stores of ATP and Creatine Phosphate in the muscles. An inadequate recovery means more reliance on the Lactic Acid energy pathway in the next set. Several factors influence the recovery period, including:

1. Type of strength you are developing
2. Number of muscle groups used in the exercise
3. The load used in the exercise
4. Your weight
5. Your condition

A recovery of three to five minutes or longer will allow almost the complete restoration of ATP/CP.

Load - Repetition Relationship

The strength training zone requires you to use loads in the range of 60% to 100% of 1 RM. The relationship of percentage loads to number of repetitions to failure are as follows:

60% - 17 reps
65% - 14 reps
70% - 12 reps
75% - 10 reps
80% - 8 reps
85% - 6 reps
90% - 5 reps
95% - 3 reps
100% - 1 reps

How Many

The number of repetitions performed to fatigue is an

important consideration in designing a strength training program. The greatest strength gains appear to result from working with 4 - 6 RM. Increasing this to 12-20RM favours the increase in muscle endurance and mass. One set of 4-6RM performed 3 days a week is a typical strength training program. The optimal number of sets of an exercise to develop muscle strength remains controversial. In a number of studies comparing multiple set programs to produce greater strength gains than a single set, the majority of studies indicate that there is not a significant difference. Handling heavy weights in the pursuit of strength will require a recovery of 3-5 minutes between sets, but only minimum recovery should be taken if strength endurance is the aim.

The majority of athletic events are fast and dynamic, and therefore this quality must be reflected in the athlete's strength work. Muscular strength is primarily developed when 8 RM or less is used in a set. How much load you use depends upon what it is you wish to develop:

1. 1 RM to 3RM - neuromuscular strength
2. 4RM to 6 RM -maximum strength by stimulating muscle hypertrophy
3. 6 RM to 12 RM -muscle size with moderate gains in strength
4. 12RM to 20RM-muscle size and endurance

Rest Interval between sessions

The energy source being used during the training session is probably the most important factor to consider. During the maximum strength phase, when you are primarily using the ATP/CP energy pathway, daily training is possible because ATP/CP restoration is completed within 24 hours. If you are training for muscular endurance then you require a 48 hour recovery as this is how long it takes to fully restore your glycogen stores. As a 'rule of thumb' 48 hours should elapse between sessions. If training strenuously, any athlete will find it extremely difficult to maintain the same level of lifting at each session, and the total poundage lifted in each session would be better to be varied each week.

Training Systems

Pyramid System

Here the load is increased and the repetitions are reduced. Pyramid lifting is only for experienced lifters who have an established good technique.

Simple sets

3 × 8 with 70% -meaning three sets of eight repetitions with a weight of 70% of maximum for one repetition. This is the system that all novice lifters should work on, because the high number of repetitions enables the lifter to learn correct technique, and thereby reduce the risk of injury.

Super Setting

This consists of performing two or three exercises continuously, without rest is between sets, until all exercises have been performed. The normal 'between sets' rest is taken before the next circuit of exercises is commenced.

What sort of weight lifting equipment?

There are variable resistance machines and free

weights. Variable resistance machines are effective tools for building strength and muscle tone and are designed to work the target muscle in isolation, without the assistance of the surrounding muscles. Free weights and machines that provide the same equal resistance to a allow you not only to target a particular muscle group but to engage other muscles that assist in the work. Once they are conditioned, these assisting muscles help you to increase the weight you use in training the target muscles in order to stimulate the most growth in muscle fibres. The assisting muscles help stabilize the body, support limbs and maintain posture during a lift. Lifting free weights improves your coordination by improving the neuromuscular pathways that connect your muscles to the central nervous system.

Training Programs

Use the above notes to assist you in the preparation of a general strength training program, to develop your general strength, and a specific strength training program to develop your specific strength to meet to the demands of your event/sport. If weight training facilities is limited to your home and a set of dumbbells then it is still possible to construct a dumbbell weight training program. To monitor progress in training you should conduct strength and muscle balance tests.

Circuit Training

Circuit training is an excellent way to simultaneously improve mobility, strength and stamina. The circuit training format utilizes a group of 6 to 10 strength exercises that are completed one exercise after another. Each exercise is performed for a specified number of repetitions or for a prescribed time period before moving on to the next exercise. The exercises within each circuit are separated by brief, timed rest intervals, and each circuit is separated by a longer rest period. The total number of circuits performed during a training session may vary from two to six depending on your training level, your period of training and your training objective.

Safety in the Weight Room

Strength training is safe when properly supervised and controlled. Every weight room should have a set of rues and regulations pertaining to safety and they should be on public display. Rules may vary from one weight room to another but some very basic rules apply to them all:

1. Follow your training schedule
2. Train only when a qualified coach is present
3. Work in pairs – one lifting the other spotting
4. Wear the correct clothing and shoes
5. No personal stereos with headphones
6. Only athletes who are working out should be in the weight room
7. No horseplay
8. No eating, drinking or smoking
9. Help and respect other athletes

Make sure you and your athletes are fully aware of the safety rules applying to the weight training room you use.

Example sessions from Owen Anderson

Warm up with 10 to 15 minutes of easy jogging, swimming or cycling, and then perform the following exercises in order. Move quickly from exercise to exercise, but don't perform the exercises themselves too quickly.

- Run 400 meters at current 5k race pace
- Complete 36 abdominal crunches
- Do 5 chin-ups
- Do 15 press-ups
- Perform 15 squat thrusts with jumps
- Run 400 metres at 5k pace again
- Complete 30 body-weight squats
- Do 12 squat and dumbbell presses
- Perform 36 low-back extensions
- Complete 15 lunges with each leg
- Repeat steps 2–13 one more time, and then cool down with about 15 minutes of light jogging, swimming, or cycling.
- Do 15 bench dips
- Run 400 meters at 5k pace again

Once your fitness and strength have increased so much that the above circuit sessions are no longer challenging, you can then move on to a more challenging circuit workout, as follows: Warm up with two miles of easy running, and then perform the following exercises in order. Move quickly from exercise to exercise, but don't perform the exercises themselves too quickly.

- Complete 8 high bench step ups with jumps
- Perform 3 series of the 6 way lunge with arm drop
- Perform 8 prone trunk extensions with arm raises
- Run 400 meters at 5k race pace
- Do 6 plyometric press ups

Repeat steps 2 to 8 once more, and then cool down with 2 miles of easy ambling.

- Complete 8 reps of the hanging scissors plus double knee raise

- Run 400 metres at 5k race pace

Half Marathon Circuit

Warm up with two miles of easy running and follow with some stretching routines and then perform the following activities in order. Move quickly from exercise to exercise, don't perform the exercises themselves too quickly.

- Run one mile at your goal half-marathon velocity
- Do 70 ab crunches
- Carry out 70 low back extensions
- Complete 15 one leg squats with your right leg and then 15 more with your left
- Carry out 30 bench dips
- Jump 100 times in place, getting your propulsive force from your ankles, not your knees, and carrying out the last 30 jumps at an especially quick tempo
- 5 × 100 meters at close to top speed, with short recoveries
- Complete 20 squat thrusts with jumps
- Perform 20 lunges with each leg, with your non lunging foot on a step or platform which is about six inches off the ground.
- Do 20 press-ups
- Run one mile at goal half marathon velocity
- Carry out 30 cross body leg swings with each leg. To do these, lean slightly forward with your hands on a wall and your full body weight on your left leg. Then, swing your right leg to the left in front of your body, pointing your toes up as your foot reaches it final point of movement. Repeat this overall motion 30 times before performing 30 reps with your left leg.
- Repeat steps 3 to 14 one more time, and then cool down with two miles of light jogging

• Run one mile at goal half-marathon velocity

Marathon Circuit

Warm up with two miles of easy running and follow with some stretching routines and then perform exercise to exercise, but don't perform the exercises themselves too quickly.

1. Complete 15 burpees
2. Do 12 one leg squats with each leg
3. Carry out 50 abdominal crunches
4. Perform 50 low back extensions
5. Do 12 feet elevated press ups
6. Carry out 12 high bench step ups
7. Repeat steps 2 to 13 twice more
8. Run 800 metres at what feels like 10K intensity
9. Perform 12 press ups
10. Run 800 metres at a little faster than marathon speed
11. Complete 12 lunges with each leg
12. Run 800 metres at a little faster than goal marathon speed
13. Cool down with two miles of easy running
14. Do 15 bench dips
15. Run 1600 metres at a little faster than goal marathon speed

These circuits build a tremendous foundation of whole body strength and fatigue resistance, both of which are critically important for marathon running. The circuits also improve efficiency while running at marathon intensity and help to raise lactate threshold.

18

PHYSICAL CONDITIONING

Training is usually defined as a systematic process of repetitive, progressive exercise or work, involving also the learning process and acclimatization. The great sports medicine pioneer Dr. S.E. Bilik concisely stated the primary objective of intense sports conditioning and training as follows: "To put the body with extreme and exceptional care under the influence of all the agents which promote its health and strength in order to enable it to meet extreme and exceptional demands upon it.

Through the use of systematic work increments, improved voluntary responses by the organs are attained, through constant repetition, the conscious movements become more automatic and more reflexive, requiring less concentration by the higher nerve centre and thus reducing the amount of energy expended, through the elimination of movements unnecessary of performance of the desired task.

Increasing the strenuousness of exercise in the ways suggested is an application of the overload principle which holds that an activity must always be upgraded to a consistently higher level through maximum or near-maximum stimulation.

In this way the metabolic level and the organic responses can be increased. Logan and Wallis identified the SAID principle, which expressly relates to sports conditioning and training. SAID is an acronym for specific adaptation to imposed demands.

The SAID principle indicates that conditioning and training are directed toward the specific demands of a given sport. "Strength, cardiovascular endurance, muscular endurance, flexibility, and neuromuscular skill may be developed by using this principle in the application of exercise."

SPECIAL PHYSIOLOGICAL CONSIDERATIONS

Physiological Stress

One area that concerns the trainer is the effect of emotional factors on physical performance. Selye has defined these diverse stimuli, which tend to induce psychological or physiological conditions that upset the internal environment of the body, as stressors.

Sport is a stressor, it upsets the haemostatic balance, with physical, psychic, and social stressors acting as an integrated whole to produce a response. The various emotional states are sustained by extensive physiological adjustments comparable to the changes evoked by work and exercise.

These changes are controlled to a great extent by the autonomic nervous system and include acceleration and straightening of the heartbeat, a rise in blood pressure, a release of glucose from the liver, the secretion of a small amount of epinephrine from the adrenal glands, and a relaxation of the muscles in the bronchial tubes, which permits easier breathing.

These changes permit the body to function more efficiently under conditions of stress. In addition to the physiological adaptation to the stress of exercise, there is an involvement of the higher centres of the nervous system. Continued repetitive acts become reflective and require less concentration on their performance. This results in improved coordination, which, in turn, is reflected in more skilful and economical performance.

Acclimatization

An increasing problem in sports is acclimatization. Today athletes and sports teams and travelling farther afield in search of competition. As a result they often encounter abrupt changes in climate. In the United States it is usual for teams to leave severe wintry conditions and engage teams enjoying as subtropical climate in which playing conditions on the stadium floor approach 100° F.

Conversely, teams from subtropical areas find themselves competing on frozen turf and encountering subfreezing temperatures. It is evident that athletes or teams competing under foreign climatic conditions will not perform as well as would be expected, unless some preliminary acclimatization takes place.

This is probably more evident when the individual moves from a cold to a hot climate. Evidence is increasing to indicate that an individual can, within a 4- to 5- day period, be completely acclimatized artificially through performing vigorous work in a hot room and that such acclimatization will suffice a minimum of 3 weeks in cold weather.

This would indicate that, when competition is scheduled for a foreign hot climate, it is necessary to provide artificial acclimatization if par performance is expected. Acclimatization of this type results in lower rectal temperatures, more stable blood pressure for any given work load, and lower work-pulse rates.

Cold does not affect performance as much as heat does. Normally, the increase in metabolic heat is the result of activity, and the necessary heat loss is carried by radiation, convection, and sweating.

The important consideration, when performing in cold environment, is to dress in such a manner as to secure heat retention during warm-up activities and rest periods and still permit heat dissipation during competition.

Training at high altitudes presents other problems of acclimatization. High altitudes often place usual demands on the body when functioning in an atmosphere where partial oxygen pressure is significantly decreased from sea level.

The ability of an athlete to use quickly and effectively the oxygen taken in is the critical factor in endurance. At an altitude of 2300 meters the partial pressure of oxygen is approximately 20% less than that at sea level.

Therefore, the athlete must take in not only a much greater volume of air, but must also effect a more efficient extraction and use of the oxygens in the ambient air if a sea-level performance is to be equalled in those events in which endurance is a requisite.

It has been shown that in running events of 800 meters or more and in swimming events greater in distance than 200 meters a decrease demand on endurance, the greater the decrement in performance.

In events that are basically anaerobic, such as sprints, no significant decrements in performance are found. In fact, the decreased density of the air gives some advantages in the sprints and field events. Recovery times in all events are considerably longer than at sea level.

If activities requiring more than 1½ minutes of constant sustained effort are to be performed at an altitude of 3000 feet or more, the athlete should undergo training for a minimum of 3 to 5 weeks at an altitude comparable to that at which the competition will be held.

Some changes in the techniques of performance also are needed, particularly in breathing patterns. This is especially true in swimming where the strokes must be adapted to a different breathing rhythm.

One advantage of altitude training has been the decided improvement of performance at sea level. Intermittent sea-level stays of as long as 11 days resulted in better performances and di not interfere with altitude acclimatization. There appears to be considerable variability between individuals in respect to acclimatization, especially in the ability to tolerate an intense performance tempo for long periods of time at high altitudes. This probably explains the failure of some top athletes to perform as well in long distance events at high altitude as they do near sea level.

Jet Lag

Jet power has made it possible to travel thousands of miles in just a few hours. Athletes and athletic teams are now quickly transported from one end of the country to the other and to foreign lands.

For some, such travel induces a particular physiological stress, resulting in a syndrome that is identified as a circadian dysrhythmia and that reflects a desychronization of one's biological and biophysical time clock.

The team circadian implies a period of time of approximately 24 hours. The body maintains many cyclic mechanisms that follow a pattern, for example, the daily rise and fall of body temperature or the tidal ebb and flow of the cortical steroid secretion.

Body mechanisms adapt at varying rates to time changes. Some, like proteins metabolism, adjust immediately whereas others take time, like the rise and fall of body temperature, which takes about 8 days. Others, such as the adrenal hormones, which regulate metabolism, and other body functions, may take as long as 3 weeks.

Even intellectual proficiency or the ability to think clearly is cyclical. Younger, although the differences are not great. The stress induced in jet travel occurs only when flying either east or west at high speed. Travel north or south has no effects on the body unless several time zones are crossed in an east or west progression.

The changes in time zones, illumination, and environment prove somewhat disruptive to the human physiological mechanisms, particularly when one flies through five or more time zones, as occurs in some international travel. Some people are much more susceptible to the syndrome than are others, but the symptoms can be sufficiently disruptive to interfere with one's ability to perform maximally in a competitive event.

The symptoms can be any one or a combination of the following: anorexia, severe headache, blurred vision, dizziness, insomnia, or extreme fatigue. For international travel a full day of recuperation should be allowed before indulging in any type of activity. It is suggested that these preventive measures be followed:

1. Plan no strenuous activities for the first 24 hours after arrival.

2. Choose daylight departures when possible.

3. Exercise moderation in eating and drinking both before and during the flight.

4. Depart well rested.

Athletes who have particular health problems such as asthma, diabetes, epilepsy, hypertension, or peptic ulcer should have medical attention if they are competing at a time of day unusual to their regular practice or competition or if travelling across time zones.

PHYSIOLOGICAL EFFECTS OF TRAINING

Proper training induces specific and identifiable physiological effects within the athlete.

Body Density

Over time, regular exercise produces density changes within the musculo-skeletal system. These physical changes are of definite, recognizable types indicative of the sport for which the training has been designed.

The muscles change in girth, showing increases in cross section and in density because of an increase in sarcoplasm. There is a reduction in the amount of adipose tissue in the body and an increase in the development of connective tissue within the muscle bundles, which adds to the general toughness of the muscle and enables it to better withstand the strains and stresses it must undergo.

As a result of the muscle activity involved in training, additional stress is put on the bones. This results is an increase in the strength of the bones and also a rearrangement of the cancellous plates of the bones in accord with the stresses to which they have been subjected, thus decreasing the susceptibility to injury.

Ligaments also become denser through proper exercise. A process of minimal stretch and release tends to strengthen connective tissue fibres, whereas constant stretch weakens the fibres.

An immediate but temporary weight loss occurs at the onset of training as a result of water loss. This weight is immediately replaced on ingestion of food and water. However, the initial true loss of weight at the start of training is caused by a reduction in the amount of fat and if followed by a slow gain in weight, resulting from an increase in muscle bulk through development.

Type of Muscle Fibres

Current opinion favours classifying muscle fibres into three basic types: the slow-twitch glycolytic fibre. Fast-twitch fibres are basically anaerobic; they do not depend on oxygen for their energy supply.

In contrast, slow-twitch fibres are aerobic; they require oxygen for continued contraction. The preponderance of one fibre over another is related to inherited genetic factors that determine sports performance potential.

Fast-twitch fibres are responsible for speed or speed-power activities such as sprinting and weight lifting. Slow-twitch muscle fibres come into play in endurance activities such as long-distance running or cross-country skiing. The FOG fibre lies somewhere in the middle, but closer to the FG than the So category.

The way in which an individual trains determines

the type of fibre developed. Slow, low-intensity work primarily uses slow-twitch fibres. Fast-twitch fibres are suited for power and speed; slow-twitch fibres contract slowly and are fatigue resistant.

Athletes in ball sports exhibit a wide variety of muscle fibre types, and tend to be somewhere in the middle of the range. In physical restoration after injury or surgery, the type of activity the athlete participates in should be considered when planning the retraining program.

Fast-twitch fibres increase in size with exercise and decrease in size with immobilization. All work of low intensity may develop the slow-twitch fibres and fail to adequately develop strength and recruit fast-twitch fibres.

Muscle Strength

Strength is defined as the capacity to exert force or as the ability to do work against resistance. The most noticeable change that takes place in the muscles as a result of regular and proper exercise is the increase in girth. However, this general rule—the girth of a muscle is proportional to the work done by it—does not always hold true.

For example, the weight training of women who engage in heavy weight training tend to develop sizable increased in strength and have very limited hypertrophy. It has bee postulated that the higher levels of testosterone found in the male are responsible for the muscle bulking.

Another important consideration is that a muscle will grow in size and strength only when a work load over and above any previous demands is placed on it. This principle of overload is one of the basic premises of strength training. Frequent repetitions, if not coincidental with increases in work load, are valueless for this purpose, although the total work load may be equal.

Size alone is not an index of the strength of a muscle, since muscles of the same size in an individual may vary considerably in strength because of the difference in the amounts of adipose or fatty tissue each contains.

In essence, it not only lacks contractile power but it also limits the speed and amount of contraction by acting as a friction brake. Muscular strength can show an increase of three times or more without a proportional increase in muscle bulk necessarily being indicated.

However, exercise must be performed against near-maximal and gradually increasing resistance. Such resistance can be obtained either by lifting, pulling, or pushing against some resistive force that requires near-maximal effort for the individual, by moving the body at an ever-increasing rate of speed that is approaching the maximum level of performance; or by a combination of the two.

It is important for the trainer to know that a number of factors are involved in strength training. The speed, duration, number of repetition, and vigour or force with which exercises are performed will determine the outcome of the program.

The variable of individual difference is another factor that will affect the final result. Two athletes of the same gender following identical programs will not develop strength at the same rate, in the same manner, or to the same degree, because of varying inherent characteristics.

General consensus favours the current theory that hypertrophy, the increase in muscle cross section, is caused by a development of the existing constituent fibres when strength exercises are employed and by an increase in the total number of capillaries called into play when exercises of endurance are employed.

In other words, a gain in strength is accompanied by a significant increase in both the size of fibres and the number of capillaries in the muscle and by a resultant gain not only in power but also in speed and endurance.

Muscle Contraction and Exercise

Exercise for the development of strength is related to the type of muscle contraction.

Isometric contraction: Performance of an isometric exercise generates heat and energy by forcefully contracting the muscle in a static position, that is, with no change in the length of the muscle or in the angle of the joint at which the contraction takes place.

Attempting to lift or push an object that cannot be moved places the muscles in a state of isometric, or static, contraction. Isometric exercise has been shown to be most effective when a maximal contraction is held for 6 seconds and the contraction repeated from five to ten times daily.

Strength gained through an isometric program is specific to the joint angle at which the contraction takes place, so it is advisable to exercise throughout the full range of joint motion during each workout.

Isotonic contraction: Shortening or lengthening the muscle through its complete range involves an isotonic contraction. Isotonic exercises involve moving a resistive force, either a part of the body or some extraneous object. This type of contraction is referred to also as a dynamic contraction, since definite and easily discerned movement takes place.

An isotonic exercise done not involve the same fibres throughout a particular movement because the load remains constant regardless of the angle of contraction or the degree of fatigue engendered; consequently, the greatest strength gain appears in those fibres used in the initial part of the movement to overcome inertia.

The least gain is at the midpoint of the contraction. The primary value of performing isotonic contraction in exercise is the increase or maintenance of joint range of motion. In addition, isotonic movements tend to promote muscular circulation and endurance.

In performing an isotonic movement against resistance, the muscle should the first placed in stretch to ensure maximal innervation of muscle fibres. After full stretch, the body part is concentrically moved as far as possible and then eccentrically moved to the beginning position.

A general rule for the most effective muscle training is to move the resistance as smoothly and quickly as possible and return it at a much slower rate. Slow, eccentric muscle contraction against resistance is known as negative resistance, enervating more muscle fibres than positive, or concentric, contraction.

Recovery from muscular fatigue is more rapid in isotonic exercises than an isometric. Isotonic exercises wherein the muscle works throughout its full range against an increasingly greater resistance are known as progressive resistance exercises and were introduced by De Lorme and Watkings.

This type of exercise, and its many variations, has been shown to be superior to the isometric form for the development of strength and endurance. The De Lorme method makes use of a series of three sets of exercises with ten repetitions each.

The first set is performed against a resistance half of one's maximum, the second at three-quarters maximum, and the final set against full maximum. When one is able to successfully complete the full series, a weight increment is progressively added to the maximum.

Numerous variations are employed today, but none has been significantly different in its effectiveness. A training program using three sets each workout produces greater strength improvement than a program using one or two sets. Workouts three to four times weekly, with four to eight repetition, produces the greatest strength.

Isokinetic contraction: Isokinetic muscle contraction occurs through an accommodating resistance exercise. It offers all the advantages of both isometric and isotonic exercises without their inherent weaknesses. This method more nearly uses total involvement of the muscle fibres, since the resistance varies according to the angle of pull and the degree of fatigue developed throughout the exercise.

The inertia of the resistance, a definite factor in the isotonic exercise, is not a factor in isokinetics, since the resistance automatically adjusts to the degree of force exerted against it, thus maintaining a constant and consistent force. Exercises can be performed throughout the entire range of the performer's speed, since most isokinetic exercise equipment has variable speed adjustments.

A decided advantage of this type of exercise is that muscle soreness does not result. It is postulated that the muscle has a brief period of relaxation between repetitions, thus allowing the blood to circulate freely throughout the fibres and cleanse away the accumulated lactic acid and metabolities from the muscle cells.

Isotonic exercises do not permit such relaxation, hence there is a buildup of fatigue products. Neither isokinetic nor isotonic resistance are superior to one another. The goal of training must be satisfied according to the SAID principle.

Over the last few years, isokinetic resistance exercising has found a valuable place in rehabilitation, whereas free weights employing isotonic principles have become increasingly popular in sports conditioning.

Plyometric exercise: For some years plyometric exercises have been in vogue in Europe. These exercises are now becoming increasingly popular in the United States. This type of exercise produces an isometric type overload, using the myotatic, or stretch, reflex.

By means of an eccentric contraction, the muscle is fully stretched immediately preceding the concentric contraction. The greater the stretch put on the muscle from its resting length immediately before the concentric contraction, the greater the load the muscle can lift or overcome. The rate of stretch is more critical than the magnitude of the stretch.

Ways of Achieving Strength

Individuals can gain strength in numerous ways. This discussion briefly describes the more prevalent ways strength is developed, they are the non-equipment, equipment, and combined nonequipment and equipment approaches.

Nonequipment approaches: Three nonequipment approaches are presently employed in sports conditioning: calisthenics, or free exercise; partner or reciprocal, resistance, and self-resistance.

Calisthenics, or free exercise, is one of the more easily available means of developing strength. Isotonic movement exercises can be graded according to intensity by using gravity as an aid, ruling gravity out, moving against gravity, or using the body or body part as a resistance against gravity.

Most calisthenics require the athlete to support the body or move the total body against the force of gravity. Push-ups are a good example of a vigorous antigravity free exercise. To be considered maximally effective, the isotonic calisthenic exercise, as in all types of exercise, must be performed in an repetitions are performed for each exercise and repeated in sets of two or three.

Some free exercises have a holding phase instead of employing a full range of motion. Examples of these are back extensions are sit-ups. When the exercise produces maximal muscle tension, it is held between 6 to 10 seconds and then repeated one to three times.

Partner, or reciprocal, resistance exercise is an excellent approach to gaining strength and flexibility, such as in neuromuscular facilitation. It requires no equipment other than a partner who is about equal in size and strength. It is often highly motivating for both participants, and all types of exercise can be engaged using this method.

When performing isokinetic resistance, the body part involved is taken into a stretched position by the partner. Resistance is accommodated through a complete range of motion. Three bouts of resistance usually are given for each exercise.

Equipment approaches: Numerous devices are designed to overload the musculature and develop strength. These range from individual pieces to entire conditioning systems and are generally categorized as isotonic/isometric and isokinetic.

Isotonic/isometric equipment are almost too numerous to mention. Some of the more standard stationary apparatus, chinning bars, parallel bars, and stall bars, have numerous possibilities for increasing strength. Another standard piece of equipment is the wall pulley weight, which progressively exercises the major joints and muscles.

Free weights are very popular and are used for developing strength through both isotonic and isometric contraction. Sports programs commonly have a variety of free weights, including dumbbells and barbells.

Dumbbells range from 2 to 2½ pounds to 50 to 75 pounds or more, and barbells range from 25 or 30 pounds to well over 200 pounds. Some people argue that free weights do not provide consistent muscle development through a full range of motion; however, they do help in the development of balance and coordination and exercise stabilizing and accessory muscles, which machine systems often do not provide.

Machine exercise systems, such as the Universal Gym, allow a variety of exercise possibilities such as sit-ups, parallel bar dips, bench presses, pull-downs, rowing exercises, knee extensions, knee curls and biceps curls, as well as arm pressing.

The Universal Gym employs graduated weights that are lifted by heavy cables as the athlete applies force against a bar.

Isokinetic machines provide an accommodating muscle resistance through a full range of motion. A maximal load is produced as the athlete dynamatically perform work. The amount of resistance depends on the extent of force applied by the athlete.

Machine designed for isokinetic resistance develop flexibility and coordination, as well as strength.

The Nautilus machine is one the newest and most popular exercise systems. Nautilus training machines provide full range of movement and direct resistance to specific muscles or muscle groups. Both concentric and eccentric muscle contraction is maximally provided by special cams and counterweights.

In this system, negative, or eccentric, work is accentuated. Although Nautilus is not an isokinetic system, it does provide some variable resistance through a full range of motion.

Each machine provides body stabilization to afford isolation of a specific muscle or muscle group. This musculature isolation emphasizes negative, or eccentric, contraction. Because the amount of resistance varies during a full range of motion, resistance is indicated by the number of plates lifted, rather than the number of pounds.

Other examples of exercise systems, such as the Mini-Gym provide opportunities for specific strength development related to sports activities. Using variables resistance devices, the athlete can concentrate on specific sports requirements.

Speed Training

Speed differs from endurance in that it requires the expenditure of an enormous amount of energy in a short time and is specific to the area developed. This requires performances of extremely short duration, such as a swim sprint, dash, or rope climb, to rely almost exclusively on the oxygen within the tissues.

The anaerobic activity depends on the immediate chemical release of oxidative energy by phosphocreatine and ATP, a high-energy phosphate compound, for instant use by the muscles.

The amount of energy released, although high, cannot meet the tremendous requirements of prolonged intensive exercise, thus calling the fast-twitch muscles into play. Age is a factor in attaining.

An individual's ability in speed reaches its peak when he or she is about 20 years of age. Speed depends not only on a considerable amount of anaerobic activity, but also on the resiliency and responsiveness of the circulatory system and reaction time, flexibility and strength.

Speed ability declines rapidly after 28 years of age because it imposes a considerable task on the heart and there is a gradual increase in loss of vascular resiliency. As previously stated, the strength gain of muscles is accompanied by a significant increase in both the size of fibres and the number of capillaries.

This gain in strength results in concomitant gains

in speed and in endurance. In training for speed one should train principally for strength by means of overload and by application of the principles employed for improving strength and power for endurance.

Speed activities should be added to the program to enable the athlete to increase the ability to produce energy more rapidly and to accumulate a greater oxygen debt.

On this basis it would be consistent to place who participate in activities that require great speed not an intensive strength program, concentrating principally on the muscle groups most called on in the particular activity. Strength training not only involves weight training or lifting, but also running and other activities to achieve the desired results since PRE makes extremely limited demands, if any at all, on the cardiorespiratory system.

Therefore, it is good practice for a sprinter to compete in cross-country in the off-season, as well as run long distances that will make heavy demands on the body during the regular competitive season. In these activities the athlete will be developing strength and endurance. A strength-endurance program of this kind must be carefully correlated with sufficient sprint activities to develop and maintain a high rate of cardiorespiratory response and efficiency.

Flexibility Training

Flexibility is defined as the range of movement of a specific joint or group of joints influenced by the associated bones and bony structures and the physiological characteristics of the muscles, tendons, ligaments, and the various other collagenous tissues surrounding the joint.

Studies have indicated that an increase in the flexibility of joints tends to decrease the injuries to those joints. In most instances it is also contended that an increase in flexibility contributes to better athletic performance. Both of these considerations are important to the trainer.

In general, the flexible athlete, is less injury prone and more likely to perform optimally when compared to the inflexible athlete. Good flexibility usually indicates that there are no adhensions or abnormalities present in or around the joints and that there are no serious muscular limitations.

This allows the body to move freely and easily through the full range of joint flexion and extension without any unnecessary restrictions in the joints or the adjacent tissues. An increase in flexibility must accompany an increase of strength, or the range of motion may be considerably affected.

Exercises of flexibility can achieve their goal without decreasing strength. Conversely, exercising for the acquisition of great strength such as is sought by some weight lifters, without the use of accompanying movements designed to maintain and increase the range of joint motion, can and will result in the condition commonly called "muscle-boundedness".

In this condition, because of the enormous bulk and inelasticity of the muscles, tendons, and ligaments, there is a decided inability to obtain complete flexibility and freedom of joint mobility. An increase in flexibility is important to the athlete.

With more flexibility the runner can increase stride,

the hurdler can effect a more economical flight, and the swimmer can produce a better leg kick and a more efficient arm stroke. The gymnast, the wrestler, and the various other athletes all depend to a large degree on good flexibility and range of motion.

Type of Flexibility Training

There is some disagreement as to the best type of stretching procedure to use for improving flexibility. The ballistic stretch, in which the body momentum forces the muscle groups into as much extensibility as can be tolerated, has been used for many years.

Evidence indicates that this type of exercise, although it will increase flexibility, may also induce muscle tears as a result of misjudging the stretch tolerance of the tissues and/or failing to control the force of the body momentum.

Therefore use of the ballistic stretch should be discouraged. The gradual stretch, in which a position of extreme stretch on a given muscle group is assumed and held for a period of time, is thought by many to be as effective as the ballistic stretch and without the possibility of pre-activity muscle strains or tears.

A convenient rule to use in setting up a flexibility program is to determine the comfortable range of motion for each joint, then set a goal to increase that range of motion in all directions. Joint flexibility may be varied or affected by a number of factors: joint problems hereditary joint structural differences, elasticity of body connective tissue, reciprocal muscle coordination, and muscle vascosity.

Hyperflexibility should be avoided. Such excessive flexibility contributes little to performance and can indeed increase susceptibility to joint injury. There appears to be no one single factor that either increases or decreases flexibility.

Although good flexibility can be attained in a relatively short time, in most instances it is lost rather quickly unless the athlete maintains a regular regimen of stretching exercises. Several objective methods are available for measuring flexibility.

The student or trainer who wishes to use such tests should refer to current books on measurement in the fields of physical education, adapted physical education, or physical therapy.

Nonmuscular Relaxation and Psychological Readiness

Relaxation is an essential aspect of any sports-conditioning program. Coordinated movement implies the ability to reciprocally contract agonist and relax antagonist muscles efficiently. This also can be called differential relaxation.

Relaxation and the reduction of abnormal muscle tension allows greater lung inspiration and expiration, making the exchange of oxygen and carbon dioxide more efficient. Establishing an attitude of readiness or "mind-set" in respect to physical performance is of utmost importance to the athlete.

The close relationship between emotions and muscles has long been recognized and has had considerable study. Thinking about a projected physician action affects the muscles involved. Motivational stressors that are based on success can induce a greater work output in the individual and serve to increase the gross mechanical and physiological efficiency, whereas motivational stressors that indicate failure may tend to promote an emotional reaction that would circumvent the increased gross mechanical efficiency.

If the emotions are developed in intensity and then properly channelled, they can be of considerable aid to physical performance. Stress reactions are similar in both sexes. A positive attitude on the part of the athlete preparing for competition aids considerably in reducing excess tension.

The champion athlete "thinks" like a champion and therefore develops a winning attitude. Relaxation also promotes better circulations, heart rate, and blood pressure. Volitional relaxation allows for neuromuscular skill learning to also take place more efficiently. An athlete who is tense and unable to relax may be more prone to a variety of musculoskeletal injuries.

Endurance and Stamina

The degree of ability to withstand fatigue is inherited, and the basis of the fatigue pattern is in each individual's constitution. Two factors modify an individual's capacity for improving endurance:

(1) The ability to endure the pain and concomitant discomforts of fatigue while endeavouring to improve the level of work tolerance, and

(2) The body's ability to effect the necessary haemostatic adjustments, which can enable an athlete to increase energy production to as much as twenty times the resting level when such a demand is made.

Endurance is the ability of the body to undergo prolonged activity or to resist stresses set up as a result of prolonged activity. Endurance involves a number of elements, each of which is partially responsible for success or failure in sustaining physical performance.

Endurance primarily depends on the various aspects of cardiac efficiency, which in turn exerts influence on the performance of the other portions of the human organism. Training or conditioning builds a given economy—an efficiency in body adaptability—which is important as the body adjusts to the continued and prolonged stresses put on it in performing an activity that requires all-out or near-maximal performance over a considerable period of time.

As a result of careful conditioning, the onset of fatigue is considerably delayed and the athlete is able to maintain a high rate of performance over a long period of time. Exercises for endurance improve muscle tonus.

The improvement is primarily caused by functional involvement of more motor units as a result of work increase. Work increase improves circulation by calling into play more capillaries, thus providing the working muscles with more oxygen and fuel and facilitating removal of the metabolic by-products of exercise.

As a muscle tires, it loses some of its ability to relax. The character of a muscle is indicated not only by its ability to produce power over a protracted period of time but also by its capacity to concurrently maintain its elasticity. As a muscle works, it restores its own oxygen and fuel supplies and disposes of lactic acid and other metabolic products.

As long as these two processes continue to operate at basically the same rate, the muscle can continue to work with efficiency. However, when an imbalance is reached in which the waste product accumulation rate is greater than the oxygen and fuel intake, physiological equilibrium is upset and fatigue sets in.

In fatigue the reaction time slows down and is accompanied by stiffening or inability of the muscle to reach a condition of relaxation. This stiffening or incomplete relaxation, coupled with a reduced ability to respond to stimulation, is one of the contributing factors to athletic injury.

Respiratory Response to Training

Training increases vital capacity and aids materially in establishing economy in the oxygen requirement. The conditioned athlete operates primarily on a "pay as you go" basis as a result of his increased stroke volume and reduced heartbeat.

An increase in the contractile power of the respiratory muscles, particularly the diaphragm, results in deeper respiration per breath. This enables the athlete to use a greater lung capacity and, consequently, to effect increased economy in the use of oxygen.

The untrained individual attempts to compensate by increasing the rate of respiration and soon reaches a state of considerable respiratory indebtedness, which severely encumbers or even halts performance. The trained individual, through aerobic endurance training is able to establish a steady state of oxygen consumption at higher rates of work because of greater mechanical efficiency in performing the required task.

This permits more work with a lower expenditure of energy or oxygen consumption. Since less oxygen is used for a given task, a greater margin of reserve and continued high-level performance for a longer period of time, without distress, can be attained.

Endurance-type exercises will produce significant changes in the cardiorespiratory system but will have little effect on muscle strength per se. Conversely, strength training brings about gains in muscular strength but has no significant influence on the cardiorespiratory systems.

Endurance training not only significantly improves maximal oxygen consumption but is a key factor in injury prevention. The fatigued athlete not only has a diminished reaction capacity but because of muscular fatigue is less able to withstand extraneous forces so that an injury can be sustained under circumstances in which a better conditioned performer will not.

Aerobic endurance training uses slow interval training. An aerobic program coupled with a good weight training program should condition the cardiorespiratory system and the neuromuscular system adequately for competition.

Anaerobic training, which enables one to sustain an oxygen debt, can be accomplished through using a fast interval program. Anaerobic capacity is vital in all athletics, since it not only permits one to sustain a greater oxygen debt but comes into play in situations where oxygen delivery may prove to be insufficient.

Cardiac and Circulatory Response to Training

Hear size will increase as the result of a training program. This is neither undesirable not indicative of any dangerous or unusual propensity for cardiac anomalies. To the contract, the increased heart size is caused by the thickening of the heart muscle.

It results in a more powerful contraction and, accordingly, a larger volume output of blood per stroke.

In other words, as a result of training or conditioning, the heart becomes considerably more efficient in its operation.

Consequently, it is capable of circulating more blood with fewer contractions. In performing a set amount of work over a period of time, the heart rate becomes slower as training progresses.

Training reduces the pulse rate, sometimes by as much as ten to twenty beats per minute, during the period between pre-training and post-training measurements. The overall efficiency of the heart is high because of the slower heart rate and the more efficient use of oxygen by the coronary arteries, although the consumption of oxygen by the heart itself rises considerably with the increase in work load.

One of the advantages of training is that whereas the heart rate does not show an immediate and rapid increase at the start of severe exercise, it does return to normal more rapidly than the heart of the untrained person. Hence, recuperative power becomes an important factor in proper conditioning.

Precluding organic or functional anomalies, there is no evidence that strenuous or severe exercise can injure the heart of a young adult. Training exerts considerable effect on blood pressure. Because of the increase in the systematic system, as a result of using blood from the splanchnic pool, there is more volume under higher pressure.

This results in better transportation of oxygen to the tissues, when it is needed, and in more efficient removal of metabolities. As the result of prolonged effort in the untrained individual, systolic pressure falls progressively, an indication of approaching exhaustion.

On the other hand, training retards this phenomenon and work can be continued for a longer time with scarcely any perceptible changes in blood pressure. During exercises of endurance, the rise in blood pressure is much greater than during exercises of speed.

Many factors tend to modify the response of blood pressure to various forms of exercise. Studies have indicated that the rate, intensity, duration, and state of training of the performer will determine the blood pressure response.

Major Principles of Physical Training

In terms of recent research, it appears that most coaches fail work their athletes hard enough. They are concerned with the problems of staleness and lack of motivation and with the fear of engendering some type of abnormal physiological condition, as a result they tend to underwork their athletes.

High school football players who participate in an exceedingly intensive preseason conditioning program for 6 to 8 weeks before the start of the playing season have much greater strength and stamina throughout the entire season than do players who begin an identical conditioning program only 2 or 3 weeks before the start of the season.

Intensity

The intensity at which an activity is performed is probably the most critical of the various factors that determine the amount of positive physical change to take place. Relatively few individuals ever approach their maximum in terms of work capacity during training.

The various physiological and psychological changes that must necessarily be effected for greater endurance will come about only through an intensive program of work based on the overload principle of progressively increasing the loads, the number of repetitions, and the rate of intensity of these repetitions.

This system applies regardless of the type of activity. There is no shortcut to attaining high standards of performance. It is a long arduous process to which athletes must dedicate themselves without reservations if they desire to become a top-flight performer.

Consistency

Athletes must train with as much regularity as possible. Depending on the requirements of the sport, training might be engaged in a number of times per week. Regularity of "workouts" is dispersed, and rest periods serve to apply the overload principle, producing a positive stress on the body.

Specificity

Physical training for a particular sport in no way guarantees that the level of fitness reached or the degree of neuromuscular skill achieved will be adequate for other sports. Repeated practice of a skill as one attempts to perfect that skill involves a biological programming and reprogramming as the skill is constantly repeated and the movement/skill pattern is developed and eventually controlled by conditioned reflexes, thus gradually eliminating conscious control.

Specificity applies to all physical activities, hence, if one wishes to improve speed, practice must be geared to speed. If endurance or strength is the objective, then practice must involve constantly raising the levels of performance in endurance or strength activities.

Practice must be related to the dominant features of the specific skill itself. Specificity means relating the specific physical requirements of an activity to a practice pattern that will elicit the specific biological responses that produce that skill. To be effective, any training program involves three considerations:

1. If one wishes to increase strength at all limb speeds, isokinetic high-speed training should be used.

2. The program must be specifically planned in terms of the sport itself.

3. The program must be geared specifically to the individual using it.

The use of mimetic training activities assists not only in developing the necessary neuromuscular skills but also in motivating the athlete.

Overload Progression

All training must apply the SAID principle, overloading the body gradually over a long period of time. Whether for power or endurance, the work should be performed with a progressively increased load. Exercise having a specific pattern in terms of either movement, force, duration, or speed is employed to produce training results that will be peculiar to that exercise alone.

THE WOMAN ATHLETE AND PHYSICAL TRAINING

Girls and women can successfully compete in strenuous athletic activities at the highest levels of physical performance without physiological or psychological harm.

Running

Many girls often have difficulty in running, particularly after adolescence. The female pelvis is frequently broader and shallower, which causes the femur to articulate at a more acute angle than does that of the male, resulting in a mechanical disadvantage; the obliquity of the femur tends to induce a lateral sway of the body in running.

Frequently failure to lift the knees sufficiently and compensation by casting the lower leg and foot out to the side in the forward-carry phase causes the femur to be rotated inwardly. The casting accentuates the trunk sway, which becomes quite pronounced.

In conditioning and coaching, good knee elevation, directly forward, coupled with straightforward foot placement, should be stressed. Many girls, as they run, tend to hug the upper arms and elbows tight against the body and swing the forearms out to the sides, meanwhile vigorously rotating the upper trunk and the shoulders in an attempt to offset the inward thigh rotation.

In addition to showing the exaggerated trunk rotation, some girls tend to keep the clenched fists tight against the chest, meanwhile alternately thrusting the elbows forward in a vigorous manner. Stressing relaxation and a proper arm swing, linked with a strong high forward knee lift, will increase the efficiency and speed of the runner.

Throwing and Support Activities

The shoulder width of the female is narrower than that of the male, and the breadth of the pelvis, augmented by the adipose pads over the hips, usually causes the arm to incline inward. Most women have a pronounced hyperextension of the elbow joint, often coupled with a decided outward angling of the forearm.

These skeletal differences create difficulties in throwing, circling, or rotatory movements of the arm as a whole. This is true also in activities involving the support of the body by the arms, as encountered in gymnastics.

In the latter the differences provide a distinct handicap, since both elbow and shoulder joints must function at somewhat unfavourable angles for weight bearing.

Feminine and Masculine Characteristics

Contrary to lay opinion, participation in sports does not masculinize women. Within a sex, the secretion of testosterone, progesterone, androgen, and oestrogen varies considerably, accounting for significant variation in terms of muscularity and general morphology among males and females.

Girls whose physiques are more masculine are stronger per unit of weight than either girls who are less masculine or boys who display considerable femininity of build.

Those who are os masculine type often enter sports and are usually quite successful because of mechanical advantages resulting from their masculine structure. However, such types are the exception; the majority of women participants in sports possess a feminine body build.

Many girls and women fear the development of unsightly, bulging muscles should they exercise vigorously. They point to the pronounced muscular definition of the quadriceps and the gastrocnemius seen in some women who have had intensive and prolonged ballet or dance training.

Actually, such overdeveloped musculature is relatively uncommon and the result of long, arduous, and concentrated training for many years. Such excessive development is not a concomitant of sports competition. One need only observe some of the outstanding girl and women athletes to obtain complete refutation of such a premise.

Indeed, physical activity develops femininity and grace. Inherent endorcionological and morphological factors, not physical activity, are responsible for femininity and masculinity.

Jumping

One of the argument frequently advanced against sports for women raises the point that activities such as the high jump or broad jump are harmful because they cause internal damage in the pelvic region as a result of the jarring forces encountered in landing.

This, it is argued, subjects the mesenteries and other supportive tissues to tearing, with concomitant trauma to the neighbouring organs.

Medical findings refute this postulate. The exercise engaged in by a woman athlete in training and in conditioning as well as in actual competition, tends to strengthen the floor of the pelvis and the surrounding tissues and brings about improved muscle tone.

Irritation or strain to the breasts can result, especially if the breasts are pendulous, unless adequate support and restraint are afforded by means of a properly designed and fitted brassiere.

Women have a lower centre of gravity than do men and hence are generally more stable. Their arms and legs are proportionately shorter than men's. Both of these factors present disadvantages in jumping.

Physiological Implications

Both structural and physiological differences emphasize the fact that women should not be compared with men in terms of performance. They should be judged in terms relative only to the performance standards of their own gender. Gender has a definite influence on training, principally because of physiological differences in the capacity to perform exercises.

Prepubertal and Pubertal Periods

During the prepubertal period, girls and the equal of, and often superior to, boys of the same age in activities requiring speed, strength, and endurance. The difference between men and women is not too apparent until after puberty. With the advent of puberty the gulf begins to widen, with the males continuing in a slower gradual increase in strength, speed, and endurance.

Circulatory Factors

In the performance of moderate exercise there is little significant difference between young men and women in respect to standards of performance, but the significance increases as the strenuousness of the activity increases. Women are subject to the same physiological law as the men.

However, they have a smaller heart and a faster pulse rate. They indicate a greater and more rapid increase in pulse rate at the beginning of exercise and a much slower recovery after exercise.

The pulse rates of trained women athletes are about ten beats per minute slower than those of non-athletes. Since the male possesses a larger heart, probably because of the fact that he has more muscle tissue, he has a larger circulation.

Since heart is proportional to body size, a larger individual will have a slower heart rate, hence the male rate is some five to eight beats slower than that of the female, resulting in a greater cardiac output at a lower cardiac cost.

At rest the average number of red blood cells in the female is 4,500,000/mm^3 as compared to 5,000,000/mm^3 in the male. Post-exercise values reflect an increase of approximately 1,000,000 for the male and a comparable rise for the female relative to the lower resting value.

This rise is indicative of the compensatory adjustment to meet the demand for an increased oxygen supply. The female also has approximately 8% less haemoglobin. At a given level of oxygen consumption women have a higher heart rate than do men.

On the other hand, at a given heart rate men can transport more oxygen during submaximal and maximal work. In both sexes the maximal heart rate bears a linear relationship with an increased work load. Exhaustion, however, is reached at a lower rate of performance in women.

Blood pressure values, both diastolic and systolic, and from 5 to 10 mm Hg lower in the female. Pubertal systolic values, although reflecting some rise, are less pronounced than those of the male and will often indicate a slight decrease, which is maintained until age 18 or 19.

After age 19 there is a slow but steady increase in both the male and female as age advances. After menopause most women show a systolic increase slightly higher than the comparable male.

Metabolism

The metabolism rate of the female at all ages is from 6% to 10% lower than that of the male of comparable size when related to body surface area. When the basal metabolic rate is related to muscle mass, however, the gender difference disappears.

This would indicate a significance to the resting heat disposition but not to muscular efficiency. The calcium metabolic rate of the female is higher than that of the male, since ossification of her bones occurs at an earlier age. However, the bones of the male are denser and more rugged because of the slower rate of ossification and the subsequent calcium retention.

Menarche

Menarche, the onset of the menses, normally occurs between the tenth and the seventeenth year, with the majority of girls usually entering it between 13 and 15 years. Menarche, like menstruation, is regular in its irregularity.

There is some indication that strenuous training and competition may delay the onset of menarche. The greatest delay appears to be related to the higher calibre competition.

In itself, a delay in the first menses does not appear to pose any significant danger to the young female athletes. The late-maturing girl commonly has longer legs, narrower hips, and less adiposity and body weight for her height, all of which are more conducive to sports.

Respiratory Function

Because of the smaller thoracic cavity, women respite more rapidly. They require less oxygen because of a lower metabolic rate and smaller body size. Trained athletes of both genders appear to use their anaerobic processes to approximately the same level.

Women breathe more shallowly, that is, with the upper part of the chest, whereas men tend to breathe deeper and hence more diaphragmatically.

Vital capacity is the volume of air moved through the lungs from a maximal inspiration to a maximal expiration. It varies between the genders, since it bears a direct relationship to body size, area, and height.

Although vital capacity does not predict performance by itself, it can be enhanced through training, and it determines performance capabilities. The vital capacity of the female is about 36% of the total.

Differences in relative amounts of muscle tissue during puberty are the result of endocrine function, which causes the fundamental sex differences in terms of weight and development.

Testosterone produces a marked increase in the weight of muscle tissue and an enlargement of the muscle fibres. Female hormones have a growth-inhibiting effect, but as with men, women's muscles develop in relation to the fundamental laws of exercise.

Adiposity

The fat is stored at various depots around the body, as well as in a rather thick subcutaneous layer that serves as protection and insulation. Because of the subcutaneous layer, women are better able to withstand heat and cold than are men.

The greater amount of adipose tissue may have some effect on the lower metabolic rate. Since fat is inert, it limits athletic performance, representing dead weight that must be carried by the athlete.

Women tend to accumulate fat on the thighs and around the hips, abdomen, and breasts, which would account generally for their greater relative weight in relation to size.

The average female has about 7 pounds more of subcutaneous fat than her male counterpart, having a ratio of 22% to 25% fat to body weight as opposed to 14% for the male. Women athletes exhibit far less adiposity than nonathletes, having a range of from 10% to 15%.

Among women distance runners, Wilmore has found values as low as 6%. The type of athletic activity in which the sports women participates seems to affect her adiposity. For example, women runners are much learner than women who compete in the weight events. Female athletes can and do approach the relative fat values attained by male athletes.

Menstruation

As interest and participation in girls and women's sports grow, the various myths that have surrounded female participation and the effects of participation as menarche, menstruation, and childbirth are gradually being dispelled.

Although the effects of sustained and strenuous training and competition on the menstrual cycle and the effects of menstruation on performance still cannot be fully explained with any degree of certainty, continued and increasing research is slowly clearing away the veil.

Some of the research in the past has been contradictory and, on occasion, open to question. Nonetheless, current research appears to be answering some of the questions, although much needs still to be done.

The menstrual cycle is considered to have four phases. These phases, based on a 28-day cycle, are as follows:

1. The menses—cycle days 1 to 5

2. Postmenstrual phase—also known as the estrogenic, proliferative, or follicular phase; cycle days 6 to 13 or 14

3. Ovulation—also known as the luteal or progesterone phase; cycle days 15 to 28

4. Postovulatory phase—also known as the premenstrual phase; cycle days 15 to 28

The majority of women tend to show some variation in the length of their cycles, these differences occurring principally because of differences in duration of the preovulatory phase rather than the premenstrual phase.

With the onset of menarche a cyclic hormone pattern commences, which establishes the menstrual cycle. These hormonal changes result from complex feedback mechanisms and specifically controlled interactions that occur between the hypothalamus, ovaries, and pituitary gland.

Two gonadotropins induce the release of the egg from the mature follicle at midcycle. They are FSH which stimulates the maturation of an ovarian follicle, and LH, which stimulates the development of the corpus luteum, and endocrine structure that secretes progesterone and estrogens.

The control and eventual inhibition of the production of FSH when the follicle reaches maturity is brought about by the estrogenic steroids produced by the ovaries. Progesterone, a steroid hormone produced within the corpus luteum—a small body that develops within a ruptured ovarian follicle after ovulation—eventually inhibits production of LH.

Estrogen is secreted principally by the luteal cells. Before onset of a new menstrual period, FSH levels are already rising, probably to initiate maturation of new follicles to reinstitute the next cycle.

For many years medical opinion held that little or no exercise should be taken during the menstrual period. In modern medical opinion the avoidance of strenuous activity is advised for only the first 2 days. During this time, the womb is quite heavy and engorged with blood.

The athlete should avoid activities involving torque or jarring forces such as jumping or twisting movements that involve the pelvis at this time. Some athletes, however, are able to participate in heavy training or competition without experiencing any distress or involvement during their menstrual period.

The best performance usually appear during the immediate postmenstrual period and the poorest performances are observed during the immediate premenstrual period. Many world-class athletes have set records during the flow phase.

As can be seen, variation is the rule, not the exception. Most authorities believe that there is little evidence that physical activities have unfavourable effects on the cycle. Variations in performance may be induced by the psychological and hormonal factors that normally accompany menstruation, and water retention.

Any athlete who is healthy gynecologically and whose menstrual cycles show no unusual or unfavourable changes either during or as the result of physical stress should be permitted to participate in sports activities at all times.

Athletic Conditioning